BASIC RIGHTS

BASIC RIGHTS

Subsistence, Affluence, and U.S. Foreign Policy

40th Anniversary Edition

HENRY SHUE

PRINCETON UNIVERSITY PRESS
PRINCETON AND OXFORD

Published by Princeton University Press, 41 William Street,
Princeton, New Jersey 08540
In the United Kingdom: Princeton University Press,
6 Oxford Street, Woodstock, Oxfordshire OX20 1TR

First published 1980

Second edition 1996

40th Anniversary Edition 2020

Paperback ISBN 9780691202280

LCCN 2019953640

British Library Cataloging-in-Publication Data is available

This book has been composed in New Caledonia

press.princeton.edu

Printed in the United States of America

To

SISTER MARIANI C. DIMARANAN, CFIC
Task Force Detainees
of the Philippines,
Quezon City

ATTORNEY YAP THIAM-HIEN, S.H.
Institute for the
Defense of Human Rights,
Jakarta

and

tous les hommes qui, ne pouvant être des
saints et refusant d'admettre les fléaux,
s'efforcent cependant d'être des médecins.
(Albert Camus)

Contents

2/26

Preface to the 40th Anniversary Edition

Charles R. Beitz, Robert E. Goodin, and Simon Caney variously remarked that although I had written about basic rights and had written about climate change, I had not at that point written systematically about basic rights and climate change.[1] This edition adds "Basic Rights and Climate Change" as an eighth chapter, in an attempt to respond explicitly to this friendly encouragement.[2] In order to streamline the book's structure, "Right-grounded Duties and the Institutional Turn," which was added in the second edition in 1996 as an afterword, has now been made a seventh chapter but is otherwise unchanged. The original seventh chapter of the first edition was omitted in 1996.

The original foreword has also been omitted, but I would like now to reaffirm the gratitude expressed there to the Ford Foundation and the Rockefeller Brothers Fund for their adventurous support for the fledgling Center for Philosophy and Public Policy of the University of Maryland at College Park, where my work on basic rights began in the late 1970s. My research on climate change, which lies behind the new eighth chapter, began at Cornell University in the early 1990s, at the insistence of the late Duane Chapman and with the assistance of him and Cornell's other far-sighted agricultural economists. Since 2002, I have been hosted by the Department of Politics and International Relations of the University of Oxford, enriched by conversation with Oxford's remarkable climate scientists and with fellow theorist Simon Caney, and supported by Merton College, Oxford, my alma mater from the early 1960s.

I am grateful to Rob Tempio of Princeton University Press for conceiving of this edition and patiently awaiting the arrival of the new chapter. Most of all, I delight in the continuing presence of Vivienne, who has been beside me for more than half a century, since years before any of this work began, and who somehow seems ready, if necessary, for even more.

Preface to the Second Edition

This edition includes as an afterword a new essay, "Right-grounded Duties and the Institutional Turn," which attempts to take another few steps along one of the paths chosen in the first edition. In order to avoid making the book longer I have omitted the original chapter 7, "Some Priorities for U.S. Foreign Policy," to make space for the new afterword. I still endorse the four recommendations made in chapter 7—and still love the concluding quotation from *The Plague*—even though the recommendations are no longer at the center of political debate. I omit them without regret, however, because they focus narrowly on the foreign policy of the United States, not on the kind of international institution-building that the afterword advocates. The remainder of the first edition has been left unchanged.

It was my long-time co-conspirator Peter G. Brown who first insisted to me that if one had not spelled out the duties, one had not really spelled out the rights. I hope he will be pleased that while I have not yet adequately dealt with the question he raised now twenty years ago, it is the one I am still working on in this afterword. Onora O'Neill, James W. Nickel, and Thomas W. Pogge have done me the honor over the years of taking some of the theses in this book seriously enough to subject them to sustained criticism. This did not seem the place to correct all errors and answer all critics, so I have not taken up many of their points. Yet grateful reflection on their penetrating arguments has often shaped what I have tried to say here. Thomas was also kind enough to critique this afterword for me.

Other debts are more diffuse. During the one glorious year that Jeremy Waldron was my colleague in Ethics & Public Life at Cornell his exuberant friendship and luminous intellect made our Thursday evening dinners thrilling reminders that philosophy at its best is exciting and surprising. Over the decades Robert K. Fullinwider has been loyal friend and philosophical conscience, reminding me—sometimes amidst cigarillo smoke or the fumes of burning NASCAR rubber—that our purpose after all was to make the best philosophy practical. I have discussed issues underlying the positions taken in the afterword with them each many times, and I hope and suspect that some of their contagious spirits are here too.

My combination of blindspots and confusions is of course my own unique contribution.

Preface to the First Edition

This is a book about the moral minimum—about the lower limits on tolerable human conduct, individual and institutional. It concerns the least that every person can demand and the least that every person, every government, and every corporation must be made to do. In this respect the bit of theory presented here belongs to one of the bottom corners of the edifice of human values. About the great aspirations and exalted ideals, saintly restraint and heroic fortitude and awesome beauties that enrich life, nothing appears here. They are not denied but simply deferred for other occasions.

This is a book only about where decent life starts. Unfortunately, for well over 1,000,000,000 human beings today the level of existence discussed here probably seems beyond reach, too far above them to be contemplated seriously. This need not be and must not continue. The original motivation for writing about basic rights was anger at lofty-sounding, but cheap and empty, promises of liberty in the absence of the essentials for people's actually exercising the promised liberty. Especially where I was angry, I have tried to be analytic. In order to lay out the structure of things carefully and clearly, I have modified traditional North Atlantic concepts where they are inadequate for the job. I have thus tried to make some contribution to the gradual evolution of a conception of rights that is not distorted by the blind spots of any one intellectual tradition. That I have my own blind spots goes without saying, and this is one of many reasons why more adequate conceptions of rights can grow only slowly and with the nurturance of many hands.

But a few things about rights are quite clear, and U.S. foreign policy has no excuse for continuing to ignore them while the debates on other points continue. In the faint hope that U.S. foreign policy might someday be brought into touch with global realities, I have concluded with a few of the most obvious implications of basic rights for current U.S. foreign policy.

This book is in every possible respect a product of the Center for Philosophy and Public Policy, on the Washington metropolitan area campus of the University of Maryland, at College Park. I am aware of no other research institute in the United States where politically informed philosophical analysis can be done on such a sustained basis. Peter G. Brown, the founding Director of the Center, had the administrative talent, foresight, and tenacity that led to the creation of the Center in 1976 and its subsequent strong development. The time for the research and writing that produced this book—all done at the Center—was made available by support from the Ford Foundation and the University of Maryland. I am grateful to Ford and Maryland for their investment of funds in an experimental institute, and to Peter Brown for the risky allocation of such a large proportion of that fledgling enterprise's total available time and energy to this study.

Virginia Smith has conquered and civilized many an untamed manuscript over the years, not only translating some from the original Amtrak squiggles but often serving as copy editor (and source of good cheer) as well as typist. Meanwhile, Elizabeth Cahoon and later Louise Collins have made it possible to keep everything else at the Center going in spite of me and my book.

Philosophy and politics, for all their differences, are haunted by the same two-headed monster: they are at once intensely lonely, and intensely public, undertakings. Only the individual philosopher can finally decide what to say—and the politician, what to do—but once it is said or done it is there for all who wish to criticize. It is not clear why any reasonable person would take up either. Those who cannot prevent themselves soon learn to be grateful for critic/friends who can save them from some of their own doubts and some of their own beliefs—people who have, in short, the rare qualities of good teachers.

In the days when the Center consisted only of Peter G. Brown and me, many a fruitful discussion was devoted not only to the substance of the issues about human rights that structure this book, but also to the even more difficult methodological issues about whether serious philosophical inquiry can be shaped so that it bears upon this or any of the rest of society's fundamental choices—and, if it can, in what way. Peter has played his chosen role of devil's advocate with insight, and with a certain unmistakable zest, and in the end not only tolerated but nurtured views he does not always share.

My next greatest debt is to the next philosopher to join the Center full-time, Douglas MacLean. There were times when he could see more potential in the early drafts of this book than I could, and he was a constant advocate of, and valuable contributor to, my not settling for less. Whatever the merits of this work, they are much greater than they would have been but for his philosophical suggestions, his moral support, and his serious commitment to expository style.

Besides the valuable support and criticism given by these two colleagues, I have received extensive and penetrating written criticisms and suggestions from Charles R. Beitz and Drew Christiansen. Others who took the trouble to read an entire draft of the manuscript at some stage and offered valuable help included Edward Johnson, Miriam Larkin, James W. Nickel, James C. Scott, Vivienne Shue, Jack Sullivan, and Mark Wicclair. And I have learned much from the hardy band of underpaid lobbyists for human rights in Washington, who are living proof that reflective people need not sell out politically and active people need not sell out intellectually. I regret that I have probably learned less from the good counsel of each than I might have.

The arguments in this book have also benefited greatly from discussion with diverse audiences in the U.S. and in Southeast Asia. In particular, I am grateful for having been able to present earlier versions of portions of the book to groups at the Law Faculty, University of Indonesia, Jakarta; the Law Center, University of the Philippines, Quezon City; the General Education Seminar, Columbia University; the University Seminar on Human Rights, Columbia University; the Project on Cultural Values and Population Policy, Institute of Society, Ethics and the Life Sciences; the Midwest Political Science Association; the New York Society for Philosophy and Public Affairs; and the Working Group on Human Rights and Security Assistance, Center for Philosophy and Public Policy, University of Maryland at College Park. An early version of portions of chapters 1 and 2 was circulated as Working Paper HRFP-1 by the Center for Philosophy and Public Policy. Particularly stirring was the experience of conducting seminars in Indonesia and the Philippines (at the expense of U.S. taxpayers through the U.S. International Communication Agency) and meeting with lonely defenders of human rights against client dictatorships also maintained partly at the expense of U.S. taxpayers—one of the smaller ironies produced by contradictions in U.S. foreign policy that are expensive at home and destructive abroad.

Vivienne was there before, will be there afterwards, and shared it all. I will not try to express my joy about that here.

BASIC RIGHTS

Through our work at the community level, we have sought to make the peasant and the worker aware that they have certain basic rights and that they are entitled to exercise those rights. To the military, that is the same thing as subversion.

Dom Alano Pena,
*Bishop of Maraba**

* Larry Rohter, "Brazil's Military, Activist Church Locked in Struggle," *Washington Post*, January 22, 1979, p. A14.

Introduction

The wisdom of a U.S. foreign policy that includes attention to "human rights" depends heavily upon which rights are in practice the focus of the attention. The major international documents on human rights include dozens of kinds of rights, often artificially divided into "civil and political" and "economic, social, and cultural" rights.[1] U.S. foreign policy probably could not, and almost certainly should not, concern itself with the performance of other governments in honoring every one of these internationally recognized human rights. The policy must in practice assign priority to some rights over others. It is not entirely clear so far either which rights are receiving priority or which rights ought to receive priority in U.S. foreign policy. The purpose of this book is to present the reasons why the most fundamental core of the so-called "economic rights," which I shall call subsistence rights, ought to be among those that receive priority. As background, a brief look at some divergent indications of what the priorities actually are now, may be useful.

The official position that is closest on the issue of subsistence rights to the one for which this book will present the reasons was enunciated as policy in 1977 by the then Secretary of State in a major address, "Human Rights Policy":

> Let me define what we mean by "human rights."
>
> *First, there is the right to be free from governmental violation of the integrity of the person.* Such violations include torture; cruel, inhuman, or degrading treatment or punishment; and arbitrary arrest or imprisonment. And they include denial of fair public trial, and invasion of the home.
>
> *Second, there is the right to the fulfillment of such vital needs as food, shelter, health care, and education.* We recognize that the fulfillment of this right will depend, in part, upon the stage of a nation's economic development. But we also know that this right can be violated by a Government's action or inaction—for example, through corrupt official processes which divert resources to an elite at the expense of the needy, or through indifference to the plight of the poor.

> *Third, there is the right to enjoy civil and political liberties.* . . .
>
> Our policy is to promote all these rights . . . I believe that, with work, all of these rights can become complementary and mutually reinforcing.[2]

The Secretary's list of "vital needs" that people have a right to have fulfilled extends even beyond what I shall include as subsistence rights.[3]

Below the level of the Secretary, however, the Department of State in 1979 suffers sharp contradictions. In particular, positions emanating from the Bureau of Legal Advisers are in opposition to policy as articulated by the Secretary and in opposition to the evolving position of the Bureau of Human Rights.[4] The advice to the President emanating from the legal advisers at the State Department is to take the same position taken by U.S. diplomats at the United Nations when the single list of human rights in the Universal Declaration was, at U.S. urging, separated into two independently ratifiable treaties: sharply split the list of rights into civil and political rights, and economic, social, and cultural rights, and declare *all* the economic, social, and cultural rights, no matter how vital their fulfillment, as less genuine rights with less binding duties.[5] It is the intellectual bankruptcy of the presuppositions of this position that this book is intended to show.

In contrast, the Bureau of Human Rights, in its annual reports on the status of rights under governments to which the U.S. government is either providing financial support in the form of grants or selling U.S. weapons and other militarily useful supplies and technologies, is gradually taking the central group of rights in the Vance trichotomy more seriously and treating these most fundamental economic and social rights more nearly equally with the most fundamental rights of other kinds. For example, the *Report on Human Rights Practices in Countries Receiving U.S. Aid* for 1978, in the case of each country, comments upon "Governmental Policies Relating to the Fulfillment of Such Vital Needs as Food, Shelter, Health Care and Education," and it gives in an appendix the positions of countries on the Physical Quality of Life Index (PQLI), which is one relatively straightforward way to quantify the extent to which a number of subsistence needs are being fulfilled.[6]

On the whole, the Department of State cannot be said to be taking rights to the fulfillment of basic economic needs very seriously. Issuing an official report that indicates, even if it does not stress, a particular government's failures to satisfy these rights is a very mild form of action, somewhat stronger than "quiet diplomacy" that criticizes violations. But "quiet diplomacy" can also be used to undercut the effects of public criticisms, and as long as major elements of the State Department deny that any economic rights are genuine, those who are criticized in public may be told in private not to worry about any serious actions being taken.

But should the Department of State, and U.S. foreign policy as finally shaped by State and others, take subsistence rights seriously and treat them as being as genuine as fundamental rights of other kinds are? This is the question I will try to answer. I will not be defending the thesis that all economic rights take priority over all other rights, a thesis as crude and implausible, I think, as its sometime rival, the thesis that all political rights take priority over all other rights. In fact, I am at least as interested in showing that although we face serious issues about priorities among rights, it is hopeless to construe the problem so broadly as a contest between the economic and the political, as I am to defend my own particular answer to the narrower problem that I think may be rationally resolvable. One of the strongest appeals I want to make is a general one in favor of slightly finer analyses that do not embrace, in one fell swoop, everything usually called economic rights and, in another, everything usually called political rights.

The common simple dichotomy between economic rights and political rights is misleading in several respects. Some rights seem to be neither economic nor political in any very strict sense. This includes not only the cultural and social rights that the partisans of political rights are inclined, in any case, to assign to the same limbo as economic rights, but also firmly entrenched rights like the right not to be tortured. Since it often needs to be asserted against governments, the right not to be tortured is frequently counted among the political rights. But most rights need to be asserted against governments, and this right can also be asserted against private individuals. Secretary Vance has enunciated official U.S. policy by means of the trichotomy quoted above. One section deals with what he (and former Congressman Donald Fraser before him) called the integrity of the person.[7] This section includes the right not to be tortured and is quite properly distinguished from both vital (economic) needs and civil and political liberties.

Other frequently asserted rights, such as the right to form labor unions or the right to own private property, are both economic and political. Each can plausibly be taken to be a liberty, and each concerns the basic structure of the economic system.

But the main reason for advocating a modestly greater degree of analysis than either the usual dichotomy, which unfortunately is enshrined in the two separate International Covenants that inadvisedly, I believe, try to split the subject-matter of the Universal Declaration, or the State Department's trichotomy is simply that even after "the integrity of the person" is separated out, the two lists remaining include items that range from the absolutely vital to the highly desirable but, if necessary, deferrable.

What I will try to show, then, is that at least one small set of what are normally counted as economic rights belongs among the rights with the highest priority. There are, if this is correct, some economic rights over which no other rights have priority, although some other rights, including some that are normally counted as political and that the Vance trichotomy treats as concerned with the integrity of the person, have equally high priority. If not all political rights are of this highest priority, some economic rights have priority over some political rights. This, I take it, is controversial enough, at least within the wealthy nations of the North Atlantic, to be worth discussing.

This book may seem to have a certain imbalance in its relative emphasis, respectively, on positive argument for the thesis that certain economic rights—namely, subsistence rights—have the highest priority and on responses to objections to the thesis. Only one of several possible lines of positive argument is given, and much attention is devoted to answering critics. This is for the following reason, which is partly strategic and partly philosophical. Virtually any argument in favor of a right will depend at bottom on emphasizing that the interest to which the right is asserted is genuinely important, fundamental, vital, indispensable, etc. But no matter how high the positive arguments are piled, the critic

can always respond by conceding it all but simply adding the objection, in effect, that recognizing the right in question would place too great a burden on all the other people with the duties to honor the right. Thus, disputes are avoided by conceding the right in theory, and costs are avoided by denying the right in practice.[8] The statement by Secretary Vance has laid the ground for such a move by following the acknowledgment of rights to the fulfillment of some vital needs with the proviso: "We recognize that the fulfillment of this right will depend, in part, upon the stage of a nation's economic development." Consequently, once some presumption has been established in favor of a right, the main task is to answer the objection that the duties involved would ask too much of others. So, I have concentrated here upon the task of responding to major variants of this potentially crippling objection.

Part I attempts to show that rights to three particular substances—subsistence, security, and liberty—are basic rights. The main conclusion is that subsistence rights are basic, but a valuable part of the case for taking subsistence to be the substance of a basic right is the demonstration that the same reasoning that justifies treating security and liberty as the substances of basic rights also supports treating subsistence as a basic right. The parallel with liberty is especially important, because the defenders of liberty usually neglect subsistence and the defenders of subsistence often neglect liberty, and each one-sided view provides its own special sustenance to the U.S. policies that support exploitative dictators who deny their subjects both liberty and subsistence. Part II then considers three of the difficulties that are most often urged against all assertions of economic rights, including—without sharply distinguishing—subsistence rights. These difficulties may be roughly summarized by the questions, what about the future poor? (chapter 4), what about me? (chapter 5), and what about the local poor? (chapter 6). Part III briefly illustrates a few of the simplest kinds of policy changes required by the recognition of subsistence rights.

·I·

THREE BASIC RIGHTS

·1·

SECURITY AND SUBSISTENCE

RIGHTS

A moral right provides (1) the rational basis for a justified demand (2) that the actual enjoyment of a substance be (3) socially guaranteed against standard threats. Since this is a somewhat complicated account of rights, each of its elements deserves a brief introductory explanation.[1] The significance of the general structure of a moral right is, however, best seen in concrete cases of rights, to which we will quickly turn.[2]

A right provides the rational basis for a justified demand. If a person has a particular right, the demand that the enjoyment of the substance of the right be socially guaranteed is justified by good reasons, and the guarantees ought, therefore, to be provided. I do not know how to characterize in general and in the abstract what counts as a rational basis or an adequate justification. I could say that a demand for social guarantees has been justified when good enough reasons have been given for it, but this simply transfers the focus to what count as good enough reasons. This problem pervades philosophy, and I could not say anything very useful about it without saying a lot. But to have a right is to be in a position to make demands of others, and to be in such a position is, among other things, for one's situation to fall under general principles that are good reasons why one's demands ought to be granted. A person who has a right has especially compelling reasons—especially deep principles—on his or her side. People can of course have rights without being able to explain them—

without being able to articulate the principles that apply to their cases and serve as the reasons for their demands. This book as a whole is intended to express a set of reasons that are good enough to justify the demands defended here. If the book is adequate, the principles it articulates are at least one specific example of how some particular demands can be justified. For now, I think, an example would be more useful than an abstract characterization.

The significance of being justified is very clear. Because a right is the basis for a justified demand, people not only may, but ought to, insist. Those who deny rights do so at their own peril. This does not mean that efforts to secure the fulfillment of the demand constituting a right ought not to observe certain constraints. It does mean that those who deny rights can have no complaint when their denial, especially if it is part of a systematic pattern of deprivation, is resisted. Exactly which countermeasures are justified by which sorts of deprivations of rights would require a separate discussion.

A right is the rational basis, then, for a justified demand. Rights do not justify merely requests, pleas, petitions. It is only because rights may lead to demands and not something weaker that having rights is tied as closely as it is to human dignity. Joel Feinberg has put this eloquently for the case of legal rights, or, in his Hohfeldian terminology, claim-rights:

> Legal claim-rights are indispensably valuable possessions. A world without claim-rights, no matter how full of benevolence and devotion to duty, would suffer an immense moral impoverishment. Persons would no longer hope for decent treatment from others on the ground of desert or rightful claim. Indeed, they would come to think of themselves as having no special claim to kindness or consideration from others, so that whenever even minimally decent treatment is forthcoming they would think themselves lucky rather than inherently deserving, and their benefactors extraordinarily virtuous and worthy of great gratitude. The harm to individual self-esteem and character development would be incalculable.
>
> A claim-right, on the other hand, can be urged, pressed, or rightly demanded against other persons. In appropriate

> circumstances the right-holder can "urgently, peremptorily, or insistently" call for his rights, or assert them authoritatively, confidently, unabashedly. Rights are not mere gifts or favors, motivated by love or pity, for which gratitude is the sole fitting response. A right is something that can be demanded or insisted upon without embarrassment or shame. When that to which one has a right is not forthcoming, the appropriate reaction is indignation; when it is duly given there is no reason for gratitude, since it is simply one's own or one's due that one received. A world with claim-rights is one in which all persons, as actual or potential claimants, are dignified objects of respect, both in their own eyes and in the view of others. No amount of love and compassion, or obedience to higher authority, or noblesse oblige, can substitute for those values.[3]

At least as much can be said for basic moral rights, including those that ought to, but do not yet, have legal protection.

That a right provides the rational basis for a justified demand for actual enjoyment is the most neglected element of many rights. A right does not yield a demand that it should be said that people are entitled to enjoy something, or that people should be promised that they will enjoy something. A proclamation of a right is not the fulfillment of a right, any more than an airplane schedule is a flight. A proclamation may or may not be an initial step toward the fulfillment of the rights listed. It is frequently the substitute of the promise in the place of the fulfillment.

The substance of a right is whatever the right is a right to. A right is not a right to enjoy a right—it is a right to enjoy something else, like food or liberty. We do sometimes speak simply of someone's "enjoying a right," but I take this to be an elliptical way of saying that the person is enjoying something or other, which is the substance of a right, and, probably, enjoying it *as* a right. Enjoying a right to, for example, liberty normally means enjoying liberty. It may also mean enjoying liberty in the consciousness that liberty is a right. Being a right is a status that various subjects of enjoyment have. Simply to enjoy the right itself, the status, rather than to enjoy the subject of the right would have to mean something like taking satisfaction that there is such a status and that something has that status. But ordinarily when we say someone is enjoying a right, we mean the person is enjoying the substance of the right.

Being socially guaranteed is probably the single most important aspect of a standard right, because it is the aspect that necessitates correlative duties.[4] A right is ordinarily a justified demand that some other people make some arrangements so that one will still be able to enjoy the substance of the right even if—actually, *especially* if—it is not within one's own power to arrange on one's own to enjoy the substance of the right. Suppose people have a right to physical security. Some of them may nevertheless choose to hire their own private guards, as if they had no right to social guarantees. But they would be justified, and everyone else is justified, in demanding that somebody somewhere make some effective arrangements to establish and maintain security. Whether the arrangements should be governmental or non-governmental; local, national, or international; participatory or non-participatory, are all difficult questions to which I may or may not be able to give definitive or conclusive answers here. But it is essential to a right that it is a demand upon others, however difficult it is to specify exactly which others.

And a right has been guaranteed only when arrangements have been made for people with the right to enjoy it. It is not enough that at the moment it happens that no one is violating the right.[5] Just as a proclamation of a right is not the fulfillment of a right and may in fact be either a step toward or away from actually fulfilling the right, an undertaking to create social guarantees for the enjoyment of various subjects of rights is by no means itself the guaranteeing and may or may not lead to real guarantees. But a right has not been fulfilled until arrangements are in fact in place for people to enjoy whatever it is to which they have the right. Usually, perhaps, the arrangements will take the form of law, making the rights legal as well as moral ones. But in other cases well-entrenched customs, backed by taboos, might serve better than laws—certainly better than unenforced laws.

The vague term "arrangements" is used in order to keep this general introductory explanation neutral on some controversial questions of interpretation. If the "arrangements" for fulfilling, for example, the duty to protect security are to be that every citizen is to be furnished a handgun and local neighborhoods are to elect residents to night patrols, then the right to security has not been socially guaranteed until the handguns have been distributed, the patrols elected, etc. (The right has still not been guaranteed if this arrangement will usually not work, as I would certainly assume would be the case.) On the other hand, if the "arrangements" are to have well-trained, tax-supported, professional police in adequate numbers, then the right has not been socially guaranteed until the police candidates have in fact been well-trained, enough public funds budgeted to hire an adequate force, etc.

I am not suggesting the absurd standard that a right has been fulfilled only if it is impossible for anyone to be deprived of it or only if no one is ever deprived of it. The standard can only be some reasonable level of guarantee. But if people who walk alone after dark are likely to be assaulted, or if infant mortality is 60 per 1000 live births, we would hardly say that enjoyment of, respectively, security or subsistence had yet been socially guaranteed. It is for the more precise specification of the reasonable level of social guarantees that we need the final element in the general structure of moral rights: the notion of a standard threat. This notion can be explained satisfactorily only after we look at some cases in detail, and I will take it up in the final section of this chapter.

That a right involves a rationally justified demand for social guarantees against standard threats means, in effect, that the relevant other people have a duty to create, if they do not exist, or, if they do, to preserve effective institutions for the enjoyment of what people have rights to enjoy.[6] From no theory like the present one is it possible to deduce precisely what sort of institutions are needed, and I have no reason to think that the same institutions would be most effective in all places and at all times. On its face, such universality of social institutions is most improbable, although some threats are indeed standard. What is universal, however, is a duty to make and keep effective arrangements, and my later threefold analysis of correlative duties will suggest that these arrangements must serve at least the functions of avoiding depriving people of the substances of their rights, protecting them against deprivation, and aiding them if they are nevertheless deprived of rights.[7] What I am now calling the duty to develop and preserve effective institutions for the fulfillment of rights is a summary of much of what is involved in performing all three of the duties correlative to typical rights, but to discuss duties now would be to jump ahead of the story.

Basic Rights

Nietzsche, who holds strong title to being the most misunderstood and most underrated philosopher of the last century, considered much of conventional morality—and not conceptions of rights only—to be an attempt by the powerless to restrain the powerful: an enormous net of fine mesh busily woven around the strong by the masses of the weak.[8] And he was disgusted by it, as if fleas were pestering a magnificent leopard or ordinary ivy were weighing down a soaring oak. In recoiling from Nietzsche's *assessment* of morality, many have dismissed too quickly his insightful *analysis* of morality. Moral systems obviously serve more than one purpose, and different specific systems serve some purposes more fully or better than others, as of course Nietzsche himself also recognized. But one of the chief purposes of morality in general, and certainly of conceptions of rights, and of basic rights above all, is indeed to provide some minimal protection against utter helplessness to those too weak to protect themselves. Basic rights are a shield for the defenseless against at least some of the more devastating and more common of life's threats, which include, as we shall see, loss of security and loss of subsistence. Basic rights are a restraint upon economic and political forces that would otherwise be too strong to be resisted. They are social guarantees against actual and threatened deprivations of at least some basic needs. Basic rights are an attempt to give to the powerless a veto over some of the forces that would otherwise harm them the most.

Basic rights are the morality of the depths. They specify the line beneath which no one is to be allowed to sink. This is part of the reason that basic rights are tied as closely to self-respect as Feinberg indicates legal claim-rights are.[9] And this helps to explain why Nietzsche found moral rights repugnant. His eye was on the heights, and he wanted to talk about how far some might soar, not about how to prevent the rest from sinking lower. It is not clear that we cannot do both.[10]

And it is not surprising that what is in an important respect the essentially negative goal of preventing or alleviating helplessness is a central purpose of something as important as conceptions of basic rights. For everyone healthy adulthood is bordered on each side by helplessness, and it is vulnerable to interruption by helplessness, temporary or permanent, at any time. And many of the people in the world now have very little control over their fates, even over such urgent matters as whether their own children live through infancy.[11] Nor is it surprising that although the goal is negative, the duties correlative to rights will turn out to include positive actions. The infant and the aged do not need to be assaulted in order to be deprived of health, life, or the capacity to enjoy active rights. The classic liberal's main prescription for the good life—do not interfere with thy neighbor—is the only poison they need. To be helpless they need only to be left alone. This is why avoiding the infliction of deprivation will turn out in chapter 2 not to be the only kind of duty correlative to basic rights.

Basic rights, then, are everyone's minimum reasonable demands upon the rest of humanity.[12] They are the rational basis for justified demands the denial of which no self-respecting person can reasonably be expected to accept. Why should anything be so important? The reason is that rights are basic in the sense used here only if enjoyment of them is essential to the enjoyment of all other rights. This is what is distinctive about a basic right. When a right is genuinely basic, any attempt to enjoy any other right by sacrificing the basic right would be quite literally self-defeating, cutting the ground from beneath itself. Therefore, if a right is basic, other, non-basic rights may be sacrificed, if necessary, in order to secure the basic right. But the protection of a basic right may not be sacrificed in order to secure the enjoyment of a non-basic right. It may not be sacrificed because it cannot be sacrificed successfully. If the right sacrificed is indeed basic, then no right for which it might be sacrificed can actually be enjoyed in the absence of the basic right. The sacrifice would have proven self-defeating.[13]

In practice, what this priority for basic rights usually means is that basic rights need to be established securely before other rights can be secured. The point is that people should be able to *enjoy*, or *exercise*, their other rights. The point is simple but vital. It is not merely that people should "have" their other rights in some merely legalistic or otherwise abstract sense compatible with being unable to make any use of the substance of the right. For example, if people have rights to free association, they ought not merely to "have" the rights to free association but also to enjoy their free association itself. Their freedom of association ought to be provided for by the relevant social institutions. This distinction between merely having a right and actually enjoying a right may seem a fine point, but it turns out later to be critical.

What is not meant by saying that a right is basic is that the right is more valuable or intrinsically more satisfying to enjoy than some other rights. For example, I shall soon suggest that rights to physical security, such as the right not to be assaulted, are basic, and I shall not include the right to publicly supported education as basic. But I do not mean by this to deny that enjoyment of the right to education is much greater and richer—more distinctively human, perhaps—than merely going through life without ever being assaulted. I mean only that, if a choice must be made, the prevention of assault ought to supersede the provision of education. Whether a right is basic is independent of whether its enjoyment is also valuable in itself. Intrinsically valuable rights may or may not also be basic rights, but intrinsically valuable rights can be enjoyed only when basic rights are enjoyed. Clearly few rights could be basic in this precise sense.

Security Rights

Our first project will be to see why people have a basic right to physical security—a right that is basic not to be subjected to murder, torture, mayhem, rape, or assault. The purpose in raising the questions why there are rights to physical security and why they are basic is not that very many people would seriously doubt either that there are rights to physical security or that they are basic. Although it is not unusual in practice for members of at least one ethnic group in a society to be physically insecure—to be, for example, much more likely than other people to be beaten by the police if arrested—few, if any, people would be prepared to defend in principle the contention that anyone lacks a basic right to physical security. Nevertheless, it can be valuable to formulate explicitly the presuppositions of even one's most firmly held beliefs, especially because these presuppositions may turn out to be general principles that will provide guidance in other areas where convictions are less firm. Precisely because we have no real doubt that rights to physical security are basic, it can be useful to see why we may properly think so.[14]

If we had to justify our belief that people have a basic right to physical security to someone who challenged this fundamental conviction, we could in fact give a strong argument that shows that if there are any rights (basic or not basic) at all, there are basic rights to physical security:

> No one can fully enjoy any right that is supposedly protected by society if someone can credibly threaten him or her with murder, rape, beating, etc., when he or she tries to enjoy the alleged right. Such threats to physical security are among the most serious and—in much of the world—the most widespread hindrances to the enjoyment of any right. If any right is to be exercised except at great risk, physical security must be protected. In the absence of physical security people are unable to use any other rights that society may be said to be protecting without being liable to encounter many of the worst dangers they would encounter if society were not protecting the rights.

A right to full physical security belongs, then, among the basic rights—not because the enjoyment of it would be more satisfying to someone who was also enjoying a full range of other rights, but because its absence would leave available extremely effective means for others, including the government, to interfere with or prevent the actual exercise of any other rights that were supposedly protected. Regardless of whether the enjoyment of physical security is also desirable for its own sake, it is desirable as part of the enjoyment of every other right. No rights other than a right to physical security can in fact be enjoyed if a right to physical security is not protected. Being physically secure is a necessary condition for the exercise of any other right, and guaranteeing physical security must be part of guaranteeing anything else as a right.

A person could, of course, always try to enjoy some other right even if no social provision were made to protect his or her physical safety during attempts to exercise the right. Suppose there is a right to peaceful assembly but it is not unusual for peaceful assemblies to be broken up and some of the participants beaten. Whether any given assembly is actually broken up depends largely on whether anyone else (in or out of government) is sufficiently opposed to it to bother to arrange an attack. People could still try to assemble, and they might sometimes assemble safely. But it would obviously be misleading to say that they are protected in their right to assemble if they are as vulnerable as ever to one of the most serious and general threats to enjoyment of the right, namely physical violence by other people. If they are as helpless against physical threats with the right "protected" as they would have been without the supposed protection, society is not actually protecting their exercise of the right to assembly.

So anyone who is entitled to anything as a right must be entitled to physical security as a basic right so that threats to his or her physical security cannot be used to thwart the enjoyment of the other right. This argument has two critical premises. The first is that everyone is entitled to enjoy something as a right.[15] The second, which further explains the first, is that everyone is entitled to the removal of the most serious and general conditions that would prevent or severely interfere with the exercise of whatever rights the person has. I take this second premise to be part of what is meant in saying that everyone is entitled to enjoy something as a right, as explained in the opening section of this chapter. Since this argument applies to everyone, it establishes a right that is universal.

Subsistence Rights

The main reason for discussing security rights, which are not very controversial, was to make explicit the basic assumptions that support the usual judgment that security rights are basic rights. Now that we have available an argument that supports them, we are in a position to consider whether matters other than physical security should, according to the same argument, also be basic rights. It will emerge that subsistence, or minimal economic security, which is more controversial than physical security, can also be shown to be as well justified for treatment as a basic right as physical security is—and for the same reasons.

By minimal economic security, or subsistence, I mean unpolluted air, unpolluted water, adequate food, adequate clothing, adequate shelter, and minimal preventive public health care. Many complications about exactly how to specify the boundaries of what is necessary for subsistence would be interesting to explore. But the basic idea is to have available for consumption what is needed for a decent chance at a reasonably healthy and active life of more or less normal length, barring tragic interventions. This central idea is clear enough to work with, even though disputes can occur over exactly where to draw its outer boundaries. A right to subsistence would not mean, at one extreme, that every baby born with a need for open-heart surgery has a right to have it, but it also would not count as adequate food a diet that produces a life expectancy of 35 years of fever-laden, parasite-ridden listlessness.

By a "right to subsistence" I shall always mean a right to at least subsistence. People may or may not have economic rights that go beyond subsistence rights, and I do not want to prejudge that question here. But people may have rights to subsistence even if they do not have any strict rights to economic well-being extending beyond subsistence. Subsistence rights and broader economic rights are separate questions, and I want to focus here on subsistence.

I also do not want to prejudge the issue of whether healthy adults are entitled to be provided with subsistence *only* if they cannot provide subsistence for themselves. Most of the world's malnourished, for example, are probably also diseased, since malnutrition lowers resistance to disease, and hunger and infestation normally form a tight vicious circle. Hundreds of millions of the malnourished are very young children. A large percentage of the adults, besides being ill and hungry, are also chronically unemployed, so the issue of policy toward healthy adults who refuse to work is largely irrelevant. By a "right to subsistence," then, I shall mean a right to subsistence that includes the provision of subsistence at least to those who cannot provide for themselves. I do not assume that no one else is also entitled to receive subsistence—I simply do not discuss cases of healthy adults who could support themselves but refuse to do so. If there is a right to subsistence in the sense discussed here, at least the people who cannot provide for themselves, including the children, are entitled to receive at least subsistence. Nothing follows one way or the other about anyone else.

It makes no difference whether the legally enforced system of property where a given person lives is private, state, communal, or one of the many more typical mixtures and variants. Under all systems of property people are prohibited from simply taking even what they need for survival. Whatever the property institutions and the economic system are, the question about rights to subsistence remains: if persons are forbidden by law from taking what they need to survive and they are unable within existing economic institutions and policies to provide for their own survival (and the survival of dependents for whose welfare they are responsible), are they entitled, as a last resort, to receive the essentials for survival from the remainder of humanity whose lives are not threatened?

The same considerations that support the conclusion that physical security is a basic right support the conclusion that subsistence is a basic right. Since the argument is now familiar, it can be given fairly briefly.

It is quite obvious why, if we still assume that there are some rights that society ought to protect and still mean by this the removal of the most serious and general hindrances to the actual enjoyment of the rights, subsistence ought to be protected as a basic right:

> No one can fully, if at all, enjoy any right that is supposedly protected by society if he or she lacks the essentials for a reasonably healthy and active life. Deficiencies in the means of subsistence can be just as fatal, incapacitating, or painful as violations of physical security. The resulting damage or death can at least as decisively prevent the enjoyment of any right as can the effects of security violations. Any form of malnutrition, or fever due to exposure, that causes severe

and irreversible brain damage, for example, can effectively prevent the exercise of any right requiring clear thought and may, like brain injuries caused by assault, profoundly disturb personality. And, obviously, any fatal deficiencies end all possibility of the enjoyment of rights as firmly as an arbitrary execution.

Indeed, prevention of deficiencies in the essentials for survival is, if anything, more basic than prevention of violations of physical security. People who lack protection against violations of their physical security can, if they are free, fight back against their attackers or flee, but people who lack essentials, such as food, because of forces beyond their control, often can do nothing and are on their own utterly helpless.[16]

The scope of subsistence rights must not be taken to be broader than it is. In particular, this step of the argument does not make the following absurd claim: since death and serious illness prevent or interfere with the enjoyment of rights, everyone has a basic right not to be allowed to die or to be seriously ill. Many causes of death and illness are outside the control of society, and many deaths and illnesses are the result of very particular conjunctions of circumstances that general social policies cannot control. But it is not impractical to expect some level of social organization to protect the minimal cleanliness of air and water and to oversee the adequate production, or import, and the proper distribution of minimal food, clothing, shelter, and elementary health care. It is not impractical, in short, to expect effective management, when necessary, of the supplies of the essentials of life. So the argument is: when death and serious illness could be prevented by different social policies regarding the essentials of life, the protection of any human right involves avoidance of fatal or debilitating deficiencies in these essential commodities. And this means fulfilling subsistence rights as basic rights. This is society's business because the problems are serious and general. This is a basic right because failure to deal with it would hinder the enjoyment of all other rights.

Thus, the same considerations that establish that security rights are basic for everyone also support the conclusion that subsistence rights are basic for everyone. It is not being claimed or assumed that security and subsistence are parallel in all, or even very many, respects. The only parallel being relied upon is that guarantees of security and guarantees of subsistence are equally essential to providing for the actual exercise of any other rights. As long as security and subsistence are parallel in this respect, the argument applies equally to both cases, and other respects in which security and subsistence are not parallel are irrelevant.

It is not enough that people merely happen to be secure or happen to be subsisting. They must have a right to security and a right to subsistence—the continued enjoyment of the security and the subsistence must be socially guaranteed. Otherwise a person is readily open to coercion and intimidation through threats of the deprivation of one or the other, and credible threats can paralyze a person and prevent the exercise of any other right as surely as actual beatings and actual protein/calorie deficiencies can.[17] Credible threats can be reduced only by the actual establishment of social arrangements that will bring assistance to those confronted by forces that they themselves cannot handle.

Consequently the guaranteed security and guaranteed subsistence are what we might initially be tempted to call "simultaneous necessities" for the exercise of any other right. They must be present at any time that any other right is to be exercised, or people can be prevented from enjoying the other right by deprivations or threatened deprivations of security or of subsistence. But to think in terms of simultaneity would be largely to miss the point. A better label, if any is needed, would be "inherent necessities." For it is not that security from beatings, for instance, is separate from freedom of peaceful assembly but that it always needs to accompany it. Being secure from beatings if one chooses to hold a meeting is part of being free to assemble. If one cannot safely assemble, one is not free to assemble. One is, on the contrary, being coerced not to assemble by the threat of the beatings.

The same is true if taking part in the meeting would lead to dismissal by the only available employer when employment is the only source of income for the purchase of food. Guarantees of security and subsistence are not added advantages over and above enjoyment of the right to assemble. They are essential parts of it. For this reason it would be misleading to construe security or subsistence—or the substance of any other basic right—merely as "means" to the enjoyment of all other rights. The enjoyment of security and subsistence is an essential part of the enjoyment of all other rights. Part of what it means to enjoy any other right is to be able to exercise that right without, as a consequence, suffering the actual or threatened loss of one's physical security or one's subsistence. And part of what it means to be able to enjoy any other right is not to be prevented from exercising it by lack of security or of subsistence. To claim to guarantee people a right that they are in fact unable to exercise is fraudulent, like furnishing people with meal tickets but providing no food.

What is being described as an "inherent necessity" needs to be distinguished carefully from a mere means to an end. If A is a means to end B and it is impossible to reach the end B without using the means A, it is perfectly correct to say that A is necessary for B. But when I describe the enjoyment of physical security, for example, as necessary for the enjoyment of a right to assemble, I do not intend to say merely that enjoying security is a means to enjoying assembly. I intend to say that part of the meaning of the enjoyment of a right of assembly is that one can assemble in physical security. Being secure is an essential component of enjoying a right of assembly, so that there is no such thing as a situation in which people do have social guarantees for assembly and do not have social guarantees for security. If they do not have guarantees that they can assemble in security, they have not been provided with assembly as a right. They must assemble and merely hope for the best, because a standard threat to assembling securely has not been dealt with. The fundamental argument is that when one fully grasps what an ordinary right is, and especially which duties are correlative to a right, one can see that the guarantee of certain things (as basic rights) is part of—is a constituent of—is an essential component of—the establishment of the conditions in which the right can actually be enjoyed. These conditions include the prevention of the thwarting of the enjoyment of the right by any "standard threat," at the explanation of which we must soon look.

A final observation about the idea of subsistence rights is, however, worth making here: subsistence rights are in no way an original, new, or advanced idea. If subsistence rights seem strange, this is more than likely because Western liberalism has had a blind spot for severe economic need.[18] Far from being new or advanced, subsistence rights are found in traditional societies that are often treated by modern societies as generally backward or primitive.

James C. Scott has shown that some of the traditional economic arrangements in Southeast Asia that were in other respects highly exploitative nevertheless were understood by both patrons and clients—to use Scott's terminology—to include rights to subsistence on the part of clients and duties on the part of patrons not only to forbear from depriving clients of subsistence but to provide assistance to any clients who were for any reason deprived:

> If the need for a guaranteed minimum is a powerful motive in peasant life, one would expect to find institutionalized patterns in peasant communities which provide for this need. And, in fact, it is above all within the village—in the patterns of social control and reciprocity that structure daily conduct—where the subsistence ethic finds social expression. The principle which appears to unify a wide array of behavior is this: "All village families will be guaranteed a minimal subsistence niche insofar as the resources controlled by villagers make this possible." Village egalitarianism in this sense is conservative not radical; it claims that all should have a place, a living, not that all should be equal. . . . Few village studies of Southeast Asia fail to remark on the informal social controls which act to provide for the minimal needs of the village poor. The position of the better-off appears to be legitimized only to the extent that their resources are employed in ways which meet the broadly defined welfare needs of villagers.[19]

As Benedict J. Kerkvliet, also writing about an Asian society, put it: "A strong patron-client relationship was a kind of all-encompassing insurance policy whose coverage, although not total and infinitely reliable, was as comprehensive as a poor family could get."[20]

Many reasons weigh in favor of the elimination of the kind of patron-client relationships that Scott and Kerkvliet have described—no one is suggesting that they should be, or could be, preserved. The point here is only that the institutionalization of subsistence rights is in no way tied to some utopian future "advanced" society. On the contrary, the real question is whether modern nations can be as humane as, in *this* regard, many traditional villages are. If we manage, we may to a considerable extent merely have restored something of value that has for some time been lost in our theory and our practice.

STANDARD THREATS

Before we turn over the coin of basic rights and consider the side with the duties, we need to establish two interrelated points about the rights side. One point concerns the final element in the account of the general structure of all rights, basic and non-basic, which is the notion of standard threats as the targets of the social guarantees for the enjoyment of the substance of a right. The other point specifically concerns basic rights and the question whether the reasoning in favor of treating security and subsistence as the substances of basic rights does not generate an impractically and implausibly long list of things to which people will be said to have basic rights. The two points are interrelated because the clearest manner by which to establish that the list of basic rights must, on the contrary, be quite short is to invoke the fact that the social guarantees required by the structure of a right are guarantees, not against all possible threats, but only against what I will call standard threats. In the end we will find a supportive coherence between the account of basic rights and the account of the general structure of most moral rights. We may begin by reviewing the reasons for taking security and subsistence to be basic rights and considering whether the same reasons would support treating many other things as basic rights. Answering that question will lead us to see the role and importance of a conception of standard threats.

Why, then, according to the argument so far, are security and subsistence basic rights? Each is essential to a normal healthy life. Because the actual deprivation of either can be so very serious—potentially incapacitating, crippling, or fatal—even the threatened deprivation of either can be a powerful weapon against anyone whose security or subsistence is not in fact socially guaranteed. People who cannot provide for their own security and subsistence and who lack social guarantees for both are very weak, and possibly helpless, against any individual or institution in a position to deprive them of anything else they value by means of threatening their security or subsistence. A fundamental purpose of acknowledging any basic rights at all is to prevent, or to eliminate, insofar as possible the degree of vulnerability that leaves people at the mercy of others. Social guarantees of security and subsistence would go a long way toward accomplishing this purpose.

Security and subsistence are basic rights, then, because of the roles they play in both the enjoyment and the protection of all other rights. Other rights could not be enjoyed in the absence of security or subsistence, even if the other rights were somehow miraculously protected in such a situation. And other rights could in any case not be protected if security or subsistence could credibly be threatened. The enjoyment of the other rights requires a certain degree of physical integrity, which is temporarily undermined, or eliminated, by deprivations of security or of subsistence. Someone who has suffered exposure or a beating is incapable of enjoying the substances of other rights, although only temporarily, provided he or she receives good enough care to recover the use of all essential faculties.

But as our earlier discussion of helplessness made clear, either the actual or the credibly threatened loss of security or subsistence leaves a person vulnerable to any other deprivations the source of the threat has in mind. Without security or subsistence one is helpless, and consequently one may also be helpless to protect whatever can be protected only at the risk of security or subsistence. Therefore, security and subsistence must be socially guaranteed, if any rights are to be enjoyed. This makes them basic rights.

In the construction of any philosophical argument, a principal challenge is to establish what needs to be established without slipping into the assertion of too much. By "too much" I mean a conclusion so inflated that, even if it is not a reduction to absurdity in the strict sense, it nevertheless strains credulity. The argument for security rights and subsistence rights may seem to suffer this malady, which might be called the weakness of too much strength. Specifically, the argument may be feared to have implicit implications that people have rights to an unlimited number of things, in addition to security and subsistence, that it is difficult to believe that people actually could justifiably demand of others.

Now it is true that we have no reason to believe that security and subsistence are the only basic rights, and chapter 3 is devoted to the question of whether some kinds of liberties are also basic rights. But as we shall see in that chapter, it is quite difficult to extend the list of basic rights, and we face little danger that the catalogue of basic rights will turn out to be excessively long. Before it becomes perhaps painfully obvious from the case of liberty, it may be helpful to see why in the abstract the list of basic rights is sharply limited even if it may have some members not considered here.

The structure of the argument that a specific right is basic may be outlined as follows, provided we are careful about what is meant by "necessary":

1. Everyone has a right to something.
2. Some other things are necessary for enjoying the first thing as a right, whatever the first thing is.
3. Therefore, everyone also has rights to the other things that are necessary for enjoying the first as a right.

Since this argument abstracts from the substance of the right assumed in the first premise, it is based upon what it normally means for anything to be a right or, in other words, upon the concept of a right. So, if the argument to establish the substances of basic rights is summarized by saying that these substances are the "other things . . . necessary" for enjoying any other right, it is essential to interpret "necessary" in the restricted sense of "made essential by the very concept of a right." The "other things" include not whatever would be convenient or useful, but only what is indispensable to anything else's being enjoyed as a right. Nothing will turn out to be necessary, in this sense, for the enjoyment of any right unless it is also necessary for the enjoyment of every right and is, for precisely this reason, qualified to be the substance of a basic right.

Since the concept of a right is a profoundly Janus-faced concept, this conceptual necessity can be explained both from the side of the bearer of the right and, as we will see more fully in chapter 2, from the side of the bearers of the correlative duties. The content of the basic rights is such that for the bearer of any right (basic or non-basic) to pursue its fulfillment by means of the trade-off of the fulfillment of a basic right is self-defeating, and such that for the bearer of duties to claim to be fulfilling the duties correlative to any right in spite of not fulfilling the duties correlative to a basic right is fraudulent. But both perspectives can be captured more concretely by the notion of common, or ordinary, and serious but remediable threats or "standard threats," which was introduced earlier as the final element in the explanation of the structure of a right.[21] Certainly from the viewpoint of the bearer of a right it would be false or misleading to assert that a right had been fulfilled unless in the enjoyment of the substance of that right, a person also enjoyed protection against the threats that could ordinarily be expected to prevent, or hinder to a major degree, the enjoyment of the initial right assumed. And certainly from the viewpoint of the bearers of the correlative duties it would be false or misleading to assert that a right had been honored unless social guarantees had been established that would prevent the most common and serious threats from preventing or acutely hindering the enjoyment of the substance of the right. On the side of duties this places especially heavy emphasis upon preventing standard threats, which, as we will see in chapter 2, is the joint function of the fulfillment of duties to avoid depriving and duties to protect against deprivation.

But the measure of successful prevention of thwarting by ordinary and serious but remediable threats is not utopian. People are neither entitled to social guarantees against every conceivable threat, nor entitled to guarantees against ineradicable threats like eventual serious illness, accident, or death. Another way to indicate the restricted scope of the argument, then, is as follows. The argument rests upon what might be called a transitivity principle for rights: If everyone has a right to *y*, and the enjoyment of *x* is necessary for the enjoyment of *y*, then everyone also has a right to *x*. But the necessity in question is analytic. People also have rights—according to this argument—only to the additional substances made necessary by the paired concepts of a right and its correlative duties. It is analytically necessary that if people are to be provided with a right, their enjoyment of the substance of the right must be protected against the typical major threats. If people are as helpless against ordinary threats as they would be on their own, duties correlative to a right are not being performed. Precisely what those threats are, and which it is feasible to counter, are of course largely empirical questions, and the answers to both questions will change as the situation changes.[22] In the argument for acknowledging security and subsistence as basic rights I have taken it to be fairly evident that the erosion of the enjoyment of any assumed right by deficiencies in subsistence is as common, as serious, and as remediable at present as the destruction of the enjoyment of any assumed right by assaults upon security.

What is, for example, eradicable changes, of course, over time. Today, we have very little excuse for allowing so many poor people to die of malaria and more excuse probably for allowing people to die of cancer. Later perhaps we will have equally little excuse to allow deaths by many kinds of cancer, or perhaps not. In any case, the measure is a realistic, not a utopian, one, and what is realistic can change. Chapter 4 returns to the question of what is realistic now in the realm of subsistence, and consideration of this concrete case will probably also provide the clearest understanding of what constitutes an ordinary and serious but remediable threat.

We noticed in an earlier section that one fundamental purpose served by acknowledging basic rights at all is, in Camus' phrase, that we "take the victim's side," and the side of the potential victims. The honoring of basic rights is an active alliance with those who would otherwise be helpless against natural and social forces too strong for them. A basic right has, accordingly, not been honored until people have been provided rather firm protection—what I am calling "social guarantees"—for enjoying the substance of their basic rights. What I am now stressing is that this protection need neither be ironclad nor include the prevention of every imaginable threat.

But the opposite extreme is to offer such weak social guarantees that people are virtually as vulnerable with their basic rights "fulfilled" as they are without them. The social guarantees that are part of any typical right need not provide impregnable protection against every imaginable threat, but they must provide effective defenses against predictable remediable threats. To try to count a situation of unrelieved vulnerability to standard threats as the enjoyment of basic rights by their bearers or the fulfillment of these rights by the bearers of the correlative duties is to engage in double-speak, or to try to behave as if concepts have no boundaries at all. To allow such practices to continue is to acquiesce in not only the violation of rights but also the destruction of the concept of rights.

Insofar as it is true that moral rights generally, and not basic rights only, include justified demands for social guarantees against standard threats, we have an interesting theoretical result. The fulfillment of both basic and non-basic moral rights consists of effective, but not infallible, social arrangements to guard against standard threats like threats to physical security and threats to economic security or subsistence. One way to characterize the substances of basic rights, which ties the account of basic rights tightly to the account of the structure of moral rights generally, is this: the substance of a basic right is something the deprivation of which is one standard threat to rights generally. The fulfillment of a basic right is a successful defense against a standard threat to rights generally. This is precisely why basic rights are basic. That to which they are rights is needed for the fulfillment of all other rights. If the substance of a basic right is not socially guaranteed, attempts actually to enjoy the substance of other rights remain open to a standard threat like the deprivation of security or subsistence. The social guarantees against standard threats that are part of moral rights generally *are the same as* the fulfillment of basic rights.[23] This is why giving less priority to any basic right than to normal non-basic rights is literally impossible.

·2·

CORRELATIVE DUTIES

"Negative" Rights and "Positive" Rights

Many Americans would probably be initially inclined to think that rights to subsistence are at least slightly less important than rights to physical security, even though subsistence is at least as essential to survival as security is and even though questions of security do not even arise when subsistence fails. Much official U.S. government rhetoric routinely treats all "economic rights," among which basic subsistence rights are buried amidst many non-basic rights, as secondary and deferrable, although the fundamental enunciation of policy concerning human rights by the then Secretary of State did appear to represent an attempt to correct the habitual imbalance.[1] Now that the same argument in favor of basic rights to both aspects of personal survival, subsistence and security, is before us, we can examine critically some of the reasons why it sometimes appears that although people have basic security rights, the right, if any, to even the physical necessities of existence like minimal health care, food, clothing, shelter, unpolluted water, and unpolluted air is somehow less urgent or less basic.

Frequently it is asserted or assumed that a highly significant difference between rights to physical security and rights to subsistence is that they are respectively "negative" rights and "positive" rights.[2] This position, which I will now try to refute, is considerably more complex than it at first appears. I will sometimes refer to it as the position that subsistence rights are *positive* and *therefore secondary*. Obviously taking the position involves holding that subsistence rights are positive in some respect in which security rights are negative and further claiming that this difference concerning positive/negative is a good enough reason to assign priority to negative rights over positive rights. I will turn shortly to the explanation of this assumed positive/negative distinction. But first I want to lay out all the premises actually needed by the position that subsistence rights are positive and therefore secondary, although I need to undercut only some—strictly speaking, only one—of them in order to cast serious doubt upon the position's conclusions.

The alleged lack of priority for subsistence rights compared to security rights assumes:

1. The distinction between subsistence rights and security rights is (a) sharp and (b) significant.[3]
2. The distinction between positive rights and negative rights is (a) sharp and (b) significant.
3. Subsistence rights are positive.
4. Security rights are negative.

I am not suggesting that anyone has ever laid out this argument in all the steps it actually needs. On the contrary, a full statement of the argument is the beginning of its refutation—this is an example of the philosophical analogue of the principle that sunlight is the best antiseptic.[4]

In this chapter I will concentrate on establishing that premises 3 and 4 are both misleading. Then I will suggest a set of distinctions among duties that accurately transmits the insight distorted by 3 and 4. Insofar as 3 and 4 are inaccurate, considerable doubt is cast upon 2, although it remains possible that someone can specify some sharply contrasting pair of rights that actually are examples of 2.[5] I will not directly attack premise 1.[6]

Now the basic idea behind the general suggestion that there are positive rights and negative rights seems to have been that one kind of rights (the positive ones) require other people to act positively—to "do something"—whereas another kind of rights (the negative ones) require other people merely to refrain from acting in certain ways—to do nothing that violates the rights. For example, according to this picture, a right to subsistence would be positive because it would require other people, in the last resort, to supply food or clean air to those unable to find, produce, or buy their own; a right to security would be negative because it would require other people merely to refrain from murdering or otherwise assaulting those with the right. The underlying distinction, then, is between acting and refraining from acting; and positive rights are those with correlative duties to act in certain ways and negative rights are those with correlative duties to refrain from acting in certain ways. Therefore, the moral significance, if any, of the distinction between positive rights and negative rights depends upon the moral significance, if any, of the distinction between action and omission of action.[7]

The ordinarily implicit argument for considering rights to subsistence to be secondary would, then, appear to be basically this. Since subsistence rights are positive and require other people to do more than negative rights require—perhaps more than people can actually do—negative rights, such as those to security, should be fully guaranteed first. Then, any remaining resources could be devoted, as long as they lasted, to the positive—and perhaps impossible—task of providing for subsistence. Unfortunately for this argument, neither rights to physical security nor rights to subsistence fit neatly into their assigned sides of the simplistic positive/negative dichotomy. We must consider whether security rights are purely negative and then whether subsistence rights are purely positive. I will try to show (1) that security rights are more "positive" than they are often said to be, (2) that subsistence rights are more "negative" than they are often said to be, and, given (1) and (2), (3) that the distinctions between security rights and subsistence rights, though not entirely illusory, are too fine to support any weighty conclusions, especially the very weighty conclusion that security rights are basic and subsistence rights are not.

In the case of rights to physical security, it may be possible *to avoid violating* someone's rights to physical security yourself by merely refraining from acting in any of the ways that would constitute violations. But it is impossible *to protect* anyone's rights to physical security without taking, or making payments toward the taking of, a wide range of positive actions. For example, at the very least the protection of rights to physical security necessitates police forces; criminal courts; penitentiaries; schools for training police, lawyers, and guards; and taxes to support an enormous system for the prevention, detection, and punishment of violations of personal security.[8] All these activities and institutions are attempts at providing social guarantees for individuals' security so that they are not left to face alone forces that they cannot handle on their own. How much more than these expenditures one thinks would be necessary in order for people actually to be reasonably secure (as distinguished from merely having the cold comfort of knowing that the occasional criminal is punished after someone's security has already been violated) depends on one's theory of violent crime, but it is not unreasonable to believe that it would involve extremely expensive, "positive" programs. Probably no one knows how much positive action would have to be taken in a contemporary society like the United States significantly to reduce the levels of muggings, rapes, murders, and other assaults that violate personal security, and in fact to make people reasonably secure.

Someone might suggest that this blurs rights to physical security with some other type of rights, which might be called rights-to-be-protected-against-assaults-upon-physical-security. According to this distinction, rights to physical security are negative, requiring others only to refrain from assaults, while rights-to-be-protected-against-assaults-upon-physical-security are positive, requiring others to take positive steps to prevent assaults.

Perhaps if one were dealing with some wilderness situation in which individuals' encounters with each other were infrequent and irregular, there might be some point in noting to someone: I am not asking you to cooperate with a system of guarantees to protect me from third parties, but only to refrain from attacking me yourself. But in an organized society, insofar as there were any such things as rights to physical security that were distinguishable from some other rights-to-be-protected-from-assaults-upon-physical-security, no one would have much interest in the bare rights to physical security. What people want and need, as even Mill partly recognized, is the protection of their rights.[9] Insofar as this frail distinction holds up, it is the rights-to-be-protected-against-assaults that any reasonable person would demand from society. A demand for physical security is not normally a demand simply to be left alone, but a demand to be protected against harm.[10] It is a demand for positive action, or, in the words of our initial account of a right, a demand for social guarantees against at least the standard threats.

So it would be very misleading to say simply that physical security is a negative matter of other people's refraining from violations. Ordinarily it is instead a matter of some people refraining from violations and of third parties being prevented from violations by the positive steps taken by first and second parties. The "negative" refraining may in a given case be less significant than the "positive" preventing—it is almost never the whole story. The end-result of the positive preventative steps taken is of course an enforced refraining from violations, not the performance of any positive action. The central core of the right is a right that others not act in certain ways. But the mere core of the right indicates little about the social institutions needed to secure it, and the core of the right does not contain its whole structure. The protection of "negative rights" requires positive measures, and therefore their actual enjoyment requires positive measures. In any imperfect society enjoyment of a right will depend to some extent upon protection against those who do not choose not to violate it.

Rights to subsistence too are in their own way considerably more complex than simply labeling them "positive" begins to indicate. In fact, their fulfillment involves at least two significantly different types of action. On the one hand, rights to subsistence sometimes do involve correlative duties on the part of others to provide the needed commodities when those in need are helpless to secure a supply for themselves, as, for example, the affluent may have a duty to finance food supplies and transportation and distribution facilities in the case of famine. Even the satisfaction of subsistence rights by such positive action, however, need not be any more expensive or involve any more complex governmental programs than the effective protection of security rights would. A food stamp program, for example, could be cheaper or more expensive than, say, an anti-drug program aimed at reducing muggings and murders by addicts. Which program was more costly or more complicated would depend upon the relative dimensions of the respective problems and would be unaffected by any respect in which security is "negative" and subsistence is "positive." Insofar as any argument for giving priority to the fulfillment of "negative rights" rests on the assumption that actually securing "negative rights" is usually cheaper or simpler than securing "positive rights," the argument rests on an empirical speculation of dubious generality.

The other type of action needed to fulfill subsistence rights is even more difficult to distinguish sharply from the action needed to fulfill security rights. Rights to physical subsistence often can be completely satisfied without the provision by others of any commodities to those whose rights are in question. All that is sometimes necessary is to protect the persons whose subsistence is threatened from the individuals and institutions that will otherwise intentionally or unintentionally harm them. A demand for the fulfillment of rights to subsistence may involve not a demand to be provided with grants of commodities but merely a demand to be provided some opportunity for supporting oneself.[11] The request is not to be supported but to be allowed to be self-supporting on the basis of one's own hard work.

What is striking is the similarity between protection against the destruction of the basis for supporting oneself and protection against assaults upon one's physical security. We can turn now to some examples that clearly illustrate that the honoring of subsistence rights sometimes involves action no more positive than the honoring of security rights does. Some cases in which all that is asked is protection from harm that would destroy the capacity to be self-supporting involve threats to subsistence of a complexity that is not usually noticed with regard to security, although the adequate protection of security would involve analyses and measures more complex than a preoccupation with police and prisons. The complexity of the circumstances of subsistence should not, however, be allowed to obscure the basic fact that essentially all that is being asked in the name of subsistence rights in these examples is protection from destructive acts by other people.

Subsistence Rights and Scarcity

The choice of examples for use in an essentially theoretical discussion that does nevertheless have implications for public policy presents an intractable dilemma. Hypothetical cases and actual cases each have advantages and disadvantages that are mirror images of each other's. A description of an actual case has the obvious advantage that it is less susceptible to being tailored to suit the theoretical point it is adduced to support, especially if the description is taken from the work of someone other than the proponent of the theoretical point. Its disadvantage is that if the description is in fact an inaccurate account of the case in question, the mistake about what is happening in that case may appear to undercut the theoretical point that is actually independent of what is happening in any single case. Thus the argument about the theoretical point may become entangled in arguments about an individual instance that was at most only one supposed illustration of the more general point.

Hypothetical cases are immune to disputes about whether they accurately depict an independent event, since, being explicitly hypothetical, they are not asserted to correspond to any one real case. But precisely because they are not constrained by the need to remain close to an independent event, they may be open to the suspicion of having been streamlined precisely in order to fit the theoretical point they illustrate and having thereby become atypical of actual cases.

The only solution I can see is to offer, when a point is crucial, an example of each kind. It is vital to the argument of this book to establish that many people's lack of the substance of their subsistence rights—of, that is, the means of subsistence like food—is a deprivation caused by standard kinds of threats that could be controlled by some combination of the mere restraint of second parties and the maintenance of protective institutions by first and third parties, just as the standard threats that deprive people of their physical security could be controlled by restraint and protection against non-restraint. So I will start with a hypothetical case in order to clarify the theoretical point before introducing the partly extraneous complexity of actual events, and then I will quote a description of some actual current economic policies that deprive people of subsistence. The hypothetical case is at the level of a single peasant village, and the actual case concerns long-term national economic strategies. Anyone familiar with the causes of malnutrition in underdeveloped countries today will recognize that the following hypothetical case is in no way unusual.[12]

Suppose the largest tract of land in the village was the property of the descendant of a family that had held title to the land for as many generations back as anyone could remember. By absolute standards this peasant was by no means rich, but his land was the richest in the small area that constituted the universe for the inhabitants of this village. He grew, as his father and grandfather had, mainly the black beans that are the staple (and chief—and adequate—source of protein) in the regional diet. His crop usually constituted about a quarter of the black beans marketed in the village. Practically every family grew part of what they needed, and the six men he hired during the seasons requiring extra labor held the only paid jobs in the village—everyone else just worked his own little plot.

One day a man from the capital offered this peasant a contract that not only guaranteed him annual payments for a 10-year lease on his land but also guaranteed him a salary (regardless of how the weather, and therefore the crops, turned out—a great increase in his financial security) to be the foreman for a new kind of production on his land. The contract required him to grow flowers for export and also offered him the opportunity, which was highly recommended, to purchase through the company, with payments in installments, equipment that would enable him to need to hire only two men. The same contract was offered to, and accepted by, most of the other larger landowners in the general region to which the village belonged.

Soon, with the sharp reduction in supply, the price of black beans soared. Some people could grow all they needed (in years of good weather) on their own land, but the families that needed to supplement their own crop with purchases had to cut back their consumption. In particular, the children in the four families headed by the laborers who lost their seasonal employment suffered severe malnutrition, especially since the parents had originally worked as laborers only because their own land was too poor or too small to feed their families.

Now, the story contains no implication that the man from the capital or the peasants-turned-foremen were malicious or intended to do anything worse than single-mindedly pursue their own respective interests. But the outsider's offer of the contract was one causal factor, and the peasant's acceptance of the contract was another causal factor, in producing the malnutrition that would probably persist, barring protective intervention, for at least the decade the contract was to be honored. If the families in the village had rights to subsistence, their rights were being violated. Society, acting presumably by way of the government, ought to protect them from a severe type of active harm that eliminates their ability even to feed themselves.

But was anyone actually harming the villagers, or were they simply suffering a regrettable decline in their fortunes? If someone was violating their rights, who exactly was the violator? Against whom specifically should the government be protecting them? For, we normally make a distinction between violating someone's rights and allowing someone's rights to be violated while simply minding our own business. It makes a considerable difference—to take an example from another set of basic rights—whether I myself assault someone or I merely carry on with my own affairs while allowing a third person to assault someone when I could protect the victim and end the assault. Now, I may have a duty not to allow assaults that I can without great danger to myself prevent or stop, as well as a duty not to assault people myself, but there are clearly two separable issues here. And it is perfectly conceivable that I might have the one duty (to avoid harming) and not the other (to protect from harm by third parties), because they involve two different types of action.[13]

The switch in land-use within the story might then be described as follows. Even if one were willing to grant tentatively that the villagers all seemed to have rights to subsistence, some of which were violated by the malnutrition that some suffered after the switch in crops, no individual or organization can be identified as the violator: not the peasant-turned-foreman, for example, because—let us assume—he did not foresee the "systemic" effects of his individual choice; not the business representative from the capital because—let us assume—although he was knowledgeable enough to know what would probably happen, it would be unrealistically moralistic to expect him to forgo honest gains for himself and the company he represented because the gains had undesired, even perhaps regretted, "side-effects"; not any particular member of the governmental bureaucracy because—let us assume—no one had been assigned responsibility for maintaining adequate nutrition in this particular village. The local peasant and the business representative were both minding their own business in the village, and no one in the government had any business with this village. The peasant and the representative may have attended to their own affairs while harm befell less fortunate villagers, but allowing harm to occur without preventing it is not the same as directly inflicting it yourself. The malnutrition was just, literally, unfortunate: bad luck, for which no one could fairly be blamed. The malnutrition was, in effect, a natural disaster—was, in the obnoxious language of insurance law, an act of God. Perhaps the village was, after all, becoming overpopulated.[14]

But, of course, the malnutrition resulting from the new choice of crop was not a natural disaster. The comforting analogy does not hold. The malnutrition was a social disaster. The malnutrition was the product of specific human decisions permitted by the presence of specific social institutions and the absence of others, in the context of the natural circumstances, especially the scarcity of land upon which to grow food, that were already given before the decisions were made. The harm in question, the malnutrition, was not merely allowed to happen by the parties to the flower-growing contract. The harm was partly caused by the requirement in the contract for a switch away from food, by the legality of the contract, and by the performance of the required switch in crops. If there had been no contract or if the contract had not required a switch away from food for local consumption, there would have been no malnutrition as things were going.[15] In general, when persons take an action that is sufficient in some given natural and social circumstances to bring about an undesirable effect, especially one that there is no particular reason to think would otherwise have occurred, it is perfectly normal to consider their action to be one active cause of the harm. The parties to the contract partly caused the malnutrition.

But the society could have protected the villagers by countering the initiative of the contracting parties in any one of a number of ways that altered the circumstances, and the absence of the appropriate social guarantees is another cause of the malnutrition. Such contracts could, for example, have already been made illegal. Or they could have been allowed but managed or taxed in order to compensate those who would otherwise predictably be damaged by them. Exactly what was done would be, *for the most part*, an economic and political question.[16] But it is possible to have social guarantees against the malnutrition that is repeatedly caused in such standard, predictable ways.

Is a right to subsistence in such a case, then, a positive right in any important ways that a right to security is not? Do we actually find a contrast of major significance? No. As in the cases of the threats to physical security that we normally consider, the threat to subsistence is human activity with largely predictable effects.[17] Even if, as we tend to assume, the motives for deprivations of security tend to be vicious while the motives for deprivations of subsistence tend to be callous, the people affected usually need protection all the same. The design, building, and maintenance of institutions and practices that protect people's subsistence against the callous—and even the merely over-energetic—is no more and no less positive than the conception and execution of programs to control violent crimes against the person. It is not obvious which, if either, it is more realistic to hope for or more economical to pursue. It is conceivable, although I doubt if anyone really knows, that the two are more effectively and efficiently pursued together. Neither looks simple, cheap, or "negative."

This example of the flower contract is important in part because, at a very simple level, it is in fact typical of much of what is happening today among the majority of the people in the world, who are poor and rural, and are threatened by forms of "economic development" that lower their own standard of living.[18] But it is also important because, once again in a very simple way, it illustrates the single most critical fact about rights to subsistence; where subsistence depends upon tight supplies of essential commodities (like food), a change in supply can have, often by way of intermediate price effects, an indirect but predictable and devastating effect on people's ability to survive. A change in supply can transport self-supporting people into helplessness and, if no protection against the change is provided, into malnutrition or death. Severe harm to some people's ability to maintain themselves can be caused by changes in the use to which other people put vital resources (like land) they control. In such cases even someone who denied that individuals or organizations have duties to supply commodities to people who are helpless to obtain them for themselves, might grant that the government ought to execute the society's duty of protecting people from having their ability to maintain their own survival destroyed by the actions of others. If this protection is provided, there will be much less need later to provide commodities themselves to compensate for deprivations.

What transmits the effect in such cases is the local scarcity of the vital commodity. Someone might switch thousands of acres from food to flowers without having any effect on the diet of anyone else where the supply of food was adequate to prevent a significant price rise in response to the cut in supply. And it goes without saying that the price rises are vitally important only if the income and wealth of at least some people is severely limited, as of course it is in every society, often for the rural majority. It is as if an abundant supply sometimes functions as a sponge to absorb the otherwise significant effect on other people, but a tight supply (against a background of limited income and wealth) sometimes functions as a conductor to transmit effects to others, who feel them sharply.

It is extremely difficult merely to mind one's own business amidst a scarcity of vital commodities. It is illusory to think that this first commandment of liberalism can always be obeyed. The very scarcity draws people into contact with each other, destroys almost all area for individual maneuver, and forces people to elbow each other in order to move forward. The tragedy of scarcity, beyond the deprivations necessitated by the scarcity itself, is that scarcity tends to make each one's gain someone else's loss. One can act for oneself only by acting against others, since there is not enough for all. Amidst abundance of food a decision to grow flowers can be at worst a harmless act and quite likely a socially beneficial one. But amidst a scarcity of food, due partly to a scarcity of fertile land, an unmalicious decision to grow flowers can cause death—unless there are social guarantees for adequate nutrition. A call for social guarantees for subsistence in situations of scarcity is not a call for intervention in what were formerly private affairs.

Two Theses About Economic Deprivation

Our actual case is an economic strategy now being followed in a considerable number of Latin American nations. As already mentioned, it also differs from the hypothetical, but very typical, example of the flower contract by being a matter of macroeconomic strategy. And the actual case differs as well in a respect that is crucial to some of the policy recommendations in chapter 7: the precise relation between the economic decisions and the resulting deprivations of subsistence. In order to be able to characterize this relation accurately we need to draw an important distinction before we look at the description of the case.

"Systemic" deprivation—deprivation resulting from the confluence of many contributing factors—of the kind already seen in the case of the flower contract may or may not be systematic. That is, deprivations that are the result of the interaction of many factors may be (a) accidental—even unpredictable—and relatively easily remediable coincidences in an economic system for which there is no plan or for which the plan does not include the deprivations; or the deprivations may be (b) inherent—perhaps predictable—and acceptable, whether or not positively desirable, elements in a consciously adopted or endorsed economic plan or policy. In the former case they are not systematic but, as I will call them, *accidental*, and in the latter case they are systematic or, I will say, *essential*: essential elements in the strategy that produces them. Essential deprivations can be eliminated only by eliminating the strategy that requires them. Accidental deprivations can be eliminated by making less fundamental changes while retaining the basic strategy, since they are not inherent in the strategy.

The thesis that particular deprivations are accidental often seems to be the explanation recommended by common sense, although we may not ordinarily think explicitly in terms of this distinction. Well-informed people are aware, for example, that the "Brazilian miracle" has left large numbers of the poorest Brazilians worse off than ever, that the Shah's "White Revolution" made relatively small inroads upon malnutrition and infant mortality, that President and Prime Minister Marcos's "New Society" is a similar failure, etc.[19] But, especially if one assumes that those who dictate economic strategy are reasonable and well-intentioned people, one may infer that these repeated failures to deal with the basic needs of the most powerless are, in spite of the regularity with which they recur, unfortunate but unpredictable byproducts of fundamentally benevolent, or anyhow enlightened, economic plans.

Alternatively, one might infer that the continuing deprivations are inherent in the economic strategies being used, and that would lead to the second kind of thesis: that the continuance of the deprivations is essential to the economic strategies. Since this thesis may be less familiar, I would like to quote an example of it at some length. Because this particular formulation is intended by the analyst, Richard Fagen, to apply only to Latin America (with the exception of Cuba and, of course, to varying degrees in various different countries), a thesis concerning essential deprivation would naturally have to be formulated differently for Africa, Asia, and elsewhere. The following is intended, then, only as one good example, formulated in specifics to cover only a single region, of the second type of thesis:

> —Aggregate economic growth in Latin America over the past decade has been above world averages. The per capita income in the region now exceeds $1,000. . . .
>
> —The actual situation with respect to income distribution and social equity is, in general, appalling. Fifty percent of the region's citizens have incomes of less than $200 per year; one-third receive less than $100. The top five percent of the population controls one-third of the total income. The emphasis on industrialization and export-led growth almost everywhere reinforces and accelerates the neglect of agriculture—at least agriculture in basic foodstuffs for domestic consumption. . . .
>
> —Related to the income distribution and social equity issues is the problem of unemployment. In some countries as many as one out of three persons in the working-age population is unable to find a job of any sort. . . .
>
> —The kind of development that has taken place is reflected in the structure of external indebtedness. Current estimates are that the countries of the region now owe approximately $80 billion in public and publicly guaranteed debt alone. . . .
>
> —The Latin American state is everywhere involved in economic development and management. It is usually the prime borrower abroad, often an important investor at home, frequently a chief partner of foreign capital, and al-

ways a source of regulations on everything from wages to import quotas. State capitalism has come to Latin America with a vengeance, and even the governments that claim to give the freest play to market forces are in fact constantly intervening to establish the rules under which "free markets" will be allowed to operate.

The above sketch of Latin American development aids in understanding the nature of contemporary authoritarianism. . . . The linkages are complex, but very largely determine the public policies that will be followed. Creditors want to be paid in dollars or in other international currencies. The international financial institutions are critically concerned with the debtor country's balance of payments. A sharp increase in exports—acknowledged to be the best way to achieve a more favorable balance and repay the debt—is very difficult to achieve in the short run. Also difficult to accomplish is a dramatic increase in capital inflows—except by borrowing even more.

This leaves imports as a natural target for those who would save hard currency. But in order to cut imports—or at least that sector of imports that is least important to ruling elites, economic managers, and most national and international business—mass consumption must be restricted. Since quotas and tariffs are seen as inappropriate policy instruments, to a large extent consumer demand must be managed through restrictions on the real purchasing power of wage-earners—and increases in unemployment.

When coupled with cutbacks in government expenditures (typically in public works and welfare-enhancing subsidies), a huge proportion of the adjustment burden is thus transferred to the working class. In an inflationary economy, the proportional burden is even greater. Needless to say, where minimal possibilities of political expression exist, this kind of adjustment medicine does not go down easily. Repression of trade unions as effective organizations and workers as individuals is in this sense "necessary" for those in charge of managing the economy and for their friends and allies abroad.

Many of these same persons may decry the extreme and

> brutal measures used in countries such as Brazil, Uruguay, Argentina, Bolivia and Chile to establish and maintain control over the labor movement and hold wages well below the inflationary spiral. Some may even take comfort in the fact that, once the most extreme measures have been used, a partial relaxation of control seems possible at a later date. But minimal honesty requires that the repression in both its physical and financial dimensions be seen as an organic aspect of what is now the prevailing mode of economic development in Latin America. Social and economic human rights do not fare well in such an environment. . . .
>
> What has evolved in Latin America (and by implication in some other areas of the Third World) is a political-economic model that has *no* historical precedent in the now more developed capitalist world. For lack of a more concise phrase, this model can be called illiberal state capitalism, a situation in which state intervention in the economy is substantial, but governmental policies tend to reinforce rather than soften or ameliorate income inequalities, class distinctions, and regional disequilibria.[20]

I take it to be evident that in various countries throughout the world deprivation is sometimes accidental and sometimes essential, and that one has no reason at all to expect that either thesis is applicable to all cases. Each continent, or rather each country, and often each regime, must be analyzed on its own. But it is fairly clear that current regimes include a number of instances of what Fagen calls "illiberal state capitalism" and that in these cases people are deprived of subsistence (and liberty) by their own government's choice of economic strategy.

In this brief theoretical work I obviously cannot attempt to establish under which governments deprivations of subsistence are essential and under which they are accidental, although I have already mentioned some cases I take to be strikingly evident. Illiberal state capitalism is only one prominent source of strategies of essential deprivation, and for us here the main point is the distinction between essential and accidental deprivation, whatever the detailed explanation for which one occurs. Especially when we come in chapter 7 to look at specific recommendations for U.S. foreign policy, it will be crucial to keep this underlying distinction between these two explanations of deprivation in mind. In most cases the formulation of policy must take the source of deprivations into account. A government that engages in essential deprivation—that follows an economic strategy in which deprivations of subsistence are inherent in the strategy—fails to fulfill even any duty merely to avoid depriving. Such systematic violation of subsistence rights is surely intolerable. Such a government is a direct and immediate threat to its own people, and they are entitled to resist it in order to defend themselves. But I am getting ahead of the theoretical story.

We turned to the actual case of illiberal state capitalism in Latin America with its macroeconomic strategies of essential deprivation, as well as to the hypothetical case of the village flower contract, which is a kind of contract encouraged by—but not dependent upon—strategies of essential deprivation, in order to see some illustrations of the inaccuracy of the philosophical doctrine that subsistence rights, like all economic rights, are positive, because their fulfillment consists largely of actively providing people with commodities like food. From these cases it is now, I hope, quite clear that the honoring of subsistence rights may often in no way involve transferring commodities to people, but may instead involve preventing people's being deprived of the commodities or the means to grow, make, or buy the commodities. Preventing such deprivations will indeed require what can be called positive actions, especially protective and self-protective actions. But such protection against the deprivation of subsistence is in all major respects like protection against deprivations of physical security or of other rights that are placed on the negative side of the conventional negative/positive dichotomy. I believe the whole notion that there is a morally significant dichotomy between negative rights and positive rights is intellectually bankrupt—that premise 2, as stated in the first section of this chapter, is mistaken. The cases we have considered establish at the very least that the dichotomy distorts when it is applied to security rights and subsistence rights—that premises 3 and 4 were mistaken. The latter is all that needed to be shown.

Avoidance, Protection, and Aid

Still, it is true that sometimes fulfilling a right does involve transferring commodities to the person with the right and sometimes it merely involves not taking commodities away. Is there not some grain of truth obscured by the dichotomy between negative and positive rights? Are there not distinctions here that it is useful to make?

The answer, I believe, is: yes, there are distinctions, but they are not distinctions between rights. The useful distinctions are among duties, and there are no one-to-one pairings between kinds of duties and kinds of rights. The complete fulfillment of each kind of right involves the performance of multiple kinds of duties. This conceptual change has, I believe, important practical implications, although it will be only in chapter 7 that the implications can begin to be illustrated. In the remainder of this chapter I would like to tender a very simple tripartite typology of duties. For all its own simplicity, it goes considerably beyond the usual assumption that for every right there is a single correlative duty, and suggests instead that for every basic right—and many other rights as well—there are three types of duties, all of which must be performed if the basic right is to be fully honored but not all of which must necessarily be performed by the same individuals or institutions. This latter point opens the possibility of distributing each of the three kinds of duty somewhat differently and perhaps confining any difficulties about the correlativity of subsistence rights and their accompanying duties to fewer than all three kinds of duties.

So I want to suggest that with every basic right, three types of duties correlate:

I. Duties to *avoid* depriving.
II. Duties to *protect* from deprivation.
III. Duties to *aid* the deprived.

This may be easier to see in the case of the more familiar basic right, the right to physical security (the right not to be tortured, executed, raped, assaulted, etc.). For every person's right to physical security, there are three correlative duties:

I. Duties not to eliminate a person's security—duties to *avoid* depriving.
II. Duties to protect people against deprivation of security by other people—duties to *protect* from deprivation.

III. Duties to provide for the security of those unable to provide for their own—duties to *aid* the deprived.

Similarly, for every right to subsistence there are:

I. Duties not to eliminate a person's only available means of subsistence—duties to *avoid* depriving.
II. Duties to protect people against deprivation of the only available means of subsistence by other people—duties to *protect* from deprivation.
III. Duties to provide for the subsistence of those unable to provide for their own—duties to *aid* the deprived.

If this suggestion is correct, the common notion that *rights* can be divided into rights to forbearance (so-called negative rights), as if some rights have correlative duties only to avoid depriving, and rights to aid (so-called positive rights), as if some rights have correlative duties only to aid, is thoroughly misguided. This misdirected simplification is virtually ubiquitous among contemporary North Atlantic theorists and is, I think, all the more pernicious for the degree of unquestioning acceptance it has now attained. It is duties, not rights, that can be divided among avoidance and aid, and protection. And—this is what matters—every basic right entails duties of all three types. Consequently the attempted division of rights, rather than duties, into forbearance and aid (and protection, which is often understandably but unhelpfully blurred into avoidance, since protection is partly, but only partly, the enforcement of avoidance) can only breed confusion.

It is impossible for any basic right—however "negative" it has come to seem—to be fully guaranteed unless all three types of duties are fulfilled. The very most "negative"-seeming right to liberty, for example, requires positive action by society to protect it and positive action by society to restore it when avoidance and protection both fail. This by no means implies, as I have already mentioned, that all three types of duties fall upon everyone else or even fall equally upon everyone upon whom they do fall. Although this tripartite analysis of duties is, I believe, perfectly general, I will focus here upon the duties correlative to subsistence rights: subsistence duties.

The Generality of the Tripartite Analysis

However, perhaps a brief word on the general issue is useful before turning to a fairly detailed analysis of the threefold duties correlative to the rights that most concern us: subsistence rights. Obviously theses of three ascending degrees of generality might be advanced:

All subsistence rights involve threefold correlative duties.

All basic rights involve threefold correlative duties.

Most moral rights involve threefold correlative duties.

I subscribe to all three theses, and I believe that the remainder of this book offers significant support for all three. But naturally the support will be most thorough for the first thesis and least thorough for the last. For the most part I am content to leave matters at that, because the only point that I am concerned fully to establish is the priority of subsistence rights, that is, their equal priority with all other basic rights. Consequently, the arguments need, strictly speaking, to be thorough only for subsistence rights. But a contrasting pair of observations are also in order.

On the one hand, the argument here is from the particular to the general, not the converse. It is not because I assumed that normal rights involve some, or threefold, duties that I concluded that subsistence rights involve some, and threefold, duties. I explored subsistence rights, as we are about to do, and found that they can be fully accounted for only by means of admitting three kinds of correlated duties. I looked at the same time at security rights and, as we will do in chapter 3, at rights to liberty and found again that an adequate explanation involves all three kinds of multiply interrelated duties, thus coming to suspect that all basic rights, at the very least, require the same tripartite analysis of the duty side of the coin.

On the other hand, on the basis of these detailed examinations of these three rights I am indeed tempted to recommend that the most general thesis be made analytically true, that is, that any right not involving the threefold duties be acknowledged to be an exceptional case. If the account of a right given at the beginning of chapter 1 were made a strict definition, then it would do just this. If a right provides the rational basis for a justified demand that the actual enjoyment of the substance of the right be socially guaranteed against standard threats, then a right provides the rational basis for insisting upon the performance, as needed, of duties to avoid, duties to protect, and duties to aid, as they will shortly be explained. This picture does seem to me to fit all the standard cases of moral rights.[21] If, however, someone can give clear counter-examples to the final step of generalization (the move from duties for basic rights to duties for moral rights generally), I can see little cause for concern, provided the admission of rights that lack some kinds of correlative duties, to the realm of non-basic rights, is not allowed to devalue the coinage of rights generally.

Subsistence Duties

The first type of subsistence duty is neither a duty to provide help nor a duty to protect against harm by third parties but is the most nearly "negative" or passive kind of duty that is possible: a duty simply not to take actions that deprive others of a means that, but for one's own harmful actions, would have satisfied their subsistence rights or enabled them to satisfy their own subsistence rights, where the actions are not necessary to the satisfaction of one's own basic rights and where the threatened means is the only realistic one.[22] Duties to avoid depriving require merely that one refrain from making an unnecessary gain for oneself by a means that is destructive for others.

Part of the relation between these subsistence duties to avoid depriving (type I) and subsistence duties to protect from deprivation (type II) is quite straightforward. If everyone could be counted upon voluntarily to fulfill duties to avoid, duties to protect would be unnecessary. But since it would be naive to expect everyone to fulfill his or her duties to avoid and since other people's very survival is at stake, it is clearly necessary that some individuals or institution have the duty of enforcing the duty to avoid. The duty to protect is, then, in part a secondary duty of enforcing the primary duty of avoiding the destruction of people's means of subsistence. In this respect it is analogous to, for example, the duty of the police to enforce the duty of parents not to starve their children.

The natural institution in many societies to have the task of enforcing those primary duties that need enforcement is the executive branch of some level of government, acting on behalf of the members of society other than the offending individuals or institutions. Which level of government takes operating responsibility is largely a practical matter and might vary among societies. Where the source of harm is, for example, a transnational corporation, protection may need to be provided by the home government or even by multilateral government action.[23] But clearly if duties to avoid depriving people of their last means of subsistence are to be taken seriously, some provision must be made for enforcing this duty on behalf of the rest of humanity upon those who would not otherwise fulfill it. Perhaps it would be worth considering nongovernmental enforcement institutions as the bearers in some cases of the secondary duty to protect, but the primary institution would normally appear to be the government of the threatened person's own nation. It is normally taken to be a central function of government to prevent irreparable harm from being inflicted upon some members of society by other individual members, by institutions, or by interactions of the two. It is difficult to imagine why anyone should pay much attention to the demands of any government that failed to perform this function, if it were safe to ignore its demands.

Duties to aid (type III) are in themselves fairly complicated, and only one kind will be discussed here. At least three sub-categories of duties to aid need to be recognized. What they have in common is the requirement that resources be transferred to those who cannot provide for their own survival. First are duties to aid (III-1) that are attached to certain roles or relationships and rest therefore upon only those who are in a particular role or relationship and are borne toward only those other persons directly involved. Some central cases are the duties of parents toward their own young children and the duties of grown children toward their own aged parents. Naturally, important issues can arise even with regard to such relatively clear duties as the duty to provide food to the helplessly young and to the helplessly old, but I have nothing to add here regarding these duties, which are not universal. By their not being universal I mean that although all parents may normally have certain duties toward their own children, no child can justifiably hold that all people, or even all parents, have *this* sort of duty toward it. All people may of course have other duties toward the child, including universal ones, and possibly including one of the other two sub-categories of duties to aid that are to be mentioned next.

The only difference between the second and third sub-categories of duties to aid is the source of the deprivation because of which aid is needed. In the second case (III-2) the deprivation is the result of failures to fulfill duties to avoid depriving and duties to protect from deprivation—some people have acted in such a way as to eliminate the last available means of subsistence for other people and the responsible government has failed to protect the victims. Thus, the need for assistance is the result of a prior twofold failure to perform duties, and the victims have been harmed by both actions and omissions of actions by other people.

In the third case (III-3) the deprivation is not the result of failures in duty and, in just this sense, the deprivation is "natural," that is, the deprivation suffered is not a case of harm primarily caused by other people. The clearest case of a natural deprivation calling for aid is a natural disaster like a hurricane or an earthquake. As always, questions arise at the borderline between cases—for example, was the death toll increased because the weather bureau or civil defense organization failed to protect with timely warnings? But uncontroversial central cases in which no human beings are much to blame are perfectly familiar, even if not so frequent as we might like to believe.

Where supplies of the necessities of life, or of the resources needed to grow or make the necessities, are scarce, duties of types I and II take on increased importance. The results of the fulfillment only of I and II would already be dramatic in the poorer areas of the world, in which most of the earth's inhabitants eke out their existences. It is easy to underestimate the importance of these two kinds of subsistence duties, which together are intended to prevent deprivation. But to eliminate the only realistic means a person has for obtaining food or other physical necessities is to cause that person, for example, the physical harm of malnutrition or of death by starvation. When physical harm but not death is caused, the effect of eliminating the only means of support can be every degree as serious as the effect of a violation of physical security by means of a bodily assault. The physical effects of malnutrition can be irreversible and far more profound than the physical effects of many an assault in fact are. And when starvation is caused, the ultimate effect of eliminating the only means of support is precisely the same as the effect of murder. Those who are helpless in the face of insuperable obstacles to their continued existence are at least one level worse off than those who are defenseless in the face of assaults upon their physical security. The defenseless will at least be able to maintain themselves if they are provided with protection against threatening assaults. If protected but otherwise left alone, they will manage. But the helpless, if simply left alone—even if they should be protected against all assaults upon their security—will die for lack of the means of subsistence. They will merely, in Coleridge's phrase, "die so slowly that none call it murder."[24]

Now of course differences between deprivations of security and deprivations of subsistence can also be noted, as already mentioned. Normally in a violation of physical security by means of assault or murder, the human agent's central intention is indeed to bring about, or at least includes bringing about, the physical harm or death that is caused for the victim, although obviously one also can injure or kill inadvertently. In the case of the elimination of the means of physical subsistence, the human agent's central intention may at least sometimes be focussed on other consequences of his or her action, such as the increased security of income that would result from a multi-year salaried contract to grow flowers rather than a precarious annual attempt to grow food. The harm to the victims may be entirely unintended. Such difference in intention between the two cases is undoubtedly relevant to any assessment of the moral stature respectively of the two persons who partly cause the harm in the two cases. But for the two victims the difference between intended physical harm and unintended physical harm may matter little, since the harmfulness of the action taken may be the same in both cases and may be even greater where unintended.

Nevertheless, it may be arbitrary to assign a role of *the* perpetrator to any one person or group in a case of the deprivation of subsistence. The deprivations in question may in fact be "systemic": the product of the joint workings of individual actions and social institutions no one of which by itself caused the harm. But what follows from this is not that no one is responsible (since everyone is). What follows is that the distinction between duties to avoid (I) and duties to protect (II), which is relatively clear in the abstract, blurs considerably in concrete reality.[25] The division of labor between individual restraint and institutional protection can be worked out in any of several acceptable ways, the full details of which would go considerably beyond the scope of this book, but between the two kinds of duties, individuals ought not to be deprived by the actions (intentional or unintentional) of others of all hope of sustaining themselves.

This means, however, that duties to protect (II) are not simply secondary duties to enforce the primary duty to avoid (I). We can mark as II-1 the duties to protect that are merely secondary duties to enforce the duty to avoid. But duties to protect also encompass the design of social institutions that do not leave individuals with duties to avoid, the fulfillment of which would necessitate superhuman qualities. This task of constructing institutions can be marked as II-2. In the original example of the flower contract, some would judge that the peasant receiving the offer to switch out of food production, in the circumstances stipulated, could reasonably have been expected to foresee the consequences of the switch and to refrain from making it. But it is probably more realistic neither to expect him to have the information and comprehension necessary to foresee the consequences nor to expect him to choose not to reduce his own insecurity—and certainly an example could readily be constructed in which an individual could not reasonably be expected to know in advance the probable bad consequences for others of his or her action or to give them more weight than improvements in his or her own precarious situation.[26]

For such cases, in which individual restraint would be too much to ask, the duty to protect (II-2) includes the design of laws and institutions that avoid reliance upon unreasonable levels of individual self-control. Many actions that are immoral ought nevertheless not to be made illegal. But one of the best possible reasons for making an act illegal is its contributing to harm as fundamental as the deprivation of someone's last available means of subsistence. And a number of intermediate steps between total prohibition and complete tolerance of an action are possible, such as tax laws that create disincentives of various strengths against the kind of action that would contribute to the deprivation of subsistence from others and create alternative sources of increased economic security for oneself. Social institutions must, at the very least, be designed to enable ordinary human beings, who are neither saints nor geniuses, to do each other a minimum of serious harm.

In sum, then, we find that the fulfillment of a basic right to subsistence involves at least the following kinds of duties:

I. To avoid depriving.
II. To protect from deprivation
   1. By enforcing duty (I) and
   2. By designing institutions that avoid the creation of strong incentives to violate duty (I).
III. To aid the deprived
   1. Who are one's special responsibility,
   2. Who are victims of social failures in the performance of duties (I), (II-1), (II-2) and
   3. Who are victims of natural disasters.

The Systematic Interdependence of Duties

Fulfillment of a basic right (and, I think, of most other moral rights as well) requires, then, performance by some individuals or institutions of each of these three general kinds of correlative duties. Duties to avoid depriving possibly come closest to failing to be essential, because duties to protect provide for the enforcement of duties to avoid. Even if individuals, organizations, and governments were otherwise inclined to violate rights to security, for example, by failing to fulfill their respective duties to avoid, forceful fulfillment of duties to protect by whomever they fell upon—presumably a national government—could probably produce behavior in compliance with duties to avoid. But reliance on duties to protect rather than duties to avoid would constitute heavy reliance on something like national police power rather than self-restraint by individuals, corporations, and lower-level governments, and would involve obvious disadvantages even if—probably, especially if—the police power were adequate actually to enforce duties to avoid upon a generally reluctant society. Unfortunately this much power to protect would also be enormous power to deprive, which is a lesson about police that even dictators sometimes have to learn the hard way.

Since duties to avoid and duties to protect taken together have only one purpose, to prevent deprivations, the reverse of what was just described is obviously also possible: if everyone who ought to fulfill duties to avoid did so, performance of duties to protect might not be necessary. Law-enforcement agencies could perhaps be disbanded in a society of restrained organizational and individual behavior. But although reliance entirely upon duties to protect is undesirable even if possible, a safe complete reliance upon duties to avoid is most improbable in the absence of at least minimal performance of duties to protect. Organizations and individuals who will voluntarily avoid deprivation that would otherwise be advantageous to them because they know that their potential victims are protected, cannot be expected to behave in the same way when they know their potential victims are without protection.

The general conclusions about duties to avoid and duties to protect, then, are, first, that strictly speaking it is essential for the guarantee of any right only that either the one or the other be completely fulfilled, but, second, that for all practical purposes it is essential to insist upon the fulfillment of both, because complete reliance on either one alone is probably not feasible and, in the case of duties to protect, almost certainly not desirable.

What division of labor is established by one's account of duties between self-restraint and restraint by others, such as police forces, will obviously have an enormous effect upon the quality of life of those living in the social system in question. I do not want to pursue the questions involved in deciding upon the division, except to note that if either duties to avoid or duties to protect are construed too narrowly, the other duty then becomes unrealistically broad. For example, if a government, in the exercise of its duty to protect, fails to impose constraints upon agribusinesses designed to prevent them from creating malnutrition, the prevention of malnutrition will then depend upon the self-restraint of the agribusinesses. But much evidence suggests that individual agribusinesses are unwilling or unable to take into account the nutritional effect of their decisions about the use of land, local credit and capital, water, and other resources. This is especially true if the agribusiness is producing export crops and most especially if it is investing in a foreign country, the nutritional level of whose people is easily considered irrelevant.[27] If indeed a particular type of corporation has demonstrated an inability to forgo projects that produce malnutrition, given their setting, it is foolish to rely on corporate restraint, and whichever governments have responsibility to protect those who are helpless to resist the corporation's activity—host governments, home government or both—will have to fulfill their duties to protect. If, on the other hand, the corporations would restrain themselves, the governments could restrain them less. How to work this out is difficult and important. The present point is simply that between the bearers of the two duties, the job of preventing deprivation ought to get done, if there is a right not to be deprived of whatever is threatened. And the side that construes its own role too narrowly, if it actually has the power to act, may be as much at fault for contributing to the violation of rights as the side that fails to take up all the resulting slack.

However, as I have already indicated, the duty to protect ought not to be understood only in terms of the maintenance of law-enforcement, regulatory, and other closely related agencies. A major and more constructive part of the duty to protect is the duty to design social institutions that do not exceed the capacity of individuals and organizations, including private and public corporations, to restrain themselves. Not only the kinds of acute threats of deprivation that police can prevent, but the kinds of chronic threats that require imaginative legislation and, sometimes, long-term planning fall under the duty to protect.[28]

Nevertheless, it is duties to aid that often have the highest urgency, because they are often owed to persons who are suffering the consequences of failures to fulfill both duties to avoid and duties to protect, that is, they are duties of type III-2. These people will have been totally deprived of their rights to subsistence if they are then not aided either. This greater urgency does not, of course, mean that duties to aid are more compelling overall than the first two types of duty, and indeed it is specifically against duties to aid that complaints that the correlative duties accompanying subsistence rights are too burdensome may seem most plausible. It is important to notice that to the extent that duties to avoid and to protect are fulfilled, duties to assist will be less burdensome. If the fulfillment of duties to protect is sufficiently inadequate, duties to assist may be overwhelming and may seem unrealistically great, as they do today to many people. For example, because the Dutch colonial empire failed to protect the people of Java against the effects of the Dutch schemes for agricultural exports, the nutritional problems of the majority of Indonesians today strike some people as almost beyond all solution.[29] The colossal failure of the Dutch colonial government in its duties to protect (or, even, to avoid deprivation) has created virtually Sisyphean duties to aid. These presumably fall to some degree upon the Dutch people who are today still profiting from their centuries of spoils. But whoever precisely has these duties to aid—there are plenty to go around—their magnitude has clearly been multiplied by past dereliction in the performance of the other two kinds of duties by the Dutch, among others. We will return in chapter 5 to some aspects of the difficult question of how to allocate duties to aid, especially when (chapter 6) they cross national boundaries.

This much, however, is already clear. The account of correlative duties is for the most part a more detailed specification of what the account of rights calls social guarantees against standard threats. Provisions for avoidance, protection, and aid are what are needed for a reasonable level of social guarantees. Making the necessary provisions for the fulfillment of subsistence rights may sometimes be burdensome, especially when the task is to recover from past neglect of basic duties. But we have no reason to believe, as proponents of the negative/positive distinction typically assert, that the performance of the duties correlative to subsistence rights would always or usually be more difficult, more expensive, less practicable, or harder to "deliver" than would the actual performance of the duties correlative to the rights that are conventionally labeled negative and that are more often announced than in fact fulfilled. And the burdens connected with subsistence rights do not fall primarily upon isolated individuals who would be expected quietly to forgo advantages to themselves for the sake of not threatening others, but primarily upon human communities that can work cooperatively to design institutions that avoid situations in which people are confronted by subsistence-threatening forces they cannot themselves handle. In spite of the sometimes useful terminology of third parties helping first parties against second parties, etc., it is worth noting, while assessing the burden of subsistence duties, that the third-party bearers of duties can also become the first-party bearers of rights when situations change. No one is assured of living permanently on one side of the rights/duties coin.

·3· LIBERTY

Not only is this book not a comprehensive theory of rights, it is also not an exhaustive discussion of basic rights. Its primary purpose is to try to rescue from systematic neglect within wealthy North Atlantic nations a kind of right that, as we have already seen, deserves as much priority as any right: rights to subsistence. But it is essential to consider briefly the right conventionally most emphatically endorsed in North Atlantic theory: rights to liberties. Some liberties merit our attention for many reasons, not the least of which is a strange convergence between supposed "friends" of liberty in the North Atlantic and rulers in the poorer countries who would share my emphasis on the priority of subsistence rights. Both groups have converged upon the "trade-off" thesis: subsistence can probably be enjoyed in poor countries only by means of "trade-offs" with liberties.[1] The only discernible difference between these friends of liberty and these particular friends of subsistence is the professed reluctance with which the friends of liberty advocate that the poor in other people's countries should be subjected to the "trade-off." The two versions might well be called the theory of reluctantly repressive development and the theory of not so reluctantly repressive development.

The Shah of Iran and his spokesmen, for example, were clumsy advocates of not so reluctantly repressive development. In an article by the Shah's representative at the International Monetary Fund and World Bank published prominently by the *New York Times* in the Sunday edition of its Op-Ed page we find the necessity of exchanging liberty for subsistence readily assumed:

> In the third world countries suffering from poverty, widespread illiteracy and a yawning gap in domestic distribution of incomes and wealth, a constitutionally guaranteed freedom of opposition and dissent may not be as significant as freedom from despair, disease and deprivation. The masses might indeed be much happier if they could put more into their mouths than empty words; if they could have a health-care center instead of Hyde Park corner; if they were assured gainful employment instead of the right to march on the capitol. The trade-offs may be disheartening and objectionable to a Western purist, but they may be necessary or unavoidable for a majority of nation states.[2]

The opposite view was put with eloquent clarity by martial-rule opponent and former Senator Diokno of the Philippines:

> Two justifications for authoritarianism in Asian developing countries are currently fashionable.
>
> One is that Asian societies are authoritarian and paternalistic and so need governments that are also authoritarian and paternalistic; that Asia's hungry masses are too concerned with providing their families with food, clothing, and shelter, to concern themselves with civil liberties and political freedoms; that the Asian conception of freedom differs from that of the West; that, in short, Asians are not fit for democracy.
>
> Another is that developing countries must sacrifice freedom temporarily to achieve the rapid economic development that their exploding populations and rising expectations demand; that, in short, government must be authoritarian to promote development.
>
> The first justification is racist nonsense. The second is a lie: authoritarianism is not needed for developing; it is needed to perpetuate the status quo.
>
> Development is not just providing people with adequate food, clothing, and shelter; many prisons do as much. Development is also people deciding what food, clothing and shelter are adequate, and how they are to be provided.[3]

Even the theory of justice of John Rawls, the depth and sincerity of whose commitment to liberty is in no way in doubt, sometimes easily assumes both the possibility and the necessity of exchanging liberty for economic growth. As Robert E. Goodin has noted, "When, as an exception to his general rule, Rawls (Sec. 82) allows that a desperately poor nation might justly sacrifice some civil liberties for some increase in economic well-being, the whole discussion presupposes that a nation *can* purchase one at the price of the other."[4] What is the place of liberty in a framework that acknowledges the importance of subsistence?

I want to show that although the advocates of repressive development profess, as I do, a strong commitment to the provision of subsistence, those theories of repressive development must be sharply distinguished from the theory of basic rights presented here. One of several major differences is the place assigned here to at least some liberties, and it is the purpose of this chapter to indicate how fundamentally the same argument that establishes security rights and subsistence rights as basic rights also justifies the acknowledgement of at least certain political liberties and certain freedom of movement as equally basic.

Enjoying Liberty for Its Own Sake

As indicated early in chapter 1, rights are basic "only if enjoyment of them is essential to the enjoyment of all other rights," irrespective of whether their enjoyment is also valuable in itself.[5] A liberty is usually valuable in itself, and liberties are usually discussed in terms of the satisfaction, if not exhilaration, that their exercise can directly and immediately bring. But the substance of a basic right can have its status only because, and so only if, its enjoyment is a constituent part of the enjoyment of every other right, as—to use our standard example—enjoying not being assaulted is a component part of the enjoyment of anything else, such as assembling for a meeting. Consequently, in this chapter liberties that are candidates for the status of substance of a basic right will be examined solely from the admittedly restricted point of view of whether they are constituents of the enjoyment of every other right. I will after this section simply set aside the consideration of any direct and immediate satisfaction that comes from enjoying the liberty in itself. But this conscious omission in no way implies any denial of any other value that liberties may have in themselves. And even the enjoyment of liberty for its own sake has an important implication concerning basic rights.

Certainly there are many liberties the exercise and enjoyment of which are valuable in themselves—and are for that reason very valuable indeed, irrespective of whether these liberties are also valuable as constituents of the enjoyment of some larger activity. And not all liberties that are valuable in themselves are especially grand. Sheer freedom of physical movement, not being forced to stand still (a common form of torture) or being kept locked in an overcrowded prison cell, but being allowed simply to walk around, may strike most people, who have never been deprived of it, as a liberty providing rather minor satisfaction by itself. And to some degree it may not be the presence of the liberty but the absence of its deprivation—the absence of walls and enforceable threats against movement—that we value. At least the intensity of the dissatisfaction from being deprived may be much greater than the intensity of the satisfaction from enjoying the liberty. But then we do not normally value things only for the intensity of the satisfaction they bring. For though it may not be especially exhilarating just to stroll out and see if the bluejays are still angry at the squirrel with the crooked tail, it can be very important and satisfying to know that if one wants to, one may (and if one doesn't want to, one need not).

If one is free to walk around, one's freedom of physical movement is of course also valuable as a mere means—of visiting friends, obtaining exercise, buying groceries, etc. It is valuable as a means in addition to its independent value in itself, and this value as a means can be called its instrumental value. But its direct satisfaction remains. In a humane prison, one's friends could visit, one could run in place or perhaps in the exercise yard, and the groceries would be not only supplied but prepared. None of this would lessen the desire to be able simply to go for a walk when and if one wished, for the sake of the walk itself and not because one needed to get somewhere.

It is true of many liberties, of course, that they are valuable not because one will be constantly—or, ever—exercising them but because they are available if wanted. Having a liberty can be valuable in itself even if one does not actually exercise it. But what may seem to be a fine distinction here is vitally important. For the people who do not in fact exercise their liberties, it must nevertheless be true that they actually could exercise them. It must not merely be the case that they comfortingly believe they could, when they could not if they were to try, because they would be prevented or hindered by common and serious but remediable threats. This provides a connection in one direction with the two basic rights already established.

People can obtain real satisfaction from false beliefs. If I am optimistic about the next few years because I believe that I am essentially healthy, my optimism is no less real if my confidence is misplaced and I have undiagnosed cancer. But the correct explanation of my confidence, then, is not my health. It is my mistaken belief that I am healthy when I am not. Similarly, people may feel content because they believe that opportunities for political participation, for example, are guaranteed to them, when in fact if they try to vote, or vote the "wrong way," they will be beaten up, arrested or fired. If so, they are not deriving satisfaction from a liberty they have but are not exercising. They are living in a fool's paradise quite different from their real situation. Illusions are not liberties.

So, it is true that people can derive satisfaction from liberties that they do not exercise but could exercise. But in order for it to be correct to attribute their satisfaction to their liberties, not to illusions about liberties, it must be true that the liberties can in fact be exercised, if the people try to exercise them, without subjection to standard threats. The belief in the usability of the liberty, on which the people's satisfaction rests, must be correct, if it is to be the liberty that is beneficial to them. Thus, it is fraudulent to comfort people with promises of liberties that they cannot actually enjoy because necessary constituents of the enjoyment, like protection for physical safety, are lacking. It is fraudulent, in other words, to promise liberties in the absence of security, subsistence, and any other basic rights.

When arguing against an imbalance in one direction (toward promised rights to liberties and away from needed constituents of the exercise not only of rights to liberties but of all other rights), it is extremely difficult not to strike a position that is unbalanced in the opposite direction.[6] Insofar as the enjoyment of rights to liberties depends upon the enjoyment of security and subsistence, the rights to security and subsistence appear to need to be established first. And it does seem to follow that if there are rights to liberties that cannot be enjoyed in the absence of security and susbistence, rights to security and rights to subsistence must be *more* basic than rights to liberties.

But this does not follow. It is also possible—and, I will now try to show, is actually the case—that not only does the enjoyment of rights to some liberties depend upon the enjoyment of security and subsistence, but the enjoyment of rights to security and subsistence depends upon the enjoyment of some liberties. A mutual dependence holds both between enjoyment of rights to some liberties and enjoyment of security and subsistence and, in the other direction, between enjoyment of rights to security and subsistence and enjoyment of some liberties. And, of course, if the enjoyment of security and subsistence is an essential component of enjoying liberties as rights, then one has a basic right to the enjoyment of security and subsistence, as we have already seen. And if, as I will now try to show, the enjoyment of some liberties is an essential component of enjoying security and subsistence as rights, then one also has equally basic rights to those liberties.

An unwelcome complication, however, is that the dependence is not completely symmetrical: the enjoyment of rights to *every liberty* is dependent upon the enjoyment of security and subsistence, but the enjoyment of rights to security and rights to subsistence is dependent upon the enjoyment of *only some liberties*. These are the liberties that, whatever the satisfaction they give in themselves (it may be considerable), are a constituent part of the enjoyment of other rights. To single out at least some of these liberties as among the basic liberties, or more properly the liberties that are the substances of basic rights, is the purpose of this chapter.

To avoid misunderstanding it is vital to keep in sharp focus the question to which I am hereafter in this chapter seeking the answer. I am not asking which are the richest or most elevated forms of liberty, judged by moral ideals of the good life or the good society.[7] Undoubtedly there are kinds of liberty that are necessary for, say, the cultural and artistic expression invaluable to the highest forms of society. But if the exercise of those liberties is not necessary for the exercise of all rights, those liberties are not basic rights, however important they are for other reasons. My concern now is to determine not the highest, but the most basic, kinds of liberty. I am here, as elsewhere in this book, working on the foundations, not the spires, of the edifice of rights. The basic liberties will turn out to include the liberty of participation.

Is Participation Universally Desired?

Much more might well be said in order to tighten up the overused concept of participation than can be said here.[8] Three points, however, are essential to mention. First, the focus of the participation I will be discussing is: the fundamental choices among the social institutions and the social policies that control security and subsistence and, where the person is directly affected, the operation of institutions and the implementation of policy. Without genuine influence over fundamental structures and strategies, influence over implementation may be to little effect. But without influence over details of implementation and operation where one's own case is affected, influence over fundamentals may be to little effect. On the other hand, it is unrealistic to say that everyone is entitled to influence upon all details. Thus, I arrive at the characterization of the focus of participation just given: all the fundamentals and the details affecting one's own case.

Second, for a right to the liberty of participation to be of any consequence, the participation must be effective and exert some influence upon outcomes. The participation must not be merely what Carole Pateman has called "pseudo participation" and "partial participation."[9] Obviously it cannot be required that genuine participation will always yield the result wanted, but it is not enough, at the other extreme, that people be heard but not listened to. I can combine these first two points by saying that we will be discussing *effective participation*, meaning genuine influence upon the fundamental choices among the social institutions and the social policies that control security and subsistence and, where the person is directly affected, genuine influence upon the operation of institutions and the implementation of policy.

Third, participation as discussed here is not construed in a narrowly political sense. One's security and subsistence, and the remainder of one's life, are at least as deeply influenced by economic organizations, like domestic corporate oligopolies and gargantuan transnational corporations, as by governments and strictly political organizations. Whether broad participation in the constraint of corporate activity can be direct or must be by way of political institutions, many of which are in any case deeply intertwined, is a question of means that can be pursued after settlement of the question about basic rights to be considered now.[10]

Two chief considerations are brought against the judgment that effective participation is a basic right. First, it is sometimes noted that many people are in fact not interested in participation in fundamental choices about social institutions or social policies, even if the fulfillment of their own rights is affected. From this observation it is then inferred that participation cannot, therefore, be a universal right. Charles Frankel maintained: "To be so characterized a right must meet two tests. First, do people everywhere think of it as a right . . . ?"[11] In quite a few traditional peasant societies, in fact, the social structure was sharply hierarchical in each community, and in each community the major landlord made the fundamental decisions even about the basic rights of security and subsistence. Moreover, in at least some of these communities the specific decisions made did actually provide both security and subsistence. The landlord saw to it that his workers were safe from want and attacks, and they were content to enjoy their security and subsistence and to be free ordinarily of concern with necessary arrangements.[12] And one can try to imagine a benevolently paternalistic dictatorship over a modern society in which people are free from deprivation or, when protection fails, are assisted in overcoming their lack of security or subsistence; institutions and policies are designed entirely by the dictator and his "experts"; and the people, as well as the dictator, are satisfied with the results of the arrangements.

But although the premise (that many people are in fact not usually interested in participation even in fundamental choices) is true, the conclusion (that participation cannot be a universal right) does not follow. It is not a necessary condition of something's being a universal right that it is universally believed to be a right. People can certainly have rights that they do not know they have. Some slaves, for example, may expect and accept beatings from their masters. They may believe that masters have a right—a duty, even— to "discipline" their slaves. If so, the slaves' beliefs are mistaken: there is no right to possess, or to violate the physical security of, another human being. Beliefs about rights can be incorrect, just as beliefs about almost all other subjects can.[13]

Which rights people have is independent of which rights they believe they have. This is a perfectly general point, applicable to any right. People's rights may be more numerous—or fewer—than they think. The same is true of duties, of course. People do not have only the duties they believe themselves to have. If that were true, no master who believed otherwise could have a duty not to "punish arrogance" with physical assaults upon his slaves. It is not "OK as long as you are sincere," and neither rights nor duties are determined subjectively.

Which rights, and correlative duties, people have is determined by weight of reasons. If the reasons for according everyone a particular right are strong enough, everyone has that right, and everyone else and all organizations and institutions ought at least to avoid violating it, and some others ought to protect it and to assist those deprived of it. If the reasons for according it are too weak, there is no such general right. In order to decide which rights there are one must assess the quality of reasoning, not measure the quantity of belief.

Saying that people can have rights regardless of whether they believe they have them, needs to be sharply distinguished from saying that people must exercise the rights they have regardless of whether they want to exercise them. The latter is ridiculous as a general thesis and has no connection with the former. That I have a right to freedom of movement, for instance, does not mean that I must constantly or, for that matter, ever move, if I do not wish to. Probably some rights actually ought to be exercised—for example, a right to a public education probably ought to be exercised, at least by everyone who cannot afford to pay for a private one that is better than the public one available. Perhaps a right to freedom of movement ought to be enjoyed by anyone able to enjoy it, because of some such consideration as the alleged broadening effects of travel. But any duty, if there is one, to take advantage of a right you have would not be a duty correlative to the right, but the quite different kind of duty that flows from a moral ideal of a rich or fulfilled life. Such ideals and their associated duties may well be important, but they are simply not part of a theory of rights. Whether people ought, as part of an ideally full life, to want to participate in the institutions and policies that control the fulfillment of their rights is an important question. But it is a different question from whether they have a basic right to participate if they do want to—and even if they choose not to.

Is Participation Universally Needed?

A second consideration against acknowledging effective participation as a basic right is much more difficult to handle than was the fact that some people do not want to participate, and it raises much more fundamental issues. This second contention is that at least some people do not need to participate in order to receive the substance of some of their rights, including even the basic rights already established: security and subsistence. Since, by definition, something can be the substance of a basic right only if enjoyment of it is essential to the enjoyment of all other rights, participation cannot be a basic right if any other rights can be enjoyed even in the absence of participation. If even only one other right can be enjoyed in the absence of participation, then the enjoyment of participation is not an essential component of enjoying something as a right and does not, strictly speaking, qualify to be the substance of a basic right. Some despotisms, which allow little or no participation, do provide security, subsistence, and some other substances of rights to their populations. Is participation actually necessary, then, for receiving other rights? Does the example of an enlightened despotism that provides security and subsistence not show that participation is not strictly necessary?

These are hard questions to answer. In order to decide about them we need a firm and sharply defined conception of what it means to enjoy a right. Clearly a paternalistic dictatorship can provide both security and subsistence. But can a dictatorship without participation provide for the enjoyment of a *right* to security and of a *right* to subsistence? We must recall exactly what some features of a right are, as introduced in the first chapter.

A right provides (1) the rational basis for a justified demand (2) that the actual enjoyment of a substance be (3) socially guaranteed against standard threats. That the enjoyment ought to be socially guaranteed means that arrangements ought to have been made by, or with (if participation is established as a basic right), others for situations in which a person otherwise could not arrange for his or her own enjoyment of what the person has a right to enjoy. An alleged right that did not include a demand for social guarantees, in the sense of arrangements made by, or with, some of or all the rest of humanity, would be a right with no correlative duties, with nothing required of others, and this would not be a normal right at all but something more like a wish, a dream, or a plea.[14]

Enjoyment of the substance of the right is socially guaranteed, as our analysis of duties in the previous chapter showed, only if all social institutions, as well as individual persons, avoid depriving people of the substance of the right, and only if some social institutions (local, national, or international) protect people from deprivation of the substance of the right and some provide, if necessary, aid to anyone who has nevertheless been deprived of the substance of the right. Enjoyment is socially guaranteed, in short, only if the three correlative duties constitutive of a right are provided for, as necessary, by social institutions. A person is actually enjoying a right only if the person is living among social institutions that are well designed to prevent violations of the right and, where prevention fails, to restore the enjoyment of the right insofar as possible. Is it, then, true that a person can in fact enjoy, most notably, rights to security and to subsistence in the absence of rights to genuine influence upon the fundamental choices among institutions and policies controlling security and subsistence and, where the person is directly affected, choices about the operation of institutions and the implementation of policy?

All things considered, the answer is no, although some qualifications must be added before we are finished. It is not possible to enjoy full rights to security or to subsistence without also having rights to participate effectively in the control of security and subsistence. A right is the basis for a certain kind of demand: a demand the fulfillment of which ought to be socially guaranteed. Without channels through which the demand can be made known to those who ought to be guaranteeing its fulfillment, when it is in fact being ignored, one cannot exercise the right.

The apparent counter-example of the benevolent dictator is a case of the enjoyment only of security and subsistence, not a case of the enjoyment of a right to security and a right to subsistence. It is the enjoyment of things that are the substances of rights (security and subsistence), but not *as* substances of rights. What is missing that keeps people under the ideally enlightened despot we are imagining from enjoying rights, and that would be supplied by rights to participate in the control of the substances of other rights, is social institutions for demanding the fulfillment of the correlative duties, especially the duty to provide one vital form of protection: protection against deprivation by the government itself, if it should become less enlightened and less benevolent, in the form of channels for protest, levers for resistance, and other types of protective action by the deprived or potentially deprived themselves. Such action is of course to some degree self-protection, not protection by others acting out of a duty to protect, but what others will have done in fulfillment of their duties in this case is to have cooperated in providing and maintaining in advance of the need for them the institutional means of self-protection through effective participation. And participation is a component not only of the prevention of deprivations of rights but also of the arrangements for securing aid when violations have occurred.

To see why the benevolent dictator cannot provide rights to security or rights to subsistence we need to look at the case more closely. The dictator may of course provide security, subsistence, or both at any given time, but simply to provide something is not the same as to provide it as a right. To provide something as a right means to provide social guarantees for its enjoyment against standard threats, and these guarantees must include adequate arrangements for the effective performance of all three types of correlative duties.

The case of duties to aid is perhaps the weakest, but still sufficient. Certainly aid might be provided to people deprived of security or subsistence even if the victims had no right to participate in any of the arrangements for security or subsistence, including the arrangements for aid. Aid might be provided by individuals and by non-governmental institutions, and it might also be provided even by the dictator's government itself. One item that would be missing without participation would be one of the best sources of information about who needed aid, which kind of aid they needed, and why they needed it. Information could be requested or spontaneously supplied without the recognition of a right to participation, of course, but it could also be suppressed relatively easily if no right to participation was recognized and institutionalized. And the information made available to the despot directly by victims of deprivation could probably be secured indirectly if the despot were for some reason sufficiently dedicated to staying fully aware of people's needs for aid. Surveys could be regularly conducted, etc., however unlikely it is that any actual despot would be so assiduous in collecting information about expensive assistance needed by people in no position to demand it.

The supplying of information, however, is barely, if at all, a form of genuine participation. A more important item that would be missing without guaranteed participation for the intended recipients of the aid would be a powerful disincentive for the kind of theft of aid supplies for which the Somoza regime in Nicaragua was notorious but which is not at all uncommon.[15] If the intended beneficiaries were not treated as passive, they could do much to restrain bureaucratic corruption. Most important, however, are the detailed knowledge of a local area and the commitment to seeing that their area obtains what it needs that local residents could bring to decision-making about the implementation of general policies.

The cases of duties to avoid and to protect are clearer still. A benevolent dictator certainly might have very efficient arrangements to protect subjects from deprivation by fellow subjects. This kind of law and order could be extremely effectively provided by a dictator who was not corrupt, however unlikely it is in fact that a dictator can for long avoid corruption. The main problem is: how are people to be protected from deprivation by the dictator? One of the critical features of dictatorship is that potential deprivation and potential protection are in the same hands. A dictator might choose to be benevolent by avoiding deprivation of security or subsistence. But even a dictator who had been self-disciplined in the past also might, for any one of a number of obvious reasons, change his or her behavior toward at least some subjects. Against deprivation by a previously benevolent dictator, no defense may be possible in the absence of established forms of participation available to intended victims.

What the absence of provisions for participation that would allow protest and mobilization of opposition against any deprivation undertaken means is, quite simply, that people who did enjoy security and subsistence would be enjoying it entirely at the discretion of the dictator. And to enjoy something only at the discretion of someone else, especially someone powerful enough to deprive you of it at will, is precisely *not* to enjoy *a right* to it. In the absence of participatory institutions that allow for the forceful raising of protest against the depredations of the authorities and allow for the at least sometimes successful requesting of assistance in resisting the authorities, the authorities become the authoritative judge of which rights there are and what it means to fulfill them, which is to say that there are no rights to anything, only benevolent or malevolent discretion, including the discretion to decide what counts as benevolent.

Other Liberties: Freedom of Physical Movement

My discussion has concentrated so far upon a kind of liberty that is normally thought of as an economic and political liberty: participation in the control of the economic and political policies and institutions that determine the fulfillment of security, subsistence, and other rights. I have left aside many other liberties, some of which will turn out to be basic rights upon thorough examination. This is not the place for a comprehensive discussion of the varieties of liberty, important as that task is. But it is worthwhile for contrast to look briefly at one very different type of liberty, freedom of physical movement, which was our initial example of a liberty that is itself very satisfying. Does freedom of physical movement also serve as a component of every other right in a way that would make it a basic right?

Most notably, freedom of physical movement is the absence of arbitrary constraints upon parts of one's body, such as ropes, chains, and straitjackets on one's limbs, and the absence of arbitrary constraints upon the movement from place to place of one's whole body, such as imprisonment, house arrest, and pass-laws (as in South Africa), at least within regional boundaries.[16] One might have hoped that something as apparently straightforward as physical movement and its prevention by others could be simple.

Of course it is not and I cannot pursue many of the complications here. But two complications need to be underlined.

First, some qualification like "arbitrary" is necessary because of cases of physical constraint that are conventionally accepted as morally legitimate, such as straitjacketing a psychotic who would otherwise mutilate himself or herself until tranquilizers have had time to take effect, and imprisoning common criminals after prompt and fair trials. But the use of "psychiatric terror" in the USSR, for example, means that even the question of "treating psychotics for their own good" must be handled with care.[17] And practically every repressive regime in the world holds that those whose rights to freedom of physical movement, among other things, it is violating are common criminals, terrorists, traitors, subversives, etc. But since these problems are widely recognized, I will not pursue them and will simply assume that we have some rough but workable notion of due process in the commitment of the allegedly psychotic or criminal to mental institutions, prisons, or house arrest.[18]

Second, the qualification "at least within regional boundaries" is needed simply to reserve for other discussions two extremely important matters that—this is the only point here—are not *simply* matters of freedom of physical movement and would therefore require extensive, separate analysis. One is the conscription, usually of youths, for public service in places they would not themselves choose to go. This includes practices like the traditional U.S. system of military conscription that sends youths outside their own country to fight and the Chinese system of peacetime conscription that sent youths to other regions within their own country to serve in agriculture, etc.[19] The other matter is the right of emigration and the relatively neglected but necessarily related right of immigration. I will simply not pursue questions about the status of these further liberties here, but will look very briefly at the simplest case: freedom of physical movement within the general area in which one is already living, free of arbitrarily imposed chains and walls.[20]

Freedom of physical movement is so clearly satisfying in itself that it is initially somewhat difficult to focus on the question whether it has the kind of value as a component of other activities that qualifies it to be the substance of a basic right. Obviously free movement has great value as a part of many kinds of enterprises, but is it actually true that the enjoyment of freedom of physical movement is necessary for the enjoyment of every other right? Examples readily come to mind of other rights that one could evidently enjoy while, for example, in prison. For instance, at least some composers could, provided they were supplied with the necessary equipment, enjoy even a particularly valuable other kind of liberty, namely freedom of expression, and perhaps create radically new musical forms. As long as the length and severity of the prison sentence was unrelated to the content and style of the composition and the composer did not need contacts unavailable in prison, some hardy souls could—indeed, some have—let their imaginations soar in spite of the imprisonment of their bodies. The followers of at least some religions, even if they were denied equipment they might prefer to have (books, altars, etc.), could—once again, often do—still believe as they wish, meditate, pray, and sing, provided that their sentences are not based upon or affected by their religion. As long as people are not being tortured, beaten, exploited for labor, or otherwise harrassed, they can enjoy quite a few activities, especially what might be called the solitary intellectual liberties, like individual creativity requiring only modest material needs and like the individual aspects of religion and contemplation.[21] We have an entire genre of prison literature, much of it fine and much of it very free in spirit. Indeed, the free spirit in the shackled body is a recurrent theme of poetry and folklore.[22]

Yet, these examples are, I hope, not very compelling. Certainly the aspiring composer can be supplied with pen and ink, with a turntable and records too perhaps. But he or she can as well so very easily be deprived of them all. The records, the writing hand, the eardrums, even the spirit, can all fairly easily be broken. And there is no need actually to break things: the materials can be politely removed, the person instructed to write nothing, and the instruction enforced, as necessary. Much can be permitted and everything can be prohibited. With contemporary drugs the most independent mind can readily be plunged into nightmare and chaos. And it is all dependent upon the wishes of people other than the prisoner, upon whoever is in power. Vulnerability and dependence, helplessness in the face of all serious deprivations, are the normal fate of at least the arbitrarily imprisoned.[23]

The argument here can be telescoped, since the argument about freedom of movement can now be seen to be the same as the argument about participation. Yes, even in the absence of a right to freedom of physical movement, people can enjoy the substances of many rights. But they cannot enjoy them as rights, only as privileges, discretions, indulgences. Deprivation can occur as readily as provision, and this is not what enjoying a right means. A right provides the basis for a demand the fulfillment of which ought to be socially guaranteed, and a right can be enjoyed only where individuals and institutions avoid deprivation, protect against deprivation, and aid any who are nevertheless deprived. A right can be enjoyed only where, to the extent that individual action will not guarantee the substance of the right, institutions are available to do it. A person is not enjoying a right when he or she is enjoying the substance of a right in total dependence upon the arbitrary will of others. To enjoy a right is to exercise it within institutions that effectively protect one against deprivation of it, especially deprivation by those with the most power in the situation. And effective protection must include channels through which those whose rightful demands have not been satisfied, can in fact repeat and insist upon their demands until they are fulfilled.

No one in the state of vulnerability and dependence of the arbitrarily imprisoned is in any position effectively to make even the demands for the things that are rights. The arbitrarily imprisoned are at the mercy of their captors. They cannot flee and they cannot fight, and they certainly cannot make demands. To be deprived of freedom of physical movement is to be deprived of the independence essential to the kind of self-protection needed as part of any adequate institutions for performance of the duty to protect. If one is in no position to make demands (deprived of freedom of movement) or if one has no channels through which to make demands (deprived of liberty of participation), one cannot effectively make known—or, more important, organize resistance to—failures in the performance of duties to avoid, duties to protect, or duties to aid. Therefore, the freedom of physical movement, as well as the liberty of economic and political participation, are basic rights, because enjoyment of them is an integral part of the enjoyment of anything as a right.

Paternalistic Dictatorship Reformed?

The varieties of liberties are so numerous that an exhaustive consideration of which liberties are basic liberties would require an extensive and, for my purposes, unnecessary further analysis. My purpose is to explore reasonably fully the structure of the fundamental argument for any judgment that something is the substance of a basic right and the specific application of that argument to subsistence, which is customarily ignored by theorists around the North Atlantic. And we have now seen that fundamentally the same argument originally given to support the judgment that security and subsistence are basic rights also supports the judgment that liberty of participation and freedom of movement are basic rights as well. Unfortunately, the argument has a weak spot, when applied to liberties, that it does not have when applied to security and subsistence. Before we leave the subject of liberty this difficulty ought to be noted, although it is not, I think, in the end fatal.

Rights provide the basis for demands, but it is useful to distinguish the content of the demand from the act of demanding, or the making of the demand. One may demand one's rights, but obviously one may in addition, or instead, demand someone else's rights—that is, demand that someone else's rights be fulfilled for him or her. Conversely, and more importantly here, someone else may demand one's own rights on one's behalf. Many a lobbying group acts on behalf of the rights of people who are not in the group.

Now this practice reflects the fact that it is not a necessary condition of obtaining fulfillment of a right that one be in a position oneself to make the demand for the substance of the right. Some controversy exists about whether animals and future generations of human beings, for example, have rights. If they were to be declared not to have rights, it could not be for so simple a reason as that they are not able to press on their own behalf the demands for the substance of their rights. On the contrary, we tend to believe that it is precisely those who are most vulnerable to deprivation and are most powerless to resist it, like the unconscious person, the torture victim, and, perhaps, animals and unborn generations, for whom it is of the greatest importance that duties to protect and to aid be performed. A major purpose of rights, after all, is to protect against deprivation those unable to protect themselves, and to aid when protection fails. It is ironical but essential that a right provides the basis for a demand sometimes made on behalf of, and often made by, those with little or no power themselves to press it upon the individuals and institutions who have the correlative duties to fulfill the right but prefer to ignore it and their own duties.

Now this fact that people do not need to have obtained the substance of a right for themselves in order to enjoy it is the source of difficulty in justifying the acknowledgment of participation and free movement as basic rights. For it seems that people would also not need to participate in obtaining something for themselves in order to be able to enjoy it as a right. The reply on behalf of accepting participation and free movement as basic rights was, in essence, (1) that full performance of the correlative duty of protection that is necessary to complete fulfillment of a right must include the building and maintaining of effective institutions for self-protection as the ultimate barrier against deprivation, and (2) that self-protection involves both physical movement and political participation.

Unfortunately for the case in favor of accepting liberties as basic rights, (2) is much more obvious than (1). Certainly self-protection, or the defense of one's own rights, depends on physical mobility and effective political influence (and possibly other liberties as well). But it is less clear that adequate protection must include mechanisms for self-protection. Why not, instead, simply make the protection so thorough and effective that no self-protection is ever called for? It might be suggested, for example, that the importance of protection merely establishes the need for some kind of system of checks and balances, which could be non-participatory. Indulging the fantasy of the benevolent and uncorrupt dictator a little further, we could perhaps imagine a dictator who established in at least partly independent form either an ombudsman or even a judicial system with some authority to protect people against abuses by the rest of the regime. Our despotic caterpillar is now on the verge of becoming a restrained butterfly, and it is progressively less certain why the government we are imagining should continue to be called a "dictatorship." But leaving aside worries about labeling the example, we can certainly note the abstract possibility of a rule of law protecting rights without any genuine influence by those with the rights on fundamental decisions about the institutions embodying the rule of law or the implementation of the institutions' policies.

The quickest way to indicate the practical inadequacy of this model of the non-participatory rule of law is simply to recall, for example, the Vorster regime in South Africa, which used an elaborate and, in many respects, rigorous system of rule of law precisely as an instrument for the deprivation of rights to both security and subsistence of members of the majority of the population, who could not effectively participate in the federal government.[24] It is barely conceivable, it might be conceded, that a paternalistic dictatorship might go so far as to establish a genuinely independent legal system that could in some respects restrain even the dictator. But what if, as in South Africa, the legal system is itself carefully designed to maintain and protect, not rights, but a systematic pattern of gross violations of security rights and subsistence rights, as well as rights to liberty?

It would appear that, however many levels of checks and balances are built into a political and legal system, institutions providing for participation are almost invaluable as the ultimate monitors and brakes upon the substantive results of the procedures. To put the point in its most abstract form, we have no reason to believe that it is possible to design non-participatory procedures that will guarantee that even basic rights are in substance respected. Consequently, whatever the non-participatory protective procedures, it will always be important to have other procedures or institutions that allow the people who have assessed the usefulness of the protective procedures (and also of the participatory procedures themselves, of course) on the basis of whether they themselves can in fact exercise their rights, to act upon their assessment in some influential way. The "bottom line" is the extent to which people's rights are enjoyed, and however many ranks of official watchdogs may be established, the crucial information lies with the people whose rights are the alleged object of all the official attention. These people may not care enough to participate effectively, even if channels are available, especially if long denials of rights have crushed their spirit. We have, however, no reason at all to suppose that the official watchdogs and official maintainers of checks and balances will in general have a deeper level of commitment to seeing that people can enjoy their rights than most of the people with the rights, and no reason not to add the ultimate check of political participation. The participatory institutions should, accordingly, be in general at least as effective as any other institutions for detecting and resisting violations of rights.

The lack of any certainty that arrangements for participation in choices among institutions and policies controlling security and subsistence will enable everyone to enjoy security and subsistence may appear to undercut this part of the argument for acknowledging participation as a basic right. The underlying argument for the importance of participation has been that participation is always essential for retaining security, subsistence, and other rights, as rights, because it is a vital component of protection. Now it is being admitted that even if rights to participation are guaranteed and used, all this may still fail to guarantee everyone's rights. This is even more obviously true of freedom of movement. Is it not being conceded that participation and free movement may not serve the purpose invoked to justify guaranteeing them?

It is indeed being granted that even the enjoyment of a right to full participation may fail to retain for people the enjoyment of their other rights—even their other basic rights. But the reason being advanced here in favor of acknowledging participation as also a basic right is not that the exercise of a basic right of participation is sufficient for the exercise of other rights, but that it is necessary. The case for judging that participation is indeed necessary, especially for the fulfillment of the duties of protection correlative to every right and for the fulfillment of the correlative duty of every government not to deprive people of the substance of their rights, has now been made. This case is in no way weakened if, in spite of being necessary, full participation is not also sufficient for creating conditions in which people can exercise their other rights. The same is true for free movement.

In general, if more than one condition is necessary, no one condition can be sufficient (because something else is also necessary). Our earlier arguments that security and subsistence are each necessary for the exercise of all other rights—and are therefore basic rights—had already established that no other condition could by itself be sufficient. In fact, we have little reason for confidence that even the enjoyment of all these basic rights—security, subsistence, participation, and freedom of movement—is sufficient, as a set, for the enjoyment of any other rights. But it is very clear that the absence of any of these basic rights is sufficient normally to allow the thwarting of the enjoyment of any other rights, and that is why each of these is a basic right.

Something of a soft spot, however, remains in this argument for participation and in the structurally identical argument for freedom of movement. At the practical level there is no room whatsoever for doubt that no non-participatory system of government will ever be so paternalistically solicitous of the safety and welfare of the population under its rule that members of the population would not find extremely valuable some very solid mechanisms for participation in the arrangements for their safety and welfare. Where are people safe and well-nourished by the grace of their self-disciplined and solicitous dictators? The Philippines? Kampuchea? Indonesia? Brazil? South Africa? Ethiopia? Haiti?

At a purely speculative level it is nevertheless imaginable that some non-participatory system of protection might somehow be as effective as the best participatory system possible in the same circumstances. Perhaps there could be something like a system of advocates, as if everyone always had a court-appointed attorney-cum-bodyguard to prevent failures in the fulfillment of his or her rights, and each person would be better looked after by his or her respective personal advocate than through any efforts at self-protection. We need not try to design a seemingly realistic institution, since the theoretical point is clear in the abstract. The one aspect of the hypothetical example that must be quite definite, however, is that it is not simply that most people happen not usually to participate actively in making arrangements for that to which they have rights. Probably most people everywhere do not in fact usually participate in making arrangements for fulfillment of their rights. What counts about the hypothetical example is that, whatever else is said about the people's enjoying rights, they do not have the right to participate in the arrangements for fulfilling the other rights that they are said to have, even if they want to participate.

What I am calling the soft spot in the argument at the theoretical level, then, is the fact that it is not utterly inconceivable that some set of institutions without a basic right to participation might turn out to protect people's other rights as well as, or better than, the most effective participatory institutions do. However unlikely this is in practice, it is not evident how to rule out the theoretical possibility within the terms of the present argument. Roughly the same is true of the right to freedom of movement. Some regime that was otherwise marvellously benign but did not want its citizens moving about freely might confine everyone to a type of house arrest—it might, say, have a permanent curfew with the requirement that everyone be in his or her appointed place every evening at curfew unless given special permission to be elsewhere—but guarantee to everyone the enjoyment of everything other than freedom of movement (and participation in decisions about whether there should be freedom of movement) to which people have rights. Once again, this does not seem to be unimaginable, although I will not pause to fill in all the details, and, because it appears to be conceivable, it cannot be ruled out as, in this sense, possible. These extraordinary hypothetical examples, however, seem to me to give little guidance for ordinary actual cases. Hence, I believe the argument for treating the two liberties I have considered as basic rights remains secure.[25]

Meanwhile, it ought to be emphasized how high a hurdle any would-be paternalistic dictator would be attempting to leap if the dictator tried to meet the terms of this argument. All that it has been necessary to concede is this: if a regime actually provided better protection for every right, including of course security rights and subsistence rights, except rights to liberties like political participation and freedom of movement, than any of those rights would receive if rights to liberties were acknowledged and honored, then the regime's failure to provide for liberties would be permissible, other things being equal.[26] *The minimum standard is a higher level of protection for every other right*. I do not expect ever to see such a regime, and I certainly would not allow any dictator with such pretensions the chance to experiment with me, given the weight of the historical evidence against success.[27]

BLEH.

·II·

THREE CHALLENGES TO SUBSISTENCE RIGHTS

·4·

REALISM AND RESPONSIBILITY

Security, subsistence, social participation, and physical movement are almost certainly not the only basic rights. The right to due process, or to a fair trial, for example, could surely be established by an argument closely resembling the argument in chapter 3 for the two liberties discussed there. But in the North Atlantic intellectual community few people would seriously challenge the importance of due process, liberty, or security, although many have challenged and do challenge the importance of subsistence rights. Therefore, as I mentioned in the introduction, I would like to concentrate in this part of the book on some of the main arguments ordinarily presented against subsistence rights, letting the positive case rest for now. In chapters 4, 5, and 6, then, I will be considering respectively the following serious and widespread contentions:

Chapter 4: The practical consequences of everyone's enjoying adequate nutrition—and especially the allegedly resultant global "population explosion"—would make the fulfillment of subsistence rights impracticable, however genuine the rights may be at a theoretical level. It would hurt the *future poor*.

Chapter 5: The fulfillment of subsistence rights would probably place inordinate, if not unlimited, burdens on everyone except the poorest. It would hurt *me*.

Chapter 6: It cannot be anyone's responsibility to fulfill the rights of strangers on the other side of the globe, however much responsibility one may have to the deprived within one's own country. It would hurt the *local poor*.

We turned for a brief look at basic rights to two liberties in order to establish that the acknowledgement of subsistence rights, far from committing us to some obscure "trade-off" of all liberty for subsistence, is deeply intertwined with the acknowledgement of rights to some important liberties, including effective social participation and physical movement. Now we return to our primary focus on basic rights to subsistence and consider the potentially crippling view that while people may in some sense or other "have" rights to subsistence, the actual provision of social guarantees for subsistence would be, in a word, impractical. This is a view that withdraws in practice what it seems to grant in theory.[1] So, let us consider some practical matters—and their theoretical presuppositions, beginning with the the general worry that the better nutrition that is a central part of subsistence would lead to larger populations that would then have worse nutrition.

A realistic look at human rights needs to consider problems about population growth, then, for at least two different reasons. First, when subsistence rights in particular are discussed, some people do in fact become concerned that "natural" constraints on "excess" population are being removed without sufficient attention to the probable consequences. Depending on exactly what form it takes, this concern is not entirely inappropriate, although it can, as I will try to show, be satisfied. Second, in an approach to human rights like the present one that is committed to examining the ramifications of people's actually having their rights protected and in fact using them, instead of merely discussing the "rights themselves" (whatever exactly that could really mean) in the abstract, a consideration of both the effects of population growth on ability to enjoy various rights and the effects of the enjoyment of the rights on population growth, which may then in turn affect people's ability to enjoy the same or other rights, is not optional or peripheral but critical and central to the overall plausibility of the view. Consequences are not all that matters morally, but they do matter very much.

One of a number of reasons that traditional theories of rights lost credibility and are inadequate intellectual support for the series of declarations and covenants on rights since World War II is, I suspect, the rather ethereal quality of their handling of many questions. Perhaps the confidence that rights were based upon natural laws that, it was assumed, were guaranteed to fit together rationally and coherently gave theorists the impression that they were relieved of any intellectual responsibility to assess thoroughly the consequences of, and the preconditions for, the general exercise of the rights hopefully declared to be universal. I, in any case, must consider the implications of everyone's exercising whatever rights he or she has, not the implications of his or her merely "having" them in some form in which they cannot be enjoyed. Consequently, it would be damaging to the position I have presented if it could be established that the enjoyment by all—or more—people of at least subsistence levels of necessities would produce too many people for any—or many—rights to be actually enjoyed by any—or many—of the people then alive.[2]

Those who advance these population objections, as I will call them, to the fulfillment of subsistence rights are in effect advancing or, more typically, assuming a third kind of thesis about the explanation of deprivation, in addition to the accidental deprivation and the essential deprivation whose characteristics I noted in chapter 2. The population objections rest upon a thesis about inevitable deprivation: deprivation that is inevitable unless population growth is slowed by means of the intentional refusal to fulfill subsistence rights. If indeed the world now has, or soon will have, an absolute shortage of vital resources—"too little food for too many people"—then some (other) people will simply have to do without the necessities for survival.[3] On this thesis about the explanation of deprivation, the unavoidable deprivations resulting from the supposed excess of people are taken to be as purely natural as any social phenomenon could be, and attempting to provide social guarantees against the resultant starvation is made to look quixotic.[4] " 'Ought' presupposes 'can,' " and since we cannot prevent deprivation of subsistence, it cannot be that we ought to try. If this hypothesis were correct, the International Covenant on Economic, Social and Cultural Rights would indeed be more like a child's letter to Santa Claus than the multilateral treaty in force that it is. It would not even be possible to avoid deprivation, except perhaps by fasting.

Someone who felt compelled to object to the universal protection and enjoyment of subsistence rights, for fear that excessive growth of population would be significantly encouraged, might attempt to draw any one of several specific conclusions. For example, the objector might try to establish that there simply are no rights to subsistence. This conclusion, however, is extremely strong and would need a correspondingly powerful set of supporting reasons, especially in the face of the case that has already been built in favor of recognizing subsistence rights and fulfilling the correlative subsistence duties.

A less extreme conclusion, which would nevertheless seriously threaten the view that there are subsistence rights and that they ought routinely to be honored, is that there may indeed be subsistence rights—they are not denied, anyhow—but subsistence rights (a) may, like other rights, sometimes be overridden and (b) ought to be overridden when the consequences of fulfilling them would probably include pressure toward excessive population. In short, subsistence rights are not absolute, and one of the grounds for insisting upon the qualification of their fulfillment is, according to the challenge, the high probability of a consequent significant contribution to overpopulation. It is this more plausible challenge that I will try to counter.[5]

I have already conceded elsewhere that no right, not even the right not to be tortured, is absolute in the sense that one cannot even conceive imaginary situations in which violation of the right would, given the alternatives, be the least evil course.[6] I have also stressed, however, that no conclusions whatsoever follow from imaginary situations, for any actual cases that are significantly different from the extraordinary cases imagined. Artificial cases make bad ethics—and even worse applied ethics. Nevertheless, in principle it is always possible to attempt to offer an adequate justification for overriding even what one fully believes to be a basic human right. Consequently, an attempt to justify the contention that subsistence rights can be overridden, when honoring them would contribute to excessive population, is perfectly in order, even for someone who grants that in happier circumstances these rights ought to be defended and enjoyed. And this particular objection is especially disturbing because, if correct, it means that attempts to fulfill subsistence rights sometimes are, in a certain sense, self-defeating. But is the objection correct? Before we can examine it, one other aspect of the objection's meaning needs to be made more precise.

The difficulty alleged against any attempt to fulfill everyone's subsistence rights could be either that the attempt is rather literally self-defeating or that it is self-defeating in a broader sense. The narrower charge would be that the very fulfillment of subsistence rights today would help to frustrate any hope of fulfilling subsistence rights later: that preventing some deaths from deprivation now is to cause more deaths from deprivation later. Children whose lives are saved today will become the parents and grandparents of even more children who will place even greater strains on the limited resources available on this planet to support human life. The rights frustrated in the future, according to this narrower version of the population objection, would be subsistence rights.

The broader charge would be that the future enjoyment of some rights, but not necessarily subsistence rights, will be frustrated by the protection now of everyone's subsistence rights. A typical recent alarmist article concludes: "In sum, the problems of food shortages by the turn of the century will ramify from the countries directly concerned. The impact on a weakened American economy could be enormous. Americans are *not* going to starve, but the average American living in the year 2000 faces, as compared with today, rampant inflation in food and energy prices; a greater chance for unemployment; and either higher taxes to meet the cost in social programs for the elderly or the curtailment of those programs." Earlier the writer has predicted: "A poorer, if still well-to-do America, will stand within a world of Hobbesian starkness." What is in question is not the particular predictions about 2000—there is "rampant inflation in food and energy prices" in 1979—but the attempt to lay all this at the feet of "this horde of idle, hungry people": "The reasons are *not* necessarily a reduction in food supplies, but, more importantly, vast increases in world population."[7] All this is presumably to happen even without any efforts to fulfill subsistence rights.

Current protection of everyone's subsistence rights would still, on the broader interpretation of the population objection, have a self-defeating character from the point of view of the general fulfillment of rights, since the protection of some rights for some people (them) would be preventing the fulfillment of the same or different rights for related or unrelated people (us). The general idea, for example, is that given limited resources, or even only a ceiling on the rate of technological advance, increases in population will at some point force reductions in the quality of life. Roughly—very roughly—speaking, quality will vary inversely with quantity, the critic assumes. To the extent that "quality of life" involves matters of rights, which is a question the objector needs to settle, the enjoyment of rights is expected to start declining at some point with increases in numbers of people. But the fact that the rights might be different and more, or less, basic introduces major additional complexities of a morally significant type into the broader objection. So the broad and the narrow versions of the objection need some separate consideration.[8]

Unfortunately, these population objections raise in an interconnected way two of the most challenging problems of political philosophy: how to allocate scarce resources across time and how to allocate scarce resources across space. These are normally referred to respectively as justice among generations and justice among nations, or international justice. But these labels carry a great deal of baggage, much of it of dubious value. In particular, they assume that it is not only intellectually useful but also morally appropriate to structure the entire discussion in terms of generational and national boundaries. This tends to shift the burden of argument onto anyone who wants to use any categories other than these traditional ones. The significance of such boundaries is, however, one of the central issues, and even if the significance will be reaffirmed in the end, it ought not merely to be built into the terms of the discussion in the beginning.[9] So one might, then, refer to these two clusters of issues more vaguely but more neutrally as temporal allocation and spatial allocation.

No major theory of justice, including *A Theory of Justice* by John Rawls, has carried the discussion of either temporal allocation or spatial allocation very far.[10] Distributive principles are normally formulated by philosophers for a single community spatially and temporally, and it is sometimes rather optimistically assumed that principles to constrain transfers among different communities, however the boundaries in time and space are to be drawn, are derivable in some straightforward manner from principles governing the distribution within a single community. But it is usually also assumed that community boundaries are morally significant to some unspecified extent, with the result that it is quite obscure how inter-community (transgenerational, transnational, or both) principles are supposed to be related to intra-community principles.

I will not remedy the lack of a truly general theory of justice. Yet the population objection quite legitimately insists that any claims about the existence of universal rights, including subsistence rights, be evaluated from global and long-term viewpoints. So we must build what we can from an intellectual heritage that has until recently largely focused on transfers within one nation during one period.

Starvation as a Method of Population Control

The first serious question for the narrow version of the population objection, however, is whether its implied cure would be acceptable, even if its diagnosis were correct. Let us suppose for now that it is reliably predictable that if the subsistence rights of everyone alive today are protected as rapidly and fully as possible, future generations of humanity will be significantly larger than if we act less decisively to protect subsistence rights or even quite consciously refrain from protecting them for at least some significant numbers of people.[11] We are talking about choosing not to prevent some preventable deaths from deprivation. We are entertaining the strategy, for example, of intentionally allowing some malnutrition and starvation that we can prevent if we choose. To be more specific—and it is essential to realistic discussion to spell out concretely the implications of our abstractions, however useful the abstractions themselves remain for some stages of discussion—we are entertaining the strategy of purposely allowing considerable numbers of children to die. Even now, half the children who die in the poorer countries die because of malnutrition.[12] In Guinea, as of 1970, for example, 36% of all children were dying (of all causes) before the age of 5 (Egypt, 25%; Guatemala, 18%).[13] We are asking, again, Ivan Karamazov's question of his brother Alyosha:

> Imagine that you are creating a fabric of human destiny with the object of making men happy in the end, giving them peace and rest at last. Imagine that you are doing this but that it is essential and inevitable to torture to death only one tiny creature—that child beating its breast with its fist, for instance—in order to found that edifice on its unavenged tears. Would you consent to be the architect on those conditions? Tell me. Tell the truth.[14]

It is small exaggeration to compare death by deprivation to death by torture. Starvation is a prolonged agony, usually shortened, if at all, only by diseases that bring their own discomforts. And Ivan's defiance was for the sake of a single child. We are contemplating deaths of a magnitude sufficient to make measurable changes in population trends.

The full horror of what is in effect a proposal to include the preventable starvation of children as a major component of a method of population control ought to be kept in focus. Those who, on the basis of population effects, object to assigning high priority to protecting subsistence rights do not say, and perhaps do not understand, that this is the policy that follows from their words. When Maurice Cranston, for example, mocks the advocates of any economic rights, repeatedly and misleadingly suggesting that holidays with pay is an example typical of all economic rights and resigning himself, without examining any alternatives, to India's managing as best she can entirely on the resources left behind by the British, the implication is that it is only practical and sensible to permit starvation to function, in India, as one major means of population control.[15] Cranston obscures, or does not see, the terrible severity of his view's implications. The fact, if it be a fact, that resulting starvation within India would be only intentionally allowed to occur, and not intentionally initiated, is of little consequence. If preventable starvation occurs as an effect of a decision not to prevent it, the starvation is caused by, among other things, the decision not to prevent it. Passive infanticide is still infanticide.

Part of the underlying logic of Cranston's position seems to be that one ought not to acknowledge any rights that fail the "test of practicability," where practicability is interpreted to be incompatible with transfers of "capital wealth."[16] The *reductio ad absurdum* of this line of reasoning occurred during the British rule of India. The British had procedures to be followed in the case of a famine, but although approximately three million persons died of starvation and starvation-induced disease in the region of Calcutta during 1943, no famine was ever declared. The explanation of the Governor of Bengal to the Viceroy was: "The Famine Code has not been applied as we simply have not the food to give the prescribed ration."[17] In other words, if you cannot perform your duty, try to obscure what is happening. "Realism" becomes denial of reality.

On the other hand, the terrible nature of the policy implied by any objection based on population effects to fulfilling subsistence rights, ought not to be thought by an advocate of protecting subsistence rights to settle the issue by itself. For, if the population objection were correct, the consequences of protecting everyone's subsistence rights will be even more terrible still. The starvation toll would simply have been pushed into the future—and encouraged to expand. Indeed, it would simply be cowardly or self-indulgent to embrace the policy that defers the dying children into the future and multiplies their numbers, merely through an inability to face up to implementing the objector's alternative, if the objector were correct. And the uncertainty of the future, since it affects both strategies equally, is neutral between them. It is, unfortunately, not clearly more rational to reject a horror in the present, even if it is certain, and accept instead a consequent probable horror of much greater magnitude in the future, if the probability of the future horror cannot be estimated.

Thomas Nagel has given the following rather complex argument, including an appeal to uncertainty but also including an essential factual assumption:

> We are . . . weighing the certainty of a present disaster against the possibility of a greater future disaster—a possibility to which no definite likelihood can be assigned. . . . Since the catastrophic results predicted by Hardin are not in-

> evitable, and can be combated directly, it would be wrong to refuse to avert certain disaster in the present on the assumption that this was the only way to prevent greater and equally certain disaster in the future. Sometimes a present sacrifice must be made to forestall even the uncertain prospect of a far greater evil in the future. But this is true only if the two evils are of different orders of magnitude. In the case at hand, the present sacrifice is too great to be subject to such calculations.[18]

But "it would be wrong to refuse to avert certain disaster in the present on the assumption that this was the only way to prevent greater and equally certain disaster in the future" only if this is in fact not the only way to prevent disaster in the future. Nagel is correct, I believe, that famine now is not the only way to prevent famine later and that the later problems can be combated directly, for the reasons I will next try to indicate. It is important, however, not to think that one can ignore this question of fact and argue *a priori* that the certainty of a present disaster should always be given more weight than the possibility of a greater future disaster. Nagel's premise about uncertainty cannot carry the weight of his conclusion without the vital (and correct) factual assumption. For if it turns out that the greater future disaster does indeed occur, and only because we chose not to allow the smaller present disaster, then we will by our unwise choice have brought about the far greater of the two evils. And insofar as the possible future disaster is uncertain, it will presumably also be uncertain whether it is or is not of a different order of magnitude. Consequently, we cannot avoid considering whether *in fact* deprivation now is the only way to avoid greater deprivation later.[19]

But fortunately we may not need to choose the lesser of two horrors, as both the population objections imply we must. In fact, we have a choice that is an alternative to both ignoring rights as a means to controlling population and protecting subsistence rights while ignoring population growth, but the correlative duties are substantial. As soon as one appreciates that starvation is by no means the only—and hardly the most humane—effective form of population control, one realizes that, however urgent the danger of overpopulation, concern with overpopulation is by itself no reason at all to deny subsistence rights. The dilemma suggested by the population objections dissolves entirely, provided that in fact poor countries have, or can obtain, means of controlling population growth that are compatible with the protection of subsistence rights. But can they? Or does the world face inevitable deprivation?

Inevitable Deprivation?

A full discussion of this issue would go considerably beyond the scope of this book and the competence of its author. Some basic points, however, are well-established. The most humane methods of controlling population growth involve decreasing the birth rate, not increasing the death rate for children already born. Overpopulation is normally one part of a vicious circle also composed of poverty and malnutrition.[20] Many of the reasons poor people have for producing large numbers of children are direct reflections of the apparent hopelessness of their economic situation.[21] Much evidence suggests that after living standards have improved enough to bring about sustained and readily perceptible reductions in infant mortality, people become considerably more receptive to the adoption of birth control measures because some of the reasons for having more children that were associated with poverty no longer apply. Whether or not improvements in living standards that reduce infant mortality are sufficient to make people more willing to control births, such improvements may be necessary, and they are undeniably extremely helpful. No nation in history is definitely known to have stabilized its birth rate for an extended period before the vast majority of its population had a minimally decent standard of living, and we have inadequate reasons for confidence that the usual historical order can often be reversed.[22]

Improvements in living standards are not, it should be emphasized, being put forward here as a substitute for direct measures of birth control, but as an extremely valuable, if not indispensable, contributing factor. The best hopes of controlling population through discouraging births, instead of encouraging deaths by refraining from protecting subsistence, depend on simultaneous, if not prior, improvements in living standards. The protection of subsistence rights, therefore, may be part of the solution, not part of the problem, as presupposed by the population objection.

If it is not entirely certain that even the combination of significant improvements in living standards and vigorous programs of birth control can slow population growth before it is too late, it is far less likely that birth control projects alone can do the job. Any cheap strategy that relied on the single factor of birth control, without the improvements in living conditions that have normally accompanied or preceded the attainment of stable or near stable growth, would recklessly court the "bigger famine later" of the narrow population objection. The only responsible alternative to starvation as a method of population control, then, is a package of measures to reduce birth rates and improve living conditions.

It is, then, reasonable to assume what can be strongly supported with factual evidence: that improvements in living standards up to at least subsistence levels are powerfully supportive complements to, if not literally necessary conditions for, effective programs of population control through reduction in birth rates. However, in presenting even a little of the case for thinking that measures to maintain subsistence are complementary to the only effective measures to control population growth that are also civilized, I have briefly taken up a burden of proof that the structure of the argument does not require me to shoulder, but places upon anyone who presses the narrow population objection. This is a fundamental feature of the overall structure of the argument, and it is worthwhile to emphasize it.

Prior to this chapter, we have seen that a number of considerations converge in support of the conclusion that everyone has a basic right to subsistence. Taken all together, these considerations establish at the very least a strong presumption in favor of subsistence rights. The population objections are introduced in an attempt to defeat the presumption in favor of subsistence rights. With a strong case already made in favor of subsistence rights, it is up to anyone who wishes to challenge subsistence rights on the basis of either population objection to show what needs to be shown in order to establish that the population objection deserves to be given the significance the challenger assigns it. For this purpose it is immaterial whether the challenge to subsistence rights is in the form of a complete denial that people have such rights or in the form of a reason for overriding the fulfillment of a right acknowledged to deserve respect in better circumstances.

The burden is upon the opponent of acknowledging or fulfilling subsistence rights, who advances the narrower objection, to demonstrate (1) that population growth will be intolerable without resort to population control by means of starvation and (2) that population growth would be made tolerable as a consequence of a resort to starvation as a method of population control. He or she must show, in other words, that no less horrible method would be effective—that it is the only way—and that the attempt to reduce the population growth rate by means of failures to honor people's subsistence claims would be effective. I believe that the weight of the evidence already cited indicates that both of the theses needed to support the challenge are false, but the structure of the argument actually requires the challenger to try to show that they are true.

The practical problem is that any package of measures seriously intended to break the syndrome of overpopulation, malnutrition, and poverty would involve large investments. Probably no one would claim to know exactly how much it would cost to enable everyone to live at no worse than subsistence levels.[23] Nevertheless, two facts are undeniable: (1) many of the poorer countries do not control, and have no foreseeable prospect of independently coming to control, the wealth necessary to make the investments that would permit the poorest of their people to enjoy adequate diets, potable water, and the other elements that may be claimed as subsistence rights; and (2) the only feasible source of the amounts now needed in addition to internal redistributions are transfers from the countries that are now wealthy: the OECD countries, some of the OPEC countries, and some of the COMECON countries.[24]

This is an issue on which what initially appears to be a sensible moderate position actually rests on sand and collapses when pressed. One can responsibly acknowledge subsistence rights, including duties to aid, only if one is willing to support, where necessary, substantial transfers of wealth or resources to those who cannot provide for their own subsistence and willing to support any structural changes necessary nationally and internationally to make those transfers possible.[25] Garrett Hardin and his followers are mistaken on many points—most, I would say—but they are correct on one point: doing too little is probably worse than doing nothing.[26] Doing too little is certainly worse than doing nothing if its effect is to exchange a smaller famine now for a larger famine later. But if, as seems evident, the dilemma can be shattered by the adequate fulfillment of duties to aid those deprived of subsistence, no such apocalyptic choice is required. Economically trivial acts of charity, however, will not enable the standard of living in areas where subsistence rights are threatened to be raised to the point at which it becomes, and can be seen by the poor themselves to be, reasonable to have fewer children. Transfers adequate actually to enable the deprived to provide for their own subsistence may need to be of a magnitude sufficient to take the edge off the affluence of the standard of living of those from whom they come. This raises in the sharpest possible form what was earlier called the broader form of the population objection.

It's Not the Principle of the Thing, It's the Money[27]

This broader objection to fulfilling—sometimes even to acknowledging—subsistence rights is based not upon a supposed clash between the subsistence rights of some people (this generation) and the subsistence rights of other people (a later generation), but upon a supposed clash between the subsistence rights of some people (the deprived) and the preferences or non-basic rights of the other people who are best able to aid the deprived.[28] The general idea behind the broader population objection is that there are (or will be, if aid is increased or, perhaps, only continued) so many deprived persons that the cost of aiding them all until they can be self-sufficient is somehow an unfair, if not impossible, burden to impose upon the affluent. In fact, most fears of any impoverishment of the affluent are laughable nonsense, for many kinds of reasons.

One kind of reason is limits upon the absorptive capacity of recipient nations and individuals. Even if the sources of aid were willing and able to make unlimited transfers, the rate at which transfers can be made would cap the maximum possible transfers at a relatively low level. For instance, if transfers of some commodity like food are what is in question, port capacities for the unloading of ships set a sharp limit on imports of the commodity. Even so wealthy a nation as the U.S.S.R. is often forced to import less grain than it would like because of limited port capacity.[29] One could, of course, consider building new ports, but that would take years and the maximum speed of port construction limits the speed at which the import limit can be changed. Alternatively, one could consider airlifts by plane and then by helicopter in cases of imminent disaster, but besides limits set by the availability of pilots and aircraft, one would still face limits on storage capacity at the end of the line to keep the grain safe from spoilage, rats, etc. And so on.

If, as is normally better, the transfers are not in kind but are of funds, the absorptive capacity of the recipient economy sets stringent limits on how much can be admitted without distortions, extreme inflation, virtually irresistible temptations to corruption, etc. The need mutually to adjust and coordinate changes in supplies of money, jobs, and the commodities apt to be wanted by those who enjoy new jobs or additional spendable income will, no matter how exactly the coordination is brought about, require time and set a limit on the speed at which even revolutionary change can occur without the chaos in which people are deprived of their basic rights.

In addition to ineradicable physical and economic limits on absorptive capacity, attempts to aid the deprived face potentially changeable but currently very real political obstacles in the form of governing elites who are indifferent or hostile to the fulfillment of the basic rights of their own citizens and who are themselves powerful members of the reluctant affluent whose objections to subsistence rights we are now considering. In many cases these elites are exploitative dictatorships with no moral right to the power they wield or the advantages they enjoy, and their opposition to efforts to fulfill subsistence rights should be defeated whenever possible. Nevertheless, insofar as the question is whether the transfers that can actually be made are so enormous that those with the duties to make them will be impoverished by the loss of the amounts involved, it is only realistic to include in the calculations the fact that, for political reasons, many transfers that ought to be made cannot in fact be made.

That it is the size of the actual transfers that are in fact likely to be made that is relevant is a result of the form of the broader objection. The objection is not that it would somehow in principle be wrong to require any transfers, but that in practice transfers of the magnitude feared to be likely by the objector would, by some standard remaining to be specified, be too large in quantity to be reasonable to require. In other words, the challenge does not deny that people have rights to subsistence at all, but maintains that in the circumstances we actually face, the rights are overridden by the burdensome expense of fulfilling them as completely as possible. Accordingly, all constraints that would in fact function to limit the size of the possible transfers are directly relevant to the question of whether the quantities likely to be involved are unreasonable.

The physical constraints, economic constraints, and political constraints mentioned so far are all limits upon the size and rate of the transfers that could be made even if the transfers needed were enormous. The most significant factors of all, however, are brakes upon the size of the transfers that are needed. It is, of course, not possible to assign a precise price tag to the fulfillment of subsistence rights throughout the world, and consequently it is difficult to judge the implications of studies of, for example, changes in per capita income for judgments about the fulfillment of subsistence rights. Nevertheless, provided that the governments of developing countries were committed to internal policies, including policies toward income distribution, that gave priority to basic rights including subsistence, one can reasonably assume that nations with a gross domestic product per capita of US$400 (in 1970 prices) could manage the fulfillment of subsistence rights. Wassily Leontief and his associates have recently directed a study for the United Nations that considered the feasibility from most major viewpoints, including that of environmental damage, of reducing the inequality in income (measured in average gross domestic product per capita) between the developed countries and the developing countries from the 12:1 ratio of 1970 to a 7:1 ratio in 2000.[30] An inequality between rich and poor nations of 7:1

would, needless to say, still be extreme, but the changes that would reduce the inequality from 12:1 to 7:1 could be used to raise the average gross domestic product of even the poorest developing countries—"non-oil Asia and Africa"—to US$400 (in 1970 prices). Accomplishing this would involve raising growth rates of domestic products to 6.9 in developing countries, restraining growth rates of developed countries to 3.6, and restraining population growth rates in developing countries to 2.0.[31]

None of this would, of course, be easy, but it is perfectly possible physically and economically. The problems, according to Leontief's UN study, are political—and therefore, I would suggest, partly moral:

> The principal limits to sustained economic growth and accelerated development are political, social and institutional in character rather than physical. No insurmountable physical barriers exist within the twentieth century to the accelerated development of the developing regions;
>
> The most pressing problem of feeding the rapidly increasing population of the developing regions can be solved by bringing under cultivation large areas of currently unexploited arable land and by doubling and trebling land productivity [in the developing countries]. Both tasks are technically feasible but are contingent on drastic measures of public policy favourable to such development and on social and institutional changes in the developing countries.[32]

Leontief's calculations strongly support the thesis of my argument: although it is essential that the affluent fulfill their duties to the poor, the most the affluent *could* do, even if they did the maximum possible, would fall far short of impoverishing them.[33]

After all, the Leontief study projects *growth* for the already developed countries at a rate of 3.6% per year, leaving them in the year 2000 still 7 times better off than the by then considerably better off developing countries. Obviously improvements for the poorest countries depend upon not only avoiding disaster in the developed countries but maintaining minimal economic health in those globe-dominating nations. The developing countries need *some* markets and sources, however high the degree of self-reliance that is ideal. Even if one believes that inequalities of 7:1 cannot be indefinitely justified—and ought never to have been allowed to build up in the first place—one could not assist the developing regions by "closing down" the developed regions, if one wanted to:

> Investment resources coming from abroad would be important but are secondary as compared to the internal sources.
>
> . . .
>
> To ensure accelerated development two general conditions are necessary: first, far-reaching internal changes of a social, political and institutional character in the developing countries, and second, significant changes in the world economic order. Accelerated development leading to a substantial reduction of the income gap between the developing and the developed countries can *only* be achieved *through* a *combination of both* these conditions. Clearly, each of them taken separately is insufficient, but when developed hand in hand, they will be able to produce the desired outcome. (emphasis added)[34]

The results of this UN study by Leontief contain for the affluent of the developed countries much good news and little bad news. The bad news is that some transfers of wealth from the affluent of the developed regions to the poor of the developing regions are essential—a "necessary" condition—but the good news is that even this redistribution takes the form of unequal growth rates, not decline for one side and growth for the other. All that is needed, or possible, is the redistribution consisting of unequal rates of growth. The *absolute* amount of growth, on the UN scenario, for the developed nations would be far greater than the growth of the developing nations, of course, because the developed start from a 12:1 advantage and thus an enormously greater base. This can hardly be considered, on the whole, a very great demand. The affluent are expected not to enjoy less, but only to acquire more at a somewhat slower rate than they would if they maximized their own interests, as narrowly construed. From a moral point of view, such a demand in the fulfillment of basic rights is mild indeed, and the demand should be kept so low, as I will argue in chapter 5, only if in fact faster or larger transfers are not possible economically.

Indeed, the nearest thing to a significant sacrifice to fall upon the affluent of the developed countries would be not directly economic, but political. The foreign policies of the governments of the developed countries would need to stop subsidizing the governments of developing countries that refused to take the "drastic measures of public policy favourable to such development." Many such regimes are maintained by vital support from the governments of developed countries, precisely because the economic policies of these developing country regimes are tilted much further toward the welfare of developed countries, as opposed to the welfare of the poor majority in their own countries, than their own subjects would want, if their rights to participation were honored, and much too far to provide for the fulfillment of their own subjects' rights to subsistence. We will return in chapter 7 to such implications for foreign policy, which are actually not duties to aid at all but mere duties to avoid complicity in the deprivation practiced by these repressive dictatorships, including the enforcers of the essential deprivations explained in chapter 2.

The empirical basis for the broader population objection, then, looks as dubious as the empirical basis for the narrower population objection. What is worse for both versions of the objection, however, is that rather than being expressions of some kind of straightforward realism, they are themselves disguised moral positions—and question-begging ones at that. Any form of the population objection must assume that the existing distribution of wealth and income among nations is morally beyond challenge. It assumes this when it takes for granted that a nation is overpopulated if it is having difficulty supporting its present population on its present wealth and income. But it is possible that instead of having too many people for its wealth, it has too little wealth for its people. This depends upon how much wealth its people ought to have, and this, in turn, depends in part upon how much they have a right to. That is what the argument is all about. To attempt to settle the argument by merely declaring certain countries to be overpopulated is in effect to declare some of their people to be "excess"—extra people with no business to be there. And this is to smuggle in a judgment about justice disguised as a fact about demography.[35] To see the strength of the implicit and unargued moral assumption, one need only ask: why is it they who have no right to be there (consuming scarce food, energy, etc.) and not I who have no right to be here (consuming scarce food, energy, etc.—at much higher rates)? Could it be that we have the same basic rights? I have tried in the first part of this book to give some good reasons for thinking so. The population objections simply assume the contradictory position without giving any good reasons.

·5·

AFFLUENCE AND RESPONSIBILITY

Why the fantasies of the pauperization of the affluent that seem to be invoked in some minds whenever transfers of wealth are mentioned have little substance is indicated in the preceding chapter. It would not be possible, and it is not necessary in order to fulfill subsistence rights, to transfer so much wealth and income from the currently affluent to the currently deprived that today's affluent will be reduced to a level only marginally better than subsistence. That already partly answers this chapter's question. Nevertheless, since no calculation of the costs of fulfilling subsistence rights universally can be precise, one cannot rule out the possibility that those with the duties to aid the deprived will suffer some decline in the quality of their lives as a result of making the required transfers. Certainly the edge might be taken off their affluence.

Suppose that the transfers of income, wealth, and resources needed to aid those who have been deprived of subsistence would cause at least an undeniable slight decline in the quality of life for those who are the sources of the transfers. Would this decline give those with the subsistence duties some cause to complain or even some basis to deny that they actually bear the duties? In general, there is no reason why the performance of duties, especially duties correlative to basic rights, should cost the bearers of the duties nothing. But, as the broader population objection complains, it is possible for the costs to be unreasonably high, particularly when large numbers of people have the kind of rights in question.[1] And if the magnitude of alleged duties is indefinite and open-ended, no one can be assured that what are said to be duties are not unacceptably excessive demands. The suspicion that any account of duties put forward is unreasonable must remain until some limit upon the duties is specified in the form of guidelines for the assignment of duties to specific bearers.[2] The previous chapter, after all, deals only in aggregates. One wants to know how the aggregate burden is distributed and how much of it any given kind of individual is expected to bear.

Unfortunately for those of us who would like to move promptly from theory to practice—at least to some general guidelines for practice—not even a general account of basic rights, a general account of the correlative duties, and a short list of specific basic rights would enable us to generate a very long list of specific positive guidelines for U.S. government policy. What is already before us will provide some guidelines, because it is clear merely from these general accounts that, for example, in the case of every right the duty to avoid deprivation (I) must be universal and therefore applies to every individual and institution, including corporations, covered by U.S. policies.

The allocation of duties to avoid the deprivation of subsistence, then, is no problem. The duty is universal. Schemes, whether "assistance" or commercial, governmental or private, short-range or long-range, that leave anyone less able to provide for subsistence, whether through absolute or relative declines, must be changed to respect subsistence rights, whatever aggregate miracles they may be achieving or whatever benefits they are expected to bestow upon the future poor. No excuse is adequate for depriving any person of subsistence, except the extraordinary situation in which someone else's subsistence cannot possibly be provided at any price by any other means.

Many deprivations, as noted in chapter 2, are systemic effects of the interaction of many factors no one or two of which can non-arbitrarily be singled out as *the* cause of the deprivation. What a transnational corporation is doing has its effect in part because of the effects of what the national government is doing, which has its effects in part because of the effects of what foreign governments are doing, etc., ad infinitum. This complexity feeds the temptation, also already mentioned, to reason that since the deprivations are the responsibility of practically everyone, they are the responsibility of no one in particular, least of all oneself. No one needs to change until after everyone else changes, it seems.[3] But where the systemic deprivations are also essential and systematic, that is, where the deprivations have been part of the economic strategy chosen by the government, the mere duty to avoid deprivation (I) already requires the government to abandon its cruel strategy of threatening the survival of its own people for a more decent strategy.[4] And presumably the responsibility for seeing that as much overall social planning as is needed (however much or little that turns out in fact to be) is done, also falls partly upon national governments, given the current organization of the world. This includes some responsibility for duty II-2, the duty to protect rights by designing (with the participation of the intended beneficiaries) institutions that avoid deprivations of rights.[5] Duty II-1 is now also conventionally left to national—and, to some extent, lower level—governments.

Accordingly, however systemic and complex the sources of deprivations are, and regardless of whether the deprivations are essential or accidental, it now is considered ultimately the business of national governments to sort out all matters of avoidance and protection or see to it that they all get sorted out, with the participation of their people. I can think of no reason why anyone owes life, fortune, sacred honor, loyalty, or much else to a comprehensive political institution that cannot arrange to refrain from and to prevent deprivations of security, subsistence, participation, freedom of movement, and the substance of any other basic rights. National governments normally have rather grand pretensions concerning the functions they serve. Preventing deprivations of rights, as well as refraining from them, would seem fairly minimal.[6]

Although interesting questions could be raised about this conventional allocation of both duties to protect, II-1 and II-2, I think it is more important to concentrate in this chapter and the next upon the controversial question of how to allocate the duties to aid that are correlative to subsistence rights—most specifically, how to allocate the duty to aid the victims of failures in the performance of duties I and II, namely duty III-2.[7] The articulation of principles to guide the assignment of duty III-2 for subsistence would add an additional layer to our analysis of basic rights and bring us one step closer to guidelines relevant to policy in a disputed area.[8]

Duties to Aid: The Priority Principle

How much sacrifice can reasonably be expected from one person for the sake of another, even for the sake of honoring the other's rights, is one of the most fundamental questions in morality, and no full or general answer will be presented here. The suggestion that can be made for subsistence duty III-2 is that the general kinds of transfers that are respectively obligatory, allowed, and forbidden are as follows.

As the figure indicates, only three types of transfers are required—and those only as necessary: the second only if the first is inadequate and the third only if the second is inadequate—and only three types are prohibited. With regard to the other ten types, one is at liberty, as far as the theory of rights is concerned, to do as one pleases or as one believes to be required by his or her own individual moral ideals. One is required to sacrifice, as necessary, anything but one's basic rights in order to honor the basic rights of others. As indicated in chapter 4, I believe that in fact it is most unlikely that anyone would need to sacrifice anything other than preferences, to which one has no right of satisfaction and which are of no cultural value, in order to honor everyone's basic rights, provided everyone with the duty to make some sacrifice of preferences does so.[9] But I believe too that in principle one could be required to sacrifice the enjoyment of cultural enrichments and even non-basic rights if, after everyone who ought to sacrifice preferences had done so, people still remained deprived of basic rights. No evidence suggests, however, that anything even approximating the sacrifice of all preferences is actually needed in order to aid all who are deprived of basic rights.

A requirement that someone sacrifice the enjoyment of his or her own basic rights in order that someone else's basic rights be enjoyed would, obviously, be a degrading inequality. No such transfer could possibly be required. Perhaps this transfer (see block 4 of the figure) ought to be prohibited, as are transfers (see blocks 8, 12, and 16) that would frustrate the basic rights of the source of

Required, Permitted, & Prohibited Transfers According to the Priority Principle

Recipient's Gain	*Source's Loss*: Preference Satisfaction	Cultural Enrichment	Non-basic Rights	Basic Rights
Basic Rights	1 Required (Primary)	2 Required (Secondary)	3 Required (Tertiary)	4 Permissible
Non-basic Rights	5 Permissible	6 Permissible	7 Permissible	8 Prohibited
Cultural Enrichment	9 Permissible	10 Permissible	11 Permissible	12 Prohibited
Preference Satisfaction	13 Permissible	14 Permissible	15 Permissible	16 Prohibited

the transfer for the sake of honoring something less than a basic right for the recipient. The reason for judging the sacrifice of one's own basic rights for the basic rights of someone else to be permissible, not prohibited, is to leave open the possibility of heroism. Although people cannot be expected to surrender their basic rights, surely they are at liberty to do so, if they choose, and we might consider a knowing and willing sacrifice of this magnitude admirable and heroic. Where food was absolutely scarce and not adequate for everyone, no one could be required not to claim the food that was his or her right. But someone might heroically choose not to make the claim so that another person could have that share.

The sacrifices represented by blocks 8, 12, and 16 might conceivably also be considered heroic and argued to be permissible, and even praiseworthy. The sacrifice of basic rights for non-basic rights (block 8) is perhaps unclear, but the sacrifices of basic rights for goods to which there is no right (blocks 12 and 16) seem to be exchanges of so much for so little as to be quite irrational and deserving of prohibition. This same is true, less strongly, of a surrender of basic rights for non-basic rights. One would be concerned that any person who was willing to make any of these three sacrifices either did not fully comprehend the stakes or suffered from an inadequte sense of self-respect, consequently needing some protection from his or her own sacrificial impulses. For these same reasons, even the transfer represented by block 15 seems highly dubious.

An alternative view would be that the prohibition of the sacrifices represented by blocks 8, 12, and 16 (or 15) is excessively paternalistic and that people who knowingly wish to sacrifice even their basic rights for lesser goods should be at liberty to do so. This view seems to me to attach an inordinate value to a kind of harmful (to the agent) liberty that is difficult to distinguish from irrational whims (like rushing into a flaming house to save your favorite bedroom slippers), but I would be willing to be persuaded that every type of transfer should be simply permissible, except those represented by the first three blocks.[10]

The case for requiring, in order and only as necessary, the transfers indicated by blocks 1, 2, and 3 will be presented in the next section. Here it is necessary only to emphasize that fairness would evidently require that no one be compelled to sacrifice more than the satisfaction of preferences until everyone else who ought to have done so has been compelled, if necessary, to sacrifice preferences.[11] Coercion would be justified in bringing about universal compliance with the requirement for the transfers represented by block 1 in order to obviate any need for anyone to make transfers represented by block 2. Otherwise one is allowing a severe inequality among bearers of the same duty.

What may seem a superfluous category, cultural enrichment, is included between rights and preferences because I believe that actions that not only satisfy preferences but also contribute in an abiding fashion to civilization are morally superior to the mere satisfaction of preferences. A full argument for this judgment would be a digression here, however. Since in both rows and columns the respective assignments for preference satisfaction, cultural enrichment, and non-basic rights are always the same, people who do not share this judgment may ignore it with no effect on the main argument by treating cultural enrichment as one more kind of preference satisfaction or of non-basic rights, as they see fit.

If one does believe that cultural enhancement is an important and distinguishable value, an additional wrinkle appears in the argument. Assuming that the development and preservation of rational morality is one form of cultural enrichment, one could contribute to civilization by insisting upon respect for the basic rights of others and, presumably even more, by contributing to the development of policies and institutions that respect rights. If so, it is not entirely clear what it would mean to sacrifice cultural enrichment for oneself in order to promote the basic rights of others, in that the acts promoting the rights might be a reaffirmation, if not a refinement, of some of the best elements in one's own culture. I shall not pursue the involutions of this argument, however, because, on such evidence as that cited earlier from Leontief, it does not seem realistic to think that the transfers needed to satisfy subsistence rights universally would require even so much as the sacrifice of all non-enriching satisfactions. Since it is unlikely that it would be necessary to move outside block 1, extensive discussion of block 2 seems pointless.

Underlying the figure and my explanation of it, then, is a fundamental principle for the assignment of the responsibility to perform duties that I will call the principle of priority for rights, or, for short, the priority principle:

1. the fulfillment of basic rights takes priority over all other activity, including the fulfillment of one's own non-basic rights;[12]
2. the fulfillment of non-basic rights takes priority over all other activity except the fulfillment of basic rights, including the enrichment of culture and the satisfaction of one's own preferences; and
3. the enrichment of culture takes priority over the satisfaction of preferences in ways that do not enrich culture.

Before we look at the reasons for the priority principle, we might glance briefly at one more of its implications, which settles an inevitable problem. How much any given individual or nation would in fact need to sacrifice in order for those deprived of subsistence in fact to enjoy the subsistence to which they have rights clearly depends upon the extent to which the rest of whoever ought to make some sacrifices make the sacrifices they ought to make. And appeals for voluntary compliance with one's duty to aid others to enjoy subsistence can be unfair, almost to the point of mild cruelty, to the responsive. For reliance on voluntary contribution allows the unresponsive totally to escape their fair share of the effort and encourages the responsive to do even more than their share. Obviously this sort of voluntarism also courts the danger of a shortfall in the amount of transfers needed and is for this reason also unfair to those currently deprived of their rights. Therefore, for the sake of fairness both to those deprived of their subsistence rights and to those who would be willing voluntarily to perform their subsistence duties to assist, the performance of these duties ought to be a legal obligation. People ought to tax themselves for the purpose, if indeed they have duties to aid those deprived of subsistence. Otherwise some people might be sacrificing more than preferences—in terms of the figure, they would be moving from block 1 to block 2—because other people had avoided sacrificing even preferences. This would violate section (3) of the priority principle. The coercion of the less responsive people is needed in order to avoid unfairness to the more responsive people.[13]

Deprivation and Degradation

In chapter 4 I deferred the question of from whom transfers ought to come by temporarily labeling those with the primary duties to aid as "the affluent." I can now be somewhat more specific about the answer to this difficult question. If the priority of transfers drawn from the priority principle and expressed in the figure is acceptable, one still vague but somewhat more specific indication of who counts as affluent is: people are affluent in proportion to the absolute amount of their consumption that consists of the satisfaction of preferences, to the satisfaction of which there is no right, rather than consisting of the enjoyment of basic rights and non-basic rights (or, I would add, of activities enriching culture as well as satisfying preferences). The affluent are those who spend absolutely large amounts in the satisfaction of mere preferences (their own or other people's). It is they upon whom duties to aid in the fulfillment of basic rights fall first, other things being equal.

Now, why? Or, more to the point, why me, assuming I am among the affluent? Why am I required to sacrifice my preferences, if necessary, in order that someone else may enjoy his or her basic rights? Why accept the priority principle? A number of quite different arguments can be given.[14] One of the strongest, I think, rests upon the still deeper and broader principle that degrading inequalities ought to be avoided. A refusal on the part of an affluent person to use any of the wealth at his or her command in order that others may be enabled to enjoy their basic rights would be an insistence upon the maintenance of a degree of inequality that is degrading: an inequality constituted by protected affluence and unprotected subsistence.

The assumption about inequality incorporated into this principle is only that there are types of inequality that are morally unacceptable, namely, inequalities that are degrading. This principle, which I will call the degradation prohibition, is not a strongly egalitarian principle. The principle does not mean that all inequality is unacceptable—it leaves open the possibility of justifying various sorts of inequalities. The principle means only that inequalities that are incompatible with self-respect—that are humiliating—are impermissible. Inequality is not prohibited by the principle but limited.[15]

It may be useful to recall as precisely as possible where we are in the overall argument of the book and what has, and has not, been established to this point. We have seen good reasons, I think, for concluding that everyone has subsistence rights or, in other words, that subsistence rights are universal. We have, second, seen that the provision of the social guarantees against standard threats that is an essential part of every moral right, or, at the very least, of every basic right, necessitates the fulfillment of all three main kinds of correlative duties. But, although everyone has a right to subsistence and every right to subsistence includes the three kinds of duties, it does not follow that toward every person with a right to subsistence, every other person bears all three kinds of duties. It does seem necessary that every person should fulfill toward everyone else the duty to avoid depriving, or that duties of avoidance (I) are universal. But none of the other duties appears to be universal, and for each of them we would need a principle for assigning responsibility.

For now I have chosen to focus on the responsibility for duty III-2, the duty to aid those deprived as a result of failures in the performance of duty I and duties II-1 and II-2. With the world in the state it is in, much is at stake in the assignment of these duties to aid the already deprived. The remaining question, then, is: given that everyone has a right to subsistence, and that every right to subsistence includes a duty to aid, who have the duties to aid? And the answer suggested is: at least the affluent, characterized as those consuming the absolutely largest amounts for the satisfaction of mere preferences (their own or other people's).[16] This is the answer dictated by the priority principle, which is itself required by the degradation prohibition. These abstract connections can also be put more concretely, as follows.

That extreme inequalities in security or subsistence are subversive of the dignity of the deprived, as well as their vitality and longevity, is readily apparent, I think, but it may be worth briefly spelling out the situation for each of these two basic rights. The conflict between self-respect and the diametrical differences in rights to liberty where some people are guaranteed liberty and some are not, will then be perfectly obvious as well, if it is not already. First, the extreme inequality created when the security of some is guaranteed and the security of others is not:

> Consider what the absence from some people of the protection of physical security accorded to other people would actually mean. Some people—call them the "superiors"—are adequately protected against all violations of their physical security, but other people—call them the "inferiors"—are not protected against violations of their security. If a "superior" were to assault another "superior," society would protect the victim (just as it would have protected the attacker if he or she had been the victim instead). If an "inferior" were to assault a "superior," society would of course also protect the victim. But whenever the victim of assault was an "inferior"—irrespective of whether the attacker was a "superior" or another "inferior"—the victim would be provided no defense by society. The "inferior" victim would be left to fend for himself or herself. "Superiors" are protected against physical assaults against which "inferiors" receive no protection. This inequality in provision for physical well-being is so profound as to be degrading to those who are denied consideration. Such a policy would add certain humiliating insult to probable physical injury.

Although I believe that it is virtually undeniable that an inequality consisting of the presence of physical protection for some and its absence from others is insulting and degrading, it is difficult to explain why, if any further explanation is actually needed. It seems to have to do with the importance of what is at stake. The less important a consideration is, the easier it is to accept inequalities with regard to it. But with regard to physical security, a minimum of which is needed for the enjoyment of every other right, an inequality that leaves some people below the minimum is morally unacceptable. By assuming that a person's physical security is not very important—not important enough for society to protect—the unequal policy described and the institutions embodying it are virtually implying: this person is not very important. For a person's physical security is not separable from the person. Indeed, one of the horrors of a rape that leaves permanent psychological damage or a beating that leaves permanent brain damage is that the person himself or herself is changed by the violence. In a real sense, the person may not survive even if he or she is not killed. This is a matter, in the apt Fraser/Vance phrase, of "the integrity of the person."[17] If physical security is important enough to be the substance of a basic right, it is too important for inequalities in social guarantees for it to be morally tolerable.

The situation created by a refusal, on the part of those with more than enough resources to provide for their own subsistence, to allow transfers to those unable to provide for their subsistence is a still more extreme inequality:

> To deny a helpless person material resources that would save the person's life or vitality in order to protect material resources controlled but not needed so desperately by one or more other persons is to inflict a profound indignity—not to mention probable death—upon the person whose urgent needs are denied. For it is not merely that the person's own preferences are to be subordinated to someone else's preferences, nor merely that the person's own needs are to be subordinated to someone else's needs, but that the person's most vital needs are to be subordinated to someone else's preferences—by accepted social practices and institutions. For social institutions to protect one person's capacity to satisfy wishes in addition to enjoying rights, at the cost of failing to protect another's capacity to enjoy any rights at all, is to place the second person in so secondary a position as to be insulting. It is not tolerable to treat one human being as so inferior to another human being that what he or she needs for a normal life can be acknowledged to be less important than what someone else wants but can do well without. This inequality in provision for physical well-being is so profound as to be degrading to those who are denied consideration. Such a policy would add certain humiliating insult to probable physical harm.

As in the case of physical security, it would be difficult to explain any further why an inequality consisting of some people's being protected in more than subsistence and other people's not being protected even in subsistence is degrading. Once again, the fulfillment of one's fundamental subsistence needs seems too important a matter on which to "compromise" by settling for less than one's vital minimum, when the total resources available are adequate to provide the minimum for all with more left over for many. A full glass for me and an empty glass for you is, in any case, not exactly a compromise—a point to which we will soon return.

And it is because an inequality that consists of some people's security being guaranteed by society and other people's security being ignored, or of some people's subsistence or liberty being guaranteed and other people's being ignored, is degrading that the priority principle presented in the preceding section is the appropriate guide for the assignment of responsibility for basic duties. The only feasible and reasonable way to avoid the inequalities condemned by the degradation prohibition is to allocate responsibility according to the priority principle.

The other way to avoid inequalities in the guarantees, of course, would be to have no social guarantees for the enjoyment of the substances of basic rights for anyone. But we have already seen too much reason to acknowledge at least three basic rights to be able to deny them to most people. All we are seeing now is (1) that if basic rights are guaranteed to some, they ought to be guaranteed to all, and (2) that if they are to be guaranteed to all, the transfers required by the priority principle are the proper ones to make. Otherwise, to deprivation is added degradation.

Deprivation and Fairness

As I understand things, the degradation prohibition is near the moral rock-bottom. If someone thought that the principle that one ought to avoid degrading inequalities were itself in need of being justified by some further principle that was still more fundamental, I would be hard put to add another level to the argument. Where one is unable to move deeper, one can sometimes move to the side, so to speak, and can show that the same conclusion is also supported by another principle, which is no less fundamental than the first. The convergence of equally fundamental principles can then be at least as good a reason for the conclusion as further direct support for the single principle initially appealed to might have been.

Accordingly, it may be worth noticing that degradingly extreme inequalities are also unfair. I suspect the reason these extreme inequalities are unfair is because they are so degrading. But perhaps, conversely, they are degrading because they are so unfair. Fortunately, for present purposes we need not decide about the relation between the humiliation and the unfairness, since the extreme inequality I have described turns out in any case to be very unfair as well as degrading. I will try now to show why it is also so unfair.[18]

A quite different way to put the thesis of this section is as follows: property laws can be morally justified only if subsistence rights are fulfilled. Social guarantees for the retention of property are unfair unless combined with social guarantees for the availability of subsistence. Throughout the world one may not simply take from others even what one genuinely needs. Conceptions of property (and of gifts) differ, and rules about property differ: it may be private, state, communal, or—usually—mixed. But whoever legally controls what, people may not just take what they need from what they do not legally control and have not received as a gift. It is possible that if the person in need asks, what is needed will be given. Still, it may not merely be seized. Stealing is as illegal under socialism as it is under capitalism and all other economic systems. Hence, this point will be a general one about property systems, not a point about any particular kind of property system.

It is often asked, taking some set of rules against stealing for granted as background, whether it is really wrong to steal a loaf of bread to feed one's starving children. But the deeper question, as the great "consent theorists" have recognized, is: is it, or on what terms is it, fair to have such rules? For rules of property, however traditional or unconscious in origins, are subject to conscious modification and are indeed constantly undergoing judicial, legislative, and customary modification. To try to have no rules about property would be lunatic. But from the fact that the elimination of all rules of property and theft is virtually impossible, it does not follow that even the best set of rules (whatever they are) are acceptable unconditionally. It may instead be the case that in order for any insistence upon compliance with even the best set of rules concerning ownership and stealing to be fair, the rules must fulfill one or more conditions.

Under what condition, then, is it fair to have property institutions that prohibit theft even by someone who is in fear of starving, or, more likely, slowly but inexorably deteriorating from nutritional insufficiencies? The answer, I think, is: only if the same set of institutions provides guarantees that the person in question will not in fact degenerate from insufficient consumption. More generally, institutions governing the ownership and transfer of property can be fair only if possession of the commodities required for the satisfaction of subsistence needs is guaranteed to those from whom compliance with the institutions is demanded. The moral acceptability of the enforcement of property rights depends upon the enforcement of subsistence rights. Why? How do we determine that this is a requirement of fairness?

A two-step argument supports the judgment that property institutions can be fair only if subsistence needs for economic commodities are guaranteed. The first step appeals to what might be called the saints-and-heroes principle: it is not fair to expect ordinary human beings to abide by rules that only a saint or a hero could reasonably be expected to obey. Judgments about what it is reasonable to expect from ordinary people, although they are regularly made in legislation, judicial decisions, and elsewhere, are notoriously slippery. I cannot imagine myself, however, simply letting myself deteriorate and die out of respect for a set of social institutions that had actually presented me only with the choice: steal or deteriorate. In fact, it may be insulting to genuine saints to suggest that they would willingly die for such an inhumane system, an act more foolish than saintly, I would think. In any case, the demand is unfair because it is a pyschologically unrealistic candidate for service as a general rule.[19]

I am of course not discussing a situation in which lazy bums are declining well-paying jobs in favor of armed robbery. The situation in question is one containing no uncorrupt legal alternative to taking what is needed except doing without. Rather than displaying heroism, a decision to lay down one's life in obedience to the rules of such a heartless system would demonstrate a lack of a healthy sense of self-respect, not to mention the absence of a normal sense of self-interest, more craven than constrained.[20]

Now it might be replied that the ultimate point about fairness is that it is not fair to demand something from people and provide them with nothing in return: nothing for something is clearly an unfair exchange. And the protection of property itself is something for those with property and nothing for those indefinitely without property.[21] But those with no property need not be receiving nothing for something. They could be receiving all sorts of other benefits of other types in fair exchange for their compliance with the rules for the protection of property, such as protection of their bodily integrity against another kind of threat: assaults by other people in the form of murder, torture, rape, etc. In short, people could be provided security rights, but not subsistence rights, in exchange for their cooperation with property rights. This is no small benefit in exchange for not stealing, and it is not clear, according to this view, that demanding compliance with rules requiring this exchange is psychologically unrealistic or unfair. Why wouldn't this be a reasonable compromise between the propertied and the property-less?[22]

But the "compromise" consists of protected affluence and unprotected subsistence. The reason for continuing to consider any such arrangement to be unfair starts from the crucial fact that the demand upon the deprived is not simply to refrain generally from stealing, but not to steal even when provided no alternative to going without the essentials of subsistence to which they have no other access. They are being asked to refrain from taking effective action in the face of a standard kind of destructive threat to their vital interests in life and bodily integrity: economic circumstances over which they have no control.

The interests that without subsistence rights are left unprotected against overwhelming economic circumstances are vital interests: health, physical vitality, physical soundness, life itself. What is unfair is to make any substantial demands of people some of whose vital interests are left unprotected against a major, common threat against which it is quite possible to protect them: it is unfair to demand of people actions the very performance of which would preclude for themselves a way of protecting a vital interest while failing to provide some other protection for that interest, when it is possible to protect it by means that do not threaten any vital interest of anyone.[23] This will be called the principle of priority for vital interests over non-vital interests, or, for short, the vital-interests principle. Thus it may be perfectly fair to insist that no one ever simply take communal property, private property of others, or any property not theirs, provided institutions are available to transfer necessities to those who cannot provide for their own subsistence. But it is unreasonable to arrange human insitutions in a way that threatens vital interests when they can be arranged in a way that does not threaten vital interests.

Failure to abide by the vital-interests principle may be a kind of unfairness because it is a case of degrading inequality: not the more obvious case of treating equals unequally, but a case of treating extreme unequals equally. To protect non-vital interests by means that preclude the satisfaction of vital interests is to treat non-vital interests as if they are as important as—actually, as more important than—vital interests. On the other hand, as I mentioned earlier, this kind of inequality may be degrading because it is patently unfair. I have no clear intuitions about which is the more primitive concept. In any case, protected affluence in the face of unprotected subsistence is clearly both degrading and unfair to those who are unable to maintain life and health. For both reasons it would be wrong for the affluent to maintain their current advantages rather than to do their fair share to aid those deprived of subsistence by the past failures of social institutions.

In this short book I have generally avoided commenting in the text on other theories. But in the face of John Rawls's theory of justice as fairness I can hardly take an opposing position on minimal economic justice, as I have in this section, without at least a very brief direct response to the Rawlsian position, which can be relied upon to have raised significant issues even when it is unacceptable.[24] Many general difficulties face hypothetical consent arguments of the kind constructed by John Rawls, since they treat like products of a voluntary decision social relationships and institutions that people not only already find themselves in when they become mature enough to make rational decisions but are deeply shaped by. Nevertheless, social-contract stories can be at least a graphic way to picture some questions about what can be rationally justified. And all that I want to establish here is that Rawls does not succeed, in his own terms, in showing that it would be rational to agree to distributive principles that guarantee no floor. Subsistence rights are such a floor.

Like someone committed to the fulfillment of subsistence rights, Rawls does focus his theory upon the fate of the worst-off. No change is an improvement by Rawlsian standards of justice unless it changes for the better the position of the worst-off. But instead of providing a floor, or, to change the metaphor, a life-preserver, Rawls provides only a rope, hitching the worst-off (in a rather loose way) to all the better-off. Whenever the better-off improve themselves, the rope of justice requires that the worst-off should be pulled upward too, by at least a little. But Rawlsian theory contains no provision that everyone's head must, for a start, be held above the surface of the water. I am reminded of Tawney's famous metaphor about the vulnerability of Chinese peasants who were said to be like "a man standing permanently up to the neck in water, so that even a ripple might drown him."[25] The Rawlsian difference principle can be fulfilled while people continue to drown but with less and less water over their heads.[26]

Rawls says little about the renunciation of violence and trickery, but a critical element in agreeing to live in accord with the Rawlsian principles would be such a surrender of alternative means for trying to satisfy one's needs, including one's subsistence needs. I do not see how Rawls could possibly demonstrate that agreeing to be governed unresistingly by a set of institutions that do not guarantee the fulfillment of one's subsistence needs is more rational than any other strategy, including a refusal to agree to anything. One alternative to agreement on principles of justice is to reserve to oneself the option of taking by stealth or force, if necessary, one's vital necessities. I am saying not that this alternative is clearly more rational but only that it is not clearly less rational.[27] It is Rawls who holds that unanimous agreement is possible on terms that are rational for everyone.

Or rather, he stipulates that there is to be a unanimous agreement and argues that his principles are superior to the alternatives on which unanimous agreement might be possible.[28] But the stipulation that there shall be unanimous agreement begs the critical question, because to stipulate that there will be an agreement is simply to stipulate that no one has any minimum demands for which it is reasonable to hold out and refuse to be cooperative. And that is not at all clear, especially when the minimum demand might be for the fulfillment of what I am calling basic rights.[29]

Rawls would need to show that abandonment of all struggle aimed at fulfilling basic rights, without receiving in exchange any guarantee that even subsistence needs will be fulfilled by the institutions to which one is expected to declare loyalty, is clearly more rational in general than continuing the struggle. On what grounds this choice could be shown generally to be more rational I cannot imagine. Surely the relative wisdom of the alternative strategies would depend in part on the prospects that the struggle would succeed, which surely would vary from one situation to another, and also in part on one's sense of dignity and whether it countenanced voluntarily settling for less than one's most basic needs—in some cultures death in a struggle for subsistence would be considered more honorable than submissively withering, and it is not apparent why this is less rational than acceptance of a radical inequality that leaves one without physical necessities.[30]

Is it clearly more rational to agree that one's fortunes may permissibly be indefinitely low, provided only that when those who are already better-off than oneself become still better-off, one's own fortunes must improve at least slightly, rather than trying, at least where there is some prospect of success, to mobilize effective opposition to any system of institutions that does not redistribute available wealth until everyone has an adequate minimum? When people have so little to lose—indeed, have no definite absolute amount to lose—it is difficult to give them motivating reasons not to resort to violence except in the form of a greater capacity for violence that makes their own violence likely to fail. This is a formula for the kind of deprivation enforced by repression that is widely followed today, a phenomenon that Rawls himself undeniably abhors.

We have, then, two fundamental reasons that separately and together support the priority principle in its requirement that the affluent take some responsibility for the fulfillment of the subsistence duty to aid (III-2). A refusal by the affluent to shoulder this responsibility would constitute an attempt to preserve inequalities that are degrading for those deprived of subsistence and are unfair to them as well. That social institutions should be used to preserve rather than to eliminate extreme and degradingly unfair inequalities is beyond rational justification. The affluent who insist on preserving such institutions are entitled to no indignation when they find the deprived being uncooperative. For the deprived will be correct in thinking that such extreme inequalities can be backed only by might, not right.

6

NATIONALITY AND RESPONSIBILITY

Any person who is already deprived of subsistence and is helpless to provide it for himself or herself will from that time never enjoy any human right, unless some other persons fulfill the duty to aid the helpless one. The helpless person may indeed not long survive and is very unlikely to survive with minimal physical and mental capacities growing, if young, or intact, if grown. If the person has been deprived of adequate subsistence since birth, death will come almost certainly early and very certainly before any human right is ever known.

But these are reasons why aid should be provided, not reasons why I should provide aid. It cannot be my duty, because it is beyond my capacity, to prevent every death and deformity caused by deprivation of uncontaminated water or nutritious food. To acknowledge this is not callous—it is only sane. Many people seem also to believe that any assignment of duties to aid that extends beyond national boundaries is for that very reason unfair, because one cannot have duties to aid toward anyone but members of one's own society, where one's own society is taken to be, roughly, national. Perhaps I have duties to aid other members of my own society, and perhaps I have duties to avoid depriving anyone, including members of other societies, but—the objection is—I surely cannot be expected as a matter of duty to provide aid to people in other societies. Charity, maybe, but duty, no.

I will call the core of this view the thesis that compatriots take priority—take it at least in the case of duties to aid.[1] The view need not completely deny that there are universal subsistence rights, but it does deny that any correlative duties to aid are universal, or even transnational. The view that compatriots take priority might accept the priority principle but restrict its application to the nation of the bearer of the duty. What I will try to do here, then, is (a) to survey some of the major kinds of reasons offered for taking national boundaries so very seriously in what is fundamentally a moral issue and (b) to indicate very briefly some reasons for doubt about each kind.

Priority for Compatriots: What Would It Mean?

First we need to glance at a few of the possible variants of the general thesis that compatriots take priority, before we canvass some of the rationales for the thesis. Naturally certain variants are more adequately supported by a given rationale than others are. A full formulation of a specific variant of the thesis must answer at least four questions (A)-(D).

Obviously it makes enormous difference (A) whether the thesis asserts that priority belongs to compatriots (1) sometimes, (2) always, or (3) never. Very likely the superficial answer is sometimes, and the interesting question is: in exactly which circumstances? Similarly, one must always determine (B) whether the thesis is that the assignment of priority to compatriots means that such priority is (1) morally required or (2) merely morally permissible—or, on the contrary, (3) morally prohibited, as it would be by a global application of the priority principle formulated in chapter 5.

Perhaps more interesting, though equally fundamental, are the closely related questions (C) whether shared nationality is being asserted to be (1) necessary, (2) sufficient, (3) both, or (4) nothing so definitive as any of these but nevertheless a consideration of some weight; and (D) whether shared nationality is seen to be (1) the source of or (2) the limit upon the moral relationship under consideration, or (3) both. It is probably worthwhile briefly to illustrate (C) and (D) and their intermingling. As a different kind of example of a type of moral relationship for which nationality is plausibly significant, consider rights and duties regarding war.

Shared nationality might be advanced as both source of and limit upon both rights and correlative duties and might be construed as either a necessary or a sufficient condition. If being compatriots is taken to be a necessary condition for certain people's having a certain right against certain other people, shared nationality is serving both as one source of rights and correlative duties and as a limit upon them. To take a specific right, suppose only fellow citizens can have respectively rights to receive protection and correlative duties to provide protection involving going to war. If shared nationality is indeed necessary, then the duty to go to war is limited by being owed, as a matter of right, only to compatriots. Thus, nationality serves as a limit upon those who can claim a right and upon those who have the corresponding duty. According to this view, one would not have a direct duty to risk one's life in battle in order to protect persons living under an allied government. And if shared nationality is only necessary (and not also sufficient) for having the duty to go to war, many compatriots of those with the right to be defended may still not have the duty to provide the defense, in virtue of failing to satisfy some additional necessary condition, such as being young and able-bodied. Thus, from the point of view of duties, shared nationality could be necessary but only necessary (and not also sufficient) for having a particular duty.

From the viewpoint of rights, it might similarly be necessary but not sufficient, as would be the case if only compatriots who had also been law-abiding were entitled to protection. More likely, shared nationality would be taken, from the viewpoint of rights, to be sufficient as well as necessary. In short, the position would be that *every* member of the nation had the right to claim protection from *some* members of the nation (and, as a matter of right, from no one else). This is, evidently, the conventional view of "military service."

So, choosing one of several plausible permutations of possible answers to questions (A)-(D), someone might advance a thesis of priority for compatriots that asserted: that shared nationality is

(A-2) always
(C-2) both necessary and sufficient for being
(B-1) morally required to go to war for the defense of
(D-3) all and only one's compatriots.

It is not necessary to ring all the changes. The point is simply that nationality's being a morally significant consideration could mean any one, or any of several combinations of more than one, thing in the general context of rights and duties. For each plausible version of the thesis, we need to ask: why? Why should exactly this priority go to compatriots?

Even if, as assumed above by way of illustration, a person has direct duties to risk his or her life in war only for compatriots, the same person may nevertheless have duties in the area of the distribution of resources—to fulfill duties to aid those deprived of subsistence, for example—among non-compatriots. Intuitively it is plausible that one might have obligations to share resources with persons for whom one would have no obligation to risk one's life. An inverse relation might hold between the degree of sacrifice one could be expected to make and the breadth of the group for whom one could be expected to make it, as we shall see in the next section.

Moral Justifications: Two Concentric-Circle Conceptions of Morality

Possible justifications for being morally required or allowed to grant priority to one's own compatriots can be superficially divided into two general groups: (1) views about the proper role of individual persons toward each other and (2) views about the proper role of such social institutions as governments and the citizens who live under them. The latter will be considered in the succeeding section.

The first grouping of justifications for granting priority to compatriots consists of a variety of moral views, otherwise dissimilar, that share the explicit implication—or, more often perhaps, the tacit assumption—that moral responsibility begins at home.[2] This cluster of views might be said to share the concentric-circle conception of morality.[3] The other people to whom one has some degree of responsibility are often conceived of as constituting a succession of concentric circles of outwardly diminishing responsibility. Responsibility is greatest to those at the center and trails off as one moves outward along a radius of the circles. According to such a view a number of compatriots take priority over other compatriots, but all compatriots take priority over non-compatriots.

Two major questions arise about theories with such a structure. The first concerns a matter on which individual theories differ sharply: the specification of the feature, or features, represented by the radii of the circle. What exactly is it of which people at the center share more and people farther from the center share less? Several kinds of answers have at least some plausibility, but here we can concentrate on two polar cases that portray the inner circles as, respectively, (1) *communities of sentiment* and (2) *communities of principle*. On the former interpretation the radii represent features like intimacy, or directness, and depth of personal involvement among the people who have responsibility for each other; on the latter the radii indicate quite different features like the extent to which the people with mutual responsibilities are committed to the same goals, principles, or basic values. Interpretation (1) might well place family and loved ones at the center and others less well and warmly known progressively farther from the center, as feelings toward them diminish in strength or significance. Interpretation (2), in contrast, might, although it need not, yield a different assignment of persons to places among the circles and a consequently different allocation of degrees of responsibility, especially if one had warm and important personal ties with people with whom one disagreed about many basic goals and values, since degree of responsibility would diminish as degree of agreement on principles diminishes. A number of variations and combinations of these two basic interpretations of the unifying element of the moral primary group, as I will call the community to which one has primary responsibilities, are of course possible. The brief discussion of nationalism in a later section of this chapter provides some concrete illustration of the interaction of sentiment and principle.

The other tantalizing question, which cuts directly across the first question about the relative weight assigned respectively to sentiment and principle, is whether (A) it is the very fact that people are compatriots, given some precise account of what being "compatriots" means, that is supposed morally to require or permit them to grant priority to each other in at least some circumstances, or (B) the grounds for the priority are some feature not intrinsically tied to nationality but as a matter of fact much more likely to be shared among compatriots than between non-compatriots. Is shared nationality (and whatever sentiments or principles shared nationality necessarily involves) the justifying grounds for the granting of priority, or is nationality simply a more or less reliable indicator that grounds of another sort are very likely, but not necessarily, available?

On the one hand, the very sharing of nationality might be taken in itself to be the grounds for some sort of moral bond: one might be taken to owe one's compatriots more than one owed other people because they are one's compatriots—and, of course, because of what being compatriots is taken to involve. Obviously several alternative accounts are available concerning which features of moral significance are taken to be exclusive to and shared among compatriots.[4] The focuses of such accounts range from emphasis on a shared history, culture, and language; to emphasis on an interdependent economy and single system of taxation and economic transfers; to participation in a social network of mutual expectations, some explicitly created and others perhaps tacit; to participation in a single political system. Such accounts need to be able to explain why participation in a single political system, for instance, creates responsibilities beyond the obligation to abide, when participating, by the prohibitions essential to the system. Should I make greater efforts to reduce malnutrition in Kentucky than in Kerala merely because Kentucky is in the American political system and Kerala is in the Indian? Why is that a good reason? What is the connection between political system and the this kind of moral responsibility?

On the other hand, one might turn out on the basis of various moral theories generally to have greater responsibility for compatriots, but *not because* they were compatriots. Several different interpretations of the radial feature that determines the degree of moral responsibility on the concentric-circle conception might have the result that those closer to the center are mostly compatriots and those farther from it are mostly not compatriots. The reason for the greater responsibility might be (1) the stronger sentiment, (2) the greater agreement upon principles, or whatever is the radial feature that dictates the allocation of people among concentric circles of responsibility, and not the shared nationality as such. It would simply be an important but contingent fact that one tended, for example, to have a greater sharing of purposes with one's compatriots, if indeed this is a fact.

If this were the outcome, national boundaries would have ethical significance, but only as indicators, not as the grounds for the moral responsibility. And the reliability of national boundaries as indicators of the presence of the morally relevant feature might turn out to vary from nation to nation or from feature to feature. This outcome, the discovery of a merely contingent and not very reliable association between shared nationality and the morally relevant shared feature, would probably be tantamount to the disintegration of the thesis that compatriots have priority.

The deepest challenges to the conviction that one has strong responsibilities to compatriots because they are compatriots, however, may lie in the rival loyalties possible toward transnational communities that include non-compatriots as well as compatriots and toward subnational communities that include some compatriots but not others. The list of alternative groupings that could with some plausibility be taken to identify those within which moral bonds are strongest—the moral primary group—is extremely long. Quite a few transnational groups, that is, groups that contain some but not all the citizens of several nations, are currently perceived to be the subject of strong allegiances.

Suppose Abdul is a Syrian and a Muslim and an Arab. Initially, it might seem at least as plausible to contend that Abdul has responsibilities to non-Syrian, non-Arab Iranian Muslims, because of their shared Islamic faith, that override his responsibilities to, say, Christian Syrians, or to contend that Abdul has responsibilities to non-Syrian Arabs to oppose Syrian policies hostile to the pan-Arab movement that override his responsibilities to fellow Syrians, as to contend that his responsibilities as a Syrian to other Syrians override his more widely shared Arab and Muslim identities. Or, if Charlotte is French and female and black, the relative strength of her respective obligations, if any, to white French males and to (at least some) non-French black women is surely somewhat unclear, given only these meager facts without a background theory of responsibility. If Abdul is a devout and strict Muslim, he might feel a strong commitment to fellow believers in what the Western press calls fundamentalist Islam, which is a powerful force across many nation-states. And Charlotte might believe that being black gives her a natural identity, not subject to voluntary renunciation, with her ancestors.

Obviously some rival pretensions to being the moral primary group can also be asserted on behalf of many subnational groups, most notably perhaps the scores of more or less ethnically defined groups with inclinations toward political separatism, such as Iraqi Kurds, Iranian Kurds, Basques, South Moluccans, East Timorese, Serbo-Croatians, French Canadians, some American Indian tribes, quite a few African tribes, Scottish Nationalists, Eritreans, et al., as well as many similar non-separatist groups that are resigned to unenthusiastic membership in confederations of convenience. The difficulty is clear without rehearsing all the variations: showing that priority goes specifically to compatriots would involve more than the merely negative step of showing that it is unreasonable to think that one has the same obligations to all mankind (apart, perhaps, from one's offspring and dearest friends) and would have to include the positive demonstration that political—not religious, ethnic, ideological, sexual, etc.—boundaries are the circumference of the moral primary group.

Naturally, not every potential loyalty mentioned deserves to be taken equally seriously. And in any given case only one claim, or combination of claims, can be granted priority. Indeed, not every instance of sharing a property is an instance of sharing membership in a morally significant group.[5] Some shared properties are morally irrelevant: red-haired people of the world will probably never unite, and they presumably owe each other, as fellow bearers of red hair, nothing. Other shared properties are morally inappropriate bases for at least some kinds of priorities: shared ancestry must for many purposes be prohibited from being allowed to count. Shared citizenship in a nation-state seems, in general, both relevant and appropriate. The question is when, and why, it should count more than other considerations. If one ignores the importance of precise specification of the characteristic(s) in virtue of which compatriots allegedly deserve priority, it is easy to slide unconsciously from the virtually undeniable conviction that members of some group smaller than all mankind have moral claims stronger than the claims of any random human being outside the smaller group, to the much more specific conviction that the smaller group with the stronger claims is, under some definition, the nation. But the general belief that one has stronger moral ties with some smaller group than one has with all the rest of humanity could be correct without that smaller group's turning out to be, in particular, one's nation.

Any justification for the assignment of priority to compatriots would, then, need to include, among other elements, two closely tied basic steps: a *specification* of what is distinctive of compatriots—what all but only compatriots have in common—and a *justification* for attaching, in at least some cases, considerable moral significance to the distinctive feature specified. If two people are starving, why should it matter, to the point of my being bound to aid the one and not bound to aid the other, that the one and not the other is my compatriot? Why should I not instead allot my aid, for example, in accord with a duty to aid those deprived of subsistence, disregarding nationality entirely or giving nationality only "tie-breaking" weight? I know of no one who has adequately answered—or even straightforwardly and systematically tackled—these questions in defense of the thesis that compatriots take priority even when the compatriots' own subsistence rights are more than adequately fulfilled and the subsistence rights of non-compatriots are ignored by those around them.[6] Priority for compatriots as a moral theory is at best unproven, however widely assumed. Meanwhile, arguments for the generality of subsistence duties, like those given in earlier chapters, seem a more adequate moral view. We must now look briefly at two political views that offer partly complementary justifications—once again, I think inadequate ones—for granting priority to compatriots even to the point of failing to acknowledge subsistence duties to non-compatriots.[7]

POLITICAL JUSTIFICATIONS: TWO CONCEPTIONS OF GOVERNMENT

The Trustee/Adversary Theory of Government. One political view is what might be called the trustee, or adversary, theory of government: the proper role of every national government is primarily or exclusively to represent and advance the interests of its own nation. This view is so widely assumed that it is ordinarily taken to be obviously correct. Various formulations of this view are possible, distinguished from each other in part by the types of constraints they acknowledge and the extent to which these constraints are allowed to override national interest. Perhaps the term "adversary" should be reserved for less constrained and more aggressive variants. Most people would presumably agree that it is reasonable to acknowledge treaties and international law generally as constraints upon the pursuit of national interest. But it is less obvious what other "rules of the game," if any, ought to be observed by governments in their sometimes bitter advocacy of national interests that are sometimes zero sum. Ought a nation ever to refrain from pressing a natural advantage out of concern for the welfare of the people of another nation—for example, ought the United States (A) actively to support an international system of food reserves that could place a ceiling on the upward volatility of world prices for commodities the U.S. exports or (B) to encourage world prices to rise as high as they will go and sell all but token amounts to whichever nations can afford to buy at the top price regardless of the levels of poverty elsewhere (assuming that selling to the highest bidder would be in the long-term U.S. national interest and that a price ceiling would not be)?

Various formulations of the trustee/adversary theory of government would also differ in the precise basis offered for the role attributed to national governments. Rarely in print but frequently in political rhetoric one finds taxation presented as the basis: the goverment is spending our money so the government ought to be serving our interests. This appeals to a principle that he who pays the piper is morally entitled to call the tune. A quite different, more strictly political basis would be an account of representative government, maintaining, roughly, that in a representative form of government individuals are entrusted with executive and legislative office precisely and explicitly in order to act on behalf of those whom they represent.[8] A decision to sacrifice the interests of constituents, or anyhow the basic interests of the nation of which the constituency is a part, would according to this view quite literally be a betrayal of a trust. A person should seek and hold a representative role only if the person is prepared faithfully to represent the interests entrusted to him or her.

Almost inevitably, faithful representation of constituent interests, where those interests do in fact conflict with the interests of other constituencies, will involve serving in an adversary role and assuming that the interests of others will be advocated by their own representatives. At the national level, then, national leaders are to be expected from this point of view to be advocates for the national interest. This may be thought to be especially appropriate at the national level. Whereas the competition of conflicting national interests may be conducted within some minimal procedural rules, looking out for the interests of other nations must generally be the business of their own leaders.

The trustee/adversary theory has two main weaknesses. The first and more important is simply that the very most that the theory could establish, even if it were fully adequate, would be that national governments have no inherent duties—no duties merely because they are national governments—directly to promote the interests of people outside the borders they control. It would remain entirely possible that some of, or all, the people served by a particular national government would, on the basis of a moral view like those considered earlier in the chapter, themselves have transnational duties and that these citizens would ask their government to act in their behalf to coordinate the performance of the citizens' duties.[9] One interest that these citizens wish to have served may be their interest in seeing their transnational duties to aid fulfilled.

The second weakness of the trustee/adversary theory affects its implicit claim that this international competition of national advocates works out best—or, at least, well enough—for everyone. Recall some of the differences between the situation within one nation and the situation among nations. Within individual nations a great deal is determined simply by the competition of adversaries representing conflicting interests, but not everything is. Institutions also exist to care for those unable to compete or unsuccessful in the competition, to provide for goods that cannot derive from competition, to regulate competition within generally beneficial rules, etc. These national institutions are in various cases defective in certain respects, but at the international level comparable institutions are virtually non-existent. The critical difference is the absence from the international arena of institutions that are designed to provide for the minimum well-being of those whose trustee/advocates prove inadequate. Suppose the national grain purchasing agency of a poor country cannot afford to outbid the Soviet trading company in the competition for U.S. wheat, or is too corrupt or incompetent to make the adequate arrangements. What is to happen to the diets of the children in the country in question?

From the existence of a need for some institution to step into the breach when a national government fails, or loses a vital competition, nothing follows about which institution that should be. It certainly does not follow that some other national government or governments should be the ones to do, or to arrange to have done, what is necessary. But it is left open that something somewhat different from a simple competition among trustee/adversaries might be better. And it is certainly left unproven that simply having each government do its utmost for its own is the best arrangement. At present no institution provides adequately for the subsistence rights of persons deprived, ignored, or ill-served by their own national government. Look, for example, at the present "haphazard, inconsistent, and badly coordinated" response to the world's 10,000,000 refugees, most of whom are children.[10]

The Comparative-Advantage Theory of Government. The second view about the role of national government is what might be called the comparative-advantage account of the significance of national boundaries. This view is, in effect, that each nation's own government (or other social institutions) are best able to care for the welfare of the people of that nation and therefore each nation ought, in effect, to care for its own. So, it is not that Americans start out with more moral responsibility for people in Kentucky than for people in Kerala because the Kentuckians are in the same political system. The argument runs in the other direction: the U.S. government is, according to this view, less likely than is the Indian government (A) to know which policies will be beneficial in Kerala (comparative advantage in comprehension) or (B) to be able to implement them effectively (comparative advantage in implementation), and therefore it has less responsibility for Indians in Kerala than the Indian government does. The basic premise adopted is (1) that a government ought to concentrate its efforts where they will do the most good. It is then taken to be the case (2) that the U.S. government can do more good in Kentucky than in Kerala and (validly) inferred (3) that the U.S. government ought to concentrate its efforts in Kentucky rather than in Kerala, given these two choices. This theory can underlie the trustee/adversary theory and be presented as the explanation why that competition is supposed to work best.

However, though the argument central to the comparative advantage view is valid, both its first (moral) premise and its second (empirical) premise are open to some doubt. The first, "do the most good," is, as stated, hopelessly vague with regard to all sorts of choices, such as the choice between doing a great deal for each of a few individuals and doing less for more (where, say, the aggregate amount accomplished would be roughly equivalent).[11] Much more serious, any calculations involving compatriots and non-compatriots would beg the crucial question, for any calculations face the following dilemma. If the welfare of compatriots and the welfare of non-compatriots are weighted equally, it is assumed that national boundaries have no moral significance. But if the welfare of compatriots is weighted more heavily, it is assumed that national boundaries do have moral significance. Rather than helping to provide an answer to the question of the proper role of a national government, this reasoning must presuppose one.

The second premise, being an empirical form of hypothesis that needs to be stated in a version specific to each case, also needs to be checked against the facts in each case. But, as we have already seen, it seems most unlikely that every domestic government is always better able to comprehend and to implement the best solutions for all the problems of its people that might concern others.[12] Comprehension of effective solutions may require managerial or technical experience not available domestically, and implementation may require capital or a will to change not found domestically. At best it is an open question of fact in each case whether a nation's own government can or will provide for even its people's most desperate needs. But even where the factual second premise needed by the comparative-advantage view is correct, the basic fault in the moral first premise—that it must beg the question of the significance of national boundaries—remains.

More fundamental arguments are needed to settle that issue. And meanwhile the priority of all and only compatriots remains to be established.

Principled Sentiments: Two Aspects of Nationalism

In addition to the two general kinds of concentric-circle moral views and the two kinds of political views, all of which are presented as positive support for the priority of compatriots, we need to consider one general counter-argument against any thesis that people have significant transnational duties: the contention that all will come to nought in the wake of nationalism. If this is true, priority might go to compatriots by default, whatever the weaknesses in the theoretical support for this priority. Certainly someone might reasonably suggest that the power of nationalism is likely to engulf and overwhelm such motives as might undergird any sense of responsibility not focused upon compatriots. Look what the fervor of nationalism has done, it is often said, even to so initially powerful-seeming an internationalist movement as Marxism, not to mention the momentum for the United Nations and other institutions of world order, with their bases in calmer passions. Does not the virility of nationalism demonstrate the impotence of any sense of extra-national responsibility? This objection, in effect, rejects the assumption that it is psychologically plausible even to consider groups other than nation-states to be moral primary groups.

Three factors indicate that the sheer strength of nationalistic forces is less decisive an objection than it might initially seem to be. Two factors are of relatively superficial philosophical interest, but a third leads toward one of the deeper problems in the philosophical psychology of morality. First, the classic studies of nationalism are indeed rich, but they are also varied—and varied at the critical points of their respective conceptions of what nationalism is, why it rather abruptly (in the scale of human history) appeared, and what factors are necessary to its continued strength.[13] Are the revolutionary nationalism of 1789, the Nazi and Fascist nationalisms of the Hitler/Mussolini period, the Zionist nationalism of Israel, the anti-colonial nationalism of Nkrumah, and the expansionist nationalism of Sukarno and

Suharto usefully categorized as fundamentally the same phenomenon? It is neither obvious that they are not nor obvious that they are. For all the insights in individual studies of nationalism, it is difficult to draw firm general conclusions from the literature as a whole.

Second, at whatever level nationalism can plausibly be pegged, it is significantly threatened by both centrifugal and centripetal forces. Undoubtedly as great as the differences among the varieties of nationalism are the differences among the varieties of regionalism. Except for the ways in which they already constrain nationalism, there may be little else in common among OPEC, the EEC, the OECD, the Group of 77, NATO, ASEAN, OAS, the Andean Pact, the Helsinki Agreement, and Islamic fundamentalism. But some forces of some degree of strength are already channeling, if not constraining, nationalistic tendencies from outside.

And the threats from inside the modern nation-state, especially in the underdeveloped countries, may be at least as profound. Geertz defined a "primordial attachment" as a loyalty based upon:

> the assumed givens . . . of social existence: immediate contiguity and kin connection mainly, but beyond them the givenness that stems from being born into a particular religious community, speaking a particular language, or even a dialect of a language, and following particular social practices. These congruities . . . are seen to have an ineffable, and at times, overpowering, coerciveness in and of themselves.[14]

Primordial sentiments, which unfortunately have come often to be called primordialism, obviously can attach to the institutions and fellow citizens of a nation-state, where the nation-state is coextensive with what is taken to be a "given" community. In these cases, primordial sentiments may actually be the deeper explanation of what is called nationalism. In scope primordial attachments also need not be unlike the commitments of what have here been called concentric-circle conceptions of morality. The main point, however, is that primordial attachments are often to groups smaller than nation-states and may indeed undermine nationalistic forces.[15]

The third consideration is philosophically more complex and interesting—indeed, here the challenge of nationalistic sentiment to the plausibility of extra-national responsibilities leads toward a critical unresolved tension in the philosophical psychology of morality. I would suggest, with apologies to Kant, that sentiments unconstrained by principles lack authority, principles unsupported by sentiments lack effect. Sentiments, both in others and in ourselves, can be judged critically. The expression in action of some sentiments is to be welcomed, the expression of others is to be discouraged. For assessing sentiments one needs principles.

Principles, on the other hand, will be adopted only if they evoke the support of some felt sentiment. Action in accord with a principle needs to be motivated, and apart from the possibility of a Kantian *Achtung* inspired somehow by the very contemplation of the principle, the principle must somehow appeal to motivational springs of action that preexist the appeal.[16]

The interaction of sentiment and principle is, then, complex. In the light of one's principles one can criticize one's sentiments, discourage them, and sometimes extinguish, sometimes suppress, them. But one cannot run ahead of oneself. Attachment to the principle must develop—it must evoke a positive response in anyone who is to be motivated to act in accord with it. The principle cannot violate all one's deepest sentiments, nor can it simply fail to connect with sentiments that would then motivate action guided by the principle.[17]

A nationalistic community can, in the terms used earlier, be a community of sentiment, a community of principle, or—most typically, of course—a combination of large measures of each. Greatly over-simplifying, I would say that one core question is: is it reasonable in the light of nationalism and other deep human feelings and motives to suggest that people break out of what I have called concentric-circle conceptions of morality and include in the universe of persons to whom they bear, out of principle, significant duties, considerable numbers of persons who are not their fellow citizens? This may depend in part upon the degree to which the circles must be taken to be communities of sentiment rather than communities of principle, for the following reason.

The concentric-circle conception of morality received its classic statement (and critique) in Hume's *Treatise:*

> Now it appears, that in the original frame of our mind, our strongest attention is confin'd to ourselves; our next is extended to our relations and acquaintance; and 'tis only the weakest which reaches to strangers and indifferent persons. This partiality, then, and unequal affection, must not only have an influence on our behaviour and conduct in society, but even on our ideas of vice and virtue; so as to make us regard any remarkable transgression of such a degree of partiality, either by too great an enlargement, or contraction of the affections, as vicious and immoral.[18]

Again over-simplifying considerably, I would epitomize the Humean view as assuming that the limits of one's "affections," or sentiments, are the limits of one's obligations. Natural communities are communities of sentiment, and natural motivation will be lacking, according to Hume, for the behavior required by any substantial enlargement of the natural boundaries of concern, which are in fact for Hume even more restricted than national boundaries. Philosophers dissatisfied with the conjunction of (1) the general principle that the limits of sentiment are the limits of obligation and (2) the particular description given by Hume of where those limits naturally fall, have responded to the Humean view (whether or not directly to Hume's *Treatise*) in a rich variety of ways (that constitute alternatives to the concentric-circle view of morality). Rousseau and Kant, for instance, provide complementary responses: Rousseau urges enlargement of the existing limits of sentiment, attacking Humean assumption (2), whereas Kant more radically suggests severing the supposed tie between sentiment and obligation, attacking Humean assumption (1).[19]

More strongly and explicitly than Hume, Rousseau challenged what he considered to be the excessive rationalism of the Lockean conception of the foundations of rights and duties:

> I would show . . . that by reason alone, unaided by conscience, we cannot establish any natural law, and that all natural right is a vain dream if it does not rest upon some instinctive need of the human heart.[20]

But for Rousseau—at least for one side of the many-sided Rousseau—an appropriate education and socialization could prevent the essentially unnatural egocentricity produced by corrupt societies:

> Extend *amour-propre* over others, we will transform it into virtue, and there is no human heart in which this virtue does not have its root. The less the object of our cares concerns ourselves immediately, the less the illusion of particular interest is to be feared; the more one generalizes this interest, the more just it becomes; and the love of the human race is in us nothing other than the love of justice. Do you wish then that Emile love the truth, do you wish him to know it; make him in his activities exist outside himself.[21]

Kant too hoped that individuals could in a sense come to exist outside themselves, not through the nurturing of a (Rousseauan) emotionally "expansive soul," but through the universality of reasoning:

> For the pure conception of duty and of the moral law generally, with no admixture of empirical inducements, has an influence on the human heart so much more powerful than all other incentives which may be derived from the empirical field that reason, in the consciousness of its dignity, despises them and gradually becomes master over them.[22]

Thus in order for a principle to lead to action no preexisting sentiment toward the people to whom the principle applies is necessary. The full comprehension of the meaning of the principle will itself motivate action in accord with the principle. And progressing through the at least superficially very different formulations of the categorical imperative, which are nevertheless said to be equivalent formulations of the content of duty, Kant arrives at a conception of a realm of ends, to which contingencies like differences of ethnic group or nationality are utterly foreign:

> By "realm" I understand the systematic union of different rational beings through common laws. Because laws determine ends with regard to their universal validity, if we abstract from the personal differences of rational beings and thus from all content of their private ends, we can think of a

> whole of all ends in systematic connection, a whole of rational beings as ends in themselves as well as of the particular ends which each may set for himself. This is a realm of ends. . . . Thus there arises a systematic union of rational beings through common objective laws.[23]

At bottom Rousseau and Hume are much closer to each other than Rousseau and Kant are.[24] For, while both Rousseau and Kant (in at least some of their respective major writings) were seeking ways to expand moral consciousness, as each understood it, Rousseau and Hume had more nearly the same understanding of the nature of moral consciousness and agreed, in particular, that the limits of sentiment are the natural limits of obligation. The on-going contemporary discussion within analytic philosophy of the nature of reasons for moral action, of "why be moral?," and especially of "internalist" and "externalist" accounts of moral motivation is to a considerable extent an elaboration and refinement of the basic conflict between Hume/Rousseau and Kant.[25]

A definitive settlement of the question of the psychological realism of expecting the fulfillment of transnational duties would depend upon the resolution of at least some of the issues raised by Hume/Rousseau and Kant. Is it impossible that, as Rousseau hoped, the sentiments can be broadened? Is it also impossible that, as Kant thought, general principles can be made persuasive? I cannot answer these questions. The proponent of the thesis that compatriots take priority is assuming, however, that both are definitely answered and that the answer to each is: yes, it is impossible. But we do not know any such thing, and until we do the priority of compatriots remains, in this respect as well, unproven.

Nationalistic principles, then, can be subjected to philosophical scrutiny in the same manner in which all principles advanced as rationally justifiable can be. The principles that survive the test of criticism can then be used to assess nationalistic sentiments. To attempt to extinguish parochial sentiments, nationalistic or primordial, would be fatuous, but to constrain them may not be. Earlier chapters have suggested why we should try. This chapter is suggesting that no one has demonstrated that it is irrational or unrealistic to try to encourage the adoption of transnational principles and to nurture a sense of transnational responsibility.

Transnational Duties to Avoid Depriving

One does not prove a thesis even by fully disproving an argument against it. I have, of course, not disproven, but only cast various doubts upon, the thesis that compatriots take priority even in matters of subsistence duties to aid. And other arguments against the generality of duties to aid those deprived of subsistence have gone not only unrefuted but unremarked. So, it has certainly not been proven that anyone has transnational duties to aid. Nevertheless, I hope to have made it seem a little less obvious that there are no economic rights at all and a little more reasonable to think that at least toward basic subsistence rights all of us who enjoy affluence have duties, including duties to provide some of the needed aid. However unclear the matter of duties to aid may have been left—much more certainly needs to be said—it may be useful in conclusion to recall how very clear is the matter of duties to avoid depriving people of the substance of their rights, even transnational duties on the part of a national government.

We need to distinguish any duties a national government A as such may have toward people living under another government *B* from duties national government A has toward the same people as an agent for members of its own population. Apart from duties to avoid depriving, which are owed to every person, relatively few duties are borne by the national government of any given nation in its own right toward persons living in other nations, as opposed to being performed by the government acting as agent for some of, or all, its own constituents. In its own right any national government has a wide range of duties toward its own people, because it is their government—and because of what this means. A full explanation of the basis and extent of the duties of a national government toward its people would of course be a major undertaking and would lead us far afield. But no one, except advocates of some view of government according to which it is not a supreme duty of government to serve the people who live under it, would deny that among the duties of a national government is service as the agent for its constituents in their pursuit of some of their interests and in their fulfillment of some of their duties, especially interests and duties that are widely shared among the constituents and require coordination in their performance.

Many of the duties toward persons outside its own jurisdiction that a national government will fulfill are therefore, strictly speaking, duties borne by the government's constituents. They are the government's duties only indirectly by way of the government's duty to its constituents to serve as their agent, when they choose, in the fulfillment of their duties. In order to have a shorthand label I will use the name "service duties" for duties correlative to rights that actually fall upon some of, or all, the people of a nation but ought to be fulfilled on behalf of the people by their national government. I will sometimes call service duties the government's duties, but I will always mean that they are duties of the government only in this indirect sense. All a government's service duties are, by this definition, derived from the duties of its people. One of the most urgent and important duties for Americans is undeniable at the theoretical level, and so is the derivative service duty for the U.S. government. In fact, this duty is extremely powerfully entailed by the theoretical structure of rights now before us, because it is fully required independently by each of two fundamental propositions, which will be recalled below, and is in this special sense a double duty.

It is clear, first, that the duty to avoid depriving is universal across individuals and institutions. Accordingly, the transnational duty to avoid depriving is one of the few duties that do fall upon governments in their own right as powerful institutions capable of causing severe deprivations when they do not restrain themselves. In the case of a superpower like the United States the capability of the national government, if it is not restrained, to cause deprivation in the farthest corners of the globe, even by its "domestic" policies, is enormous. A change in "domestic" U.S. farm policy, for example, can almost immediately raise the price of bread in New Delhi.

But individual Americans, of course, also share in the universal duty not to deprive others of their basic rights. A clear practical implication of this duty is that Americans, like people of every other nationality, ought to restrain not only themselves as individuals but also the government that is their agent from depriving anyone, including people of other countries, of their rights. Thus, the U.S. government has a second, service duty owed to its constituents to avoid contributing to deprivations of rights, just as it is required in its own right as a powerful social institution to avoid depriving people of the substance of their rights. Therefore, a government that does violate, or assist in violating, the rights of people outside its own territory is failing in its duties both to the victims of the deprivation and, as an agent with service duties, to its own population. It would be difficult to imagine a much stronger case against one government's complicity in violations of rights by other governments. This has strong implications for U.S. foreign policy, and we can now briefly consider a few examples.

·III·

NEW CHALLENGES TO BASIC RIGHTS

·7·

RIGHT-GROUNDED DUTIES AND THE INSTITUTIONAL TURN

As far as I can tell, one of the most useful effects of the first edition of *Basic Rights* was to help to throw open a number of issues about the duties that need to be performed if rights are in fact to be secure. Or perhaps I should say "help to throw into confusion." In any case, during the subsequent years I along with others, some of whom I will mention below, have continued to struggle with issues about both the specification and the assignment of right-grounded duties, two intertwined complexes of problems concerning the "division of moral labor."[1] Here I would like to rework once again some of the persistent questions about rights and their duties, indicating a little about how my picture of them has evolved so far.

John Locke had taken for granted that the right to accumulate private property was limited by a universal right to subsistence.[2] A balanced picture of rights of this kind, including guarantees for both liberties and subsistence, had been reaffirmed by various U.S. political leaders, most powerfully perhaps by Franklin Delano Roosevelt.[3] In the first year of the Carter Administration (1977), Secretary of State Cyrus Vance announced a balanced view as the basis for the enhanced attention that, it was promised, would be given to human rights in U.S. foreign policy.[4] The secretary of state's affirmation of rights nevertheless quickly came under philosophical attack, including a politically influential critique in 1978 by Charles Frankel, maintaining that "the list proposed by Secretary Vance, and particularly the economic and social rights of which it speaks, must be characterized as somewhat puzzling."[5] My discussion of duties in chapter 2 was initially intended primarily to assist, by portraying a little more realistically how rights function in practice, with the refutation of some bad arguments against balanced accounts of rights like those embraced by Locke, Roosevelt, and Carter/Vance, and of course embodied in international law. Several bad arguments depended upon, among other things, a highly overabstracted and thereby oversimplified picture of rights as falling into two neat types: "negative rights" and "positive rights." (To this day many theorists portray this crude polarity as a distinction crucial to the architecture of all rights.) The supposed "negative" and "positive" rights were being forced into this simplistic abstract dichotomy on the basis, not of the nature of the substance of the right (what the right was a right to), but of the supposed nature of the duties required to fulfill the right, which were in turn being given only half-hearted attention.

Each of a number of rights has as its substance one of the varieties of liberty, for example. If everything must simply be divided into negative and positive, some liberties are clearly "positive"; for example, many political liberties involve active participation in self-government, which is a highly active, and in that sense positive, undertaking. So even if one did concentrate on the substance of liberty rights themselves, and one was determined to label everything either positive or negative, some rights would turn out to be positive because some liberties are positive. But other liberties, looked at simply in themselves, would indeed turn out to be "negative"; some types of liberty consist mainly in being left alone by all other persons, not in, say, participating actively in one's own self-government. So one could have reasonably said that a right to a liberty of noninterference was a negative right in the sense that what is protected when this right is protected is negative: the protected liberty consists at its core in not being interfered with. This obviously leaves out all that must be done to protect, and otherwise provide for, even such a negative liberty, which is by no means mainly negative, but to take implementation seriously is precisely to turn to duties.

Yet an appeal to the core substance of rights was not the kind of argument being made two decades ago. When Charles Frankel, for example, attacked Cyrus Vance's balanced list of rights for including the economic and social rights that are entrenched in the international law of human rights, Frankel did not argue that the protected content of all economic and social rights is more like positive rights to political liberties than it is like negative rights to noninterference. Instead, he emphasized the onerousness and alleged impracticality of the duties allegedly distinctively involved in fulfilling economic and social rights—the supposed "dangerously utopian overtones" of seriously attempting to honor them.[6]

The picture underlying such criticisms seemed, then, fundamentally to be that rights are negative if the duties necessary to fulfill them are (exclusively) negative, and rights are positive if the duties necessary to fulfill them are (at least partly) positive. It was then announced that the performance of the positive duties would be too much reasonably to ask of people, if not literally impossible for them to bear, and that, accordingly, the positive so-called rights to which these onerous duties were correlative would have to be disqualified from being genuine rights, although they could be kept as the goals of aspirations. Most critics of the balanced view simply helped themselves as well to the crucial, and false, assumptions that all economic and social rights are positive and no civil and political rights are positive, on the basis of one or two quick examples.

Against this I suggested, in chapter 2, that while some duties are at the negative end of the spectrum and others are at the positive (and many are in between), no right can, if one looks at social reality, be secured by the fulfillment of only one duty, or only one kind of duty. If one looks concretely at specific rights and the particular arrangements that it takes to defend or fulfill them, it always turns out in concrete cases to involve a mixed bag of actions and omissions. Two points became evident. First, in general, while one can line up particular duties correlative to various rights on a spectrum running from onerous actions to costless omissions, what one cannot find in practice is a right that is fully honored, or merely even adequately protected, only by negative duties or only by positive duties. It is impossible, therefore, meaningfully and exhaustively to split all rights into two kinds based upon the nature of their implementing duties, because the duties are always a mixture of positive and negative ones.

Second, specifically concerning the economic and social rights that are the intended target of the dismissive dichotomy, it is simply not the case that all, or most, civil and political rights can be fulfilled entirely or mostly by negative duties, while all, or most, economic and social rights must be fulfilled entirely or mostly by positive duties. This second point is true for a myriad of reasons, not least that civil and political rights, on the one hand, and economic and social rights, on the other, often cannot be fulfilled separately from each other.

The main point so far is simply that duties are complicated, far beyond anything reducible to, or helpfully summarized as, negative/positive. Duties do not come in only two kinds, but in several, and the provisions for the secure enjoyment of any one thing that people have a right to will involve duties of several kinds. Jeremy Waldron has recently captured this in the apt image of "successive waves of duty": "Each right is best thought of not as correlative to one particular duty (which might then be classified as a duty of omission or as a positive duty of action or assistance), but as generating successive waves of duty, some of them duties of omission, some of them duties of commission, some of them too complicated to fit easily under either heading."[7] We may, for example, first tell others not to interfere with what a person has a right to. When we find that some are interfering anyway, we establish police to stop them. Then when the police turn out to be corrupt, we reeducate the police and go after the drug dealers who corrupted them. Going after the drug dealers may be possible only after defeating the incumbent politicians, which may depend upon an uncorrupt judiciary. And so forth, until the person actually enjoys what Thomas W. Pogge nicely calls "secure access" to the substance of her right.[8] The only way to be safe from interference in one's private life may be first to become politically active, as many a ghetto resident has reluctantly discovered. That requires usable political rights, the implementation of which depends upon the performance by a wide range of people of another wide range of duties. The need for such second, third, and further waves of duties is readily foreseeable. Adequate arrangements to secure any right will include advance provisions for Waldron's predictably necessary successive waves.

The intricate interweaving of rights of diverse kinds also suggests the image of a fabric, especially one of those rough fabrics with threads of different sizes and strengths. Some of the threads are stronger and more crucial than others—the basic rights—but even the strong threads support each other and support and are supported by the weaker threads. A seeker of privacy will be more secure in a society in which rights of political participation are well protected, because the addicts will keep breaking in as long as the politicians ignore the drug trade. The privacy seeker will also do better, other things being equal, if there is a free press and due process.

One pitfall for philosophers is already evident here: the danger of drifting into unhelpfully saying merely that no right can be safely enjoyed unless numberless people perform innumerable duties. One strategy I employed in the first edition to guard against this danger was the strategy of attempting to identify some of the basic rights. While I never intended to suggest, as some people have misunderstood me, that the three basic rights I discussed at greater length—physical security, subsistence, and liberty (taken to include both social participation and physical movement)—were *the only* basic rights, I would still defend the attempt to identify strategically critical rights.[9] However, I do not want to pursue that here but instead to stick with issues about duties.

Unfortunately for us theorists, while it would indeed be unhelpful to say *merely* that no right can be safely enjoyed unless numberless people perform innumerable duties, this is in fact the case. Indeed, notoriously, most people whom we ever actually encounter must perform their negative duties if we are to enjoy even a reasonable level of physical safety. Anyone who has ever blundered into a situation in which it was entirely unclear whether large numbers of the strangers present had peaceable intentions can testify to the level of insecurity, psychological and physical, that arises from actually not being able to count upon negative duties generally being performed, as those of us in fortunate situations normally can. Theorists, however, must find more to say than that it is all complicated and that a lot of people, including total strangers, bear a lot of duties toward each other.

In chapter 2 I suggested my "very simple tripartite typology of duties" (p. 52), shortly adding a few subcategories (p. 60). Evidently, chapter 2 in general and the tripartite typology in particular have been by far the most discussed portions of the book. A number of elaborations seem now to be called for. First, the practical focus of this book is, as indicated in the subtitle, the foreign policy of the United States. The two most prominent ways that consideration of human rights is built into the legislation governing U.S. foreign policy are both sections of the Foreign Assistance Act: Section 116, usually referred to as the "Harkin Amendment," after its sponsor Senator Tom Harkin of Iowa; and Section 502B. Both Section 116, which governs economic assistance including food aid, and Section 502B, which governs "security assistance"—that is, military weapons and training—take the form of requiring the cessation of foreign aid to regimes whose violations of human rights are especially egregious. Both these sections were inserted into foreign policy legislation in attempts by Congress to rein in the policy, regularly practiced by Henry Kissinger and others, of subsidizing any regime with an anti-Communist foreign policy no matter how outrageous its domestic policies of torture, arbitrary execution, imprisonment of dissidents, and so on.[10] This meant that the portion of U.S. foreign policy on which consideration of human rights was getting what little bite it ever got was the relatively small portion concerned with foreign aid.

In order for me to focus at the time on the relevant portion of foreign policy, then, I needed to focus on foreign assistance. Actually the focus, for the sake of direct relevance, needed to be on foreign aid for two independent reasons. The less important reason was that, since the action required by the two relevant amendments was the *cessation* of aid, it was useful to be aware of any countervailing reasons for continuing aid that might flow from some duty to aid. Far more important was the fact that the United States was an active accomplice in many of the worst violations of human rights on the anti-Communist side of the Cold War because we were lavishing assistance upon governments hated by their own people in attempts to buy these governments' support of U.S. foreign policy goals. In some notorious cases, like Iran and Guatemala, the Central Intelligence Agency had literally put the governments into power through "covert" action, and in many others, like South Korea and the Philippines, U.S. weapons and training were pouring in to dictators who had helped themselves to power. Much of the outrage in Congress was because congressional hearings in the 1970s, prior to the Carter presidency, had revealed the fact that, for example, arbitrary executions and torture were being carried out by military officers not only armed but trained in special schools by the United States.[11]

Of the three general categories of duties I had suggested, then, it was the third, duties to aid, that I thought I needed to concentrate on (p. 113) in chapters 5 and 6, in spite of the fact that duties to aid become relevant only after failures to perform the first two general kinds of duty. Thus the figure (p. 115), as indicated by the sub-title of this section of the chapter (p. 114), is specifically about duties to aid people whose rights have already been violated, which, I believe, makes the position embodied in it less extreme than it may otherwise seem.[12]

From a more purely theoretical point of view, my concentration of attention on duties to aid, which are, in Waldron's image, one of the last waves of duties—what you must do when you have not done anything else you should have done—was unfortunate.[13] Devoting so much attention to duties to aid was unfortunate above all because it obscured the importance of the second general kind of duty, the duty to protect, and most specifically what I labeled duty II-2, the duty to protect people from violation of their rights by the design of better institutions (p. 60). While I fairly prominently mentioned a duty to create effective institutions (for example, pp. 17, 59–60, and 198) and analyzed some ways that rights deprivations are essential to, or inherent in, institutionalized economic strategies (pp. 46–51), I gave the creation of better institutions designed to ensure that rights are respected in the first place less attention than I now believe it deserves.

Worse, I conceived of duty II-2 much too negatively and much too narrowly. Duty II-2 is said to be "to protect from deprivation . . . by designing institutions that avoid the creation of strong incentives to violate duty I [which is to avoid depriving people of what they have a right to]" (p. 60). Certainly it is a good thing to produce institutions that avoid incentives to violate rights; this is why the CIA, for example, ought to be totally transformed or abolished. The CIA systematically generates temptations for its employees to violate fundamental human rights to which they routinely succumb. Merely eliminating evil (and phenomenally wasteful, corrupt, and incompetent) institutions like the CIA is, however, far too negative and narrow. Accordingly, some scholar/activists have retained my suggested three underlying categories (avoid depriving, protect from deprivation, and aid the deprived) and given broader and more positive content to the second duty to protect.[14] Others have proposed a typology containing a more constructive third category, "to respect, to protect, and to fulfill," where to fulfill rights clearly involves more than aiding those whose rights one has already violated and includes the creation of more effective institutions to see that rights are honored in the first instance.[15]

Now, almost everyone involved in these discussions realizes that typologies are not the point. Typologies are at best abstract instruments for temporarily fending off the complexities of concrete reality that threaten to overwhelm our circuits. Be they dichotomous or trichotomous, typologies are ladders to be climbed and left behind, not monuments to be caressed or polished. Thus, there is no ultimately significant question of the form, how many kinds of duties are involved in honoring rights? Three? Four? A dozen? Waldron is closer to the mark in saying "successive waves of duty." How many waves? Lots—more sometimes than others.

The "very simple tripartite typology of duties," then, was not supposed to become a new frozen abstraction to occupy the same rigid conceptual space previously held by "negative rights" and "positive rights." The critical point was: do not let any theorist tell you that the concrete reality of rights enforcement is so simple that all the implementation of any right can usefully be summed up as either positive or negative. The constructive point was: look at what it actually takes to enable people to be secure against the standard, predictable threats to their rights—focus on the duties required to implement the right.

This form of analysis means treating the securing of rights as ends and arriving at adequate arrangements through means/end, or strategic, reasoning.[16] James W. Nickel has put it this way: "Where human rights violations are deep and systematic, rights advocates must devise strategies for political change that are not in the scopes of human rights. Here respect for and implementation of human rights becomes a goal, and something like consequentialist reasoning must be used to pursue this goal."[17] I have quoted a negative point and a positive point from Nickel. The negative point is that "strategies . . . are not in the scopes of human rights." He had earlier noted that "rights are *to* some freedom or benefit. We can say that the *scope* of a right specifies what it is to."[18] The point is, then, that knowledge of *what* a right is to is insufficient to tell us *how* to guarantee it, and I take this to entail that conceptual analysis alone (of the scope, substance, or content of a right) provides inadequate information for grounding judgments about implementation. It is necessary, but not sufficient, to understand the conception of the right and what the right is to. Knowing how to protect the right against violation, or to restore the right after violation, depends as well on historical and empirical understanding of the relevant social, economic, political, legal, and psychological factors. As long as theorists remain narrow specialists, adequate analysis of how to institutionalize a right requires interdisciplinary collaboration. It is certainly nothing that ethical theory alone can settle.[19]

Nickel's positive point is put: "something like consequentialist reasoning must be used to pursue this goal." The emphasis ought to go on "something like," or this phrasing can be misleading. Better, I think, simply to say that means/end, instrumental, or strategic reasoning is needed.[20] One's goal is for everyone to enjoy everything they have a right to enjoy. One's next task is to figure out how this can be arranged and how to allocate the tasks involved in the establishment and operation of the arrangements. One must, in short, help to design social institutions that protect and fulfill rights.

Thomas Pogge suggests what he calls an institutional understanding of human rights, which he contrasts with what he labels the interactional understanding.[21] On the interactional understanding, which he notes found its canonical expression in Hohfeld's ritualistically invoked diagram, each human "right entails certain directly corresponding duties."[22] On Pogge's recommended institutional

> understanding, too, human rights (conceptually) entail moral duties—but these are not corresponding duties in any simple

> way: The human right not to be subjected to cruel or degrading treatment gives me a duty to help ensure that those living in my society need not endure such treatment. Depending on context, this duty may . . . generate obligations to advocate and support programs to improve literacy and unemployment benefits when such programs are necessary to secure the object of this human right for a class of my compatriots (domestic servants).[23]

Earlier in the article Pogge has explained the connection between literacy and unemployment benefits and protection against cruel and degrading treatment:

> In some of these societies, inhuman or degrading treatment of domestic servants by their employers is perfectly legal. In others, certain legal prohibitions are in place but ineffective: Most of the servants, often illiterate, are ignorant of their legal rights, convictions for mistreatment are extremely difficult if not impossible to obtain, punishments are negligible. Moreover, servants are also often forced to endure illegal conduct on account of economic necessity: They do not dare file complaints against their employers for fear of being fired. This fear is both justified and substantial, because they have only minimal financial reserves, there is a general oversupply of servants and/or they have reason to believe that their present employer would refuse to issue them the positive reference requisite to find new employment.[24]

Pogge has a number of separable theses, not all of them relevant here. One, which might be called the indirection thesis, is that duties are not "directly corresponding" to rights and "are not corresponding duties in any simple way": the route to the fulfillment of a right is often not the direct route through a supposed corresponding, Hohfeldian duty. The simple, direct picture Pogge is rejecting is the one, I believe, that leads people to think that the right not to be subject to cruel and degrading treatment is a purely negative right because its fulfillment is completely constituted by the noninterference prescribed by a purely negative duty.[25] If employers are molesting their maids, one simply says, in effect: "keep your hands off your maid"—or, in the language of duty, "you have a duty not to deprive your maid of her physical security" (especially since, if she lives-in, she is basically trapped, having no other home to flee to if she wants to earn a living). If employers would keep their hands off their live-in maids, there would naturally be no problem.

The real problem, Pogge correctly sees, is that many employers do not in fact leave their maids alone, and this will in fact not be changed merely by the proclamation of duties of noninterference. Nor will the police in fact be checking the homes of the well-to-do to see whether their owners are respecting the rights of their live-in servants and to protect any servants who need protection. In reality, live-in servants will be secure only if they are, in a word, empowered—made agents in their own rescue. The servants must be taught their rights, taught how to demand them, and provided with some third alternative to submission inside the employer's house or starvation outside in the streets. Learning about the rights may require first being taught to read and write, and having a viable third option may require being provided with unemployment insurance, as Pogge is rightly indicating. In reality the route to physical security against inhuman or degrading treatment often runs indirectly through primary education and minimal economic security.

James Nickel emphasizes the same web of interdependent rights and duties, and consequent importance of the agency of victims, in the case of Third World hunger:

> Most people who experience hunger and malnutrition are functional, are getting water and a little food, and are capable of doing things to find food such as moving or seeking work. If we think of hungry and malnourished people as agents, albeit agents with limited capacities and options, we will avoid assuming that self-help is impossible and that only donated foreign food or money can address the problem. Further, viewing hungry people as agents is a more respectful stance that provides a barrier to the paternalistic attitude that it is mainly rich people from the First World who are competent to address problems of hunger in poorer countries. The purpose of reframing the problem of world hunger is not to

get people in rich countries off the hook, but to have a better idea of which hook they should be on.[26]

The "hook" that the rich-country folk need to be on may be the urgency of ceasing military assistance to a regime that denies its own people avenues of protest while supporting the rich country's foreign policy goals, that is, a nonintervention hook that allows domestic agency to work, not an international intervention hook. While there certainly is a right to food, the more urgent rights for many hungry people are the right to peaceful assembly and the right to vote. Figuring out what is urgent in a particular context depends upon the means/end or strategic reasoning that Nickel had earlier recommended in *Making Sense of Human Rights*.

I said earlier simply that duties are complicated. I have been emphasizing one particular respect in which that is true. One cannot stay at the purely conceptual level, reasoning simply that if there is a right to have *x*, there must be a duty for others to provide *x*. There may instead be a duty to stay out of people's way while they take *x* for themselves, or a duty to teach them to read so they can figure out how to make or grow *x*, or a duty to let them form a political party so that they can effectively demand that the government stop exporting *x* (instead of having the CIA arm their police so that they can suppress all dissent). Sometimes there is a duty to provide *x* to them, conditionally or unconditionally. Positively put, which duties there are depends upon means/end reasoning in which secure enjoyment of the substance of the right in question is the end. Means/end reasoning must be not simply what philosophers like to call "empirical," but strategic, involving judgments about policies and institutions. Often the means to the fulfillment of one right will include the fulfillment of other rights, because rights may be of great instrumental value in the fulfillment of other rights regardless of whether they are of intrinsic value as well.

Moreover, one certainly cannot definitively allocate duties among potential bearers—determine who ought to do what—until means/end reasoning has established what needs to be done, or at the very least, what are the most promising ways to accomplish what needs to be done if the rights in question are to be enjoyed.

In other words, the allocation of duties among bearers depends upon the specification of which duties need to be performed, and hence allocated. Unfortunately, which duties can reasonably be specified also depends upon which allocations of duties among bearers are generally reasonable and, most specifically, fair. The depth of the difficulty here emerges from one aspect of Pogge's contrast, as I understand it, between the institutional and the interactional perspectives. This difficulty has two elements.

First, one can reason, as it were, from either end of the problem. On the one hand, one can take an institutional perspective on the honoring of rights by asking: what institutions would need to be functioning effectively in order for people generally to have secure access to what they have rights to? This is the strategic reasoning that Nickel and I—but not, I gather, Pogge, who is concentrating on institutions that are already in place—are advocating: taking adequate provision for rights as the goal to be reached, one asks which institutional means are needed in order to get there from here. The specification of adequate institutions is then one basis for an assignment of duties to individuals: the assignment of duties to individuals must be an assignment—more than one different assignment may satisfy this test—that enables an adequate set of institutions—more than one set may do the job—to function. The institutions specified are one test for allocations of duties among individuals.

On the other hand, one can ask: which allocations of right-grounded duties would be fair to individual duty-bearers?[27] I intend to invoke this perspective when I say that we should not forget that for the duty-bearers too this is the only life they will live, by which I mean that, however terrible the prospects from the point of view of potential right-bearers if certain rights are not acknowledged and implemented, the point of view of the bearers of the duties implicated by those rights also should be taken into account before one decides whether those rights should, all things considered, be acknowledged. What the latter point of view may reasonably be naturally would have to be spelled out much more fully than I am doing here, but the central thought is that some test of fairness to individual duty-bearers must be satisfied by any allocation of duties, however effectively that allocation would serve the purpose of honoring otherwise reasonable-seeming rights. From this other point of view, then, fair assignments of duties to individuals are one basis for the specification of institutions. The duties permitted by fairness are one test for acceptable institutions.

The reasoning from these two opposite directions is not a contradiction. It is perfectly possible for a necessary condition of the specification of acceptable institutions to be that at least one assignment of the duties the institutions require for their successful operation be fair to individual duty-bearers *and* a necessary condition of an acceptable assignment of duties to be that they enable the successful operation of at least one set of the institutions specified. In short, one wants institutions that function effectively to honor rights while imposing only duties that make fair demands of those who bear them.

The second element of the difficulty here, however, is that while these reciprocal requirements are not contradictory, there unfortunately is also no guarantee that they can both be satisfied simultaneously in fact. It is like digging a tunnel under a river by having two teams work simultaneously, one from each side, planning to meet in the middle—the nightmare is that they will not arrive at the same place. In practice, it may be that in the situation we actually face the only institutions adequate to secure even the most minimal set of rights for everyone could function only by demanding far more than is fair of many duty-bearers. Given a precise understanding of a fair allocation of duties, this would be an empirical question about the workings of the various institutions we could conceive. *Institutional adequacy,* as the duties are specified, and *individual fairness,* as the duties are assigned, are each a test that cannot in principle be surrendered.[28] We simply must find out whether both can be satisfied together in practice, being as imaginative as we can.[29]

An Institutional Turn for Conceptions of Human Rights

Several important considerations come together, then, to recommend an institutional turn in thinking about human rights. First, in order to take the implementation of rights seriously at all, one must think strategically. Taking the honoring of the rights as the goal, one needs to look for genuinely effective means, rather than quickly declaring the rights to be utopian or impractical. Second, any effective means to a goal as ambitious as the honoring of fundamental rights requires a division of moral labor. Neither can rights ordinarily be protected one at a time, nor can any one right be honored by small numbers of individuals acting alone. Waves of duties may need to be performed and—to switch images—webs of duty-bearers may need to become involved at various stages. Where the tasks to be performed are predictable, they often should be allocated in advance. Whether the division of moral labor is formal or informal, it must presumably be fair. Third, the ineliminable need for varieties of duty-bearers must not obscure the fact that, when it is possible, the most effective arrangement is to empower the victim. The best arrangement is often one that allows victims of rights violations to become the agents of their own salvation, but this often depends upon institutions that support empowerment.

Complementary considerations about the third point need to be kept in balance. My primary contention has been that taking rights seriously means taking duties seriously. This is of course a thesis about what people other than the right-bearer ought to do on behalf of the right-bearer. This is a vital consideration because in the worst cases of rights violations the right-bearer may have been turned into an at least temporarily helpless victim, who is doomed unless others act in accord with their duties. However, this should in no way obscure, and is not at all in conflict with, the contention that a major part of the means, as well as the goal, of providing for people's rights is bringing it about that they are in a position to look out for themselves as much as possible. The best institutions for implementing rights will do both.

Theories of rights have been alternately criticized for being statist and for being asocial. Some theories fail in the one direction, and others, in the other, but neither failure is necessary if the complementary considerations just above are held together. An account of rights may be statist, or overly bureaucratic, or even paternalistic, if it allocates more of the work than necessary to people other than the right-bearers. The very first wave of action normally should be responsibility or initiative on the part of the right-bearer himself or herself. Arrangements for fulfilling rights should never be arrangements to do for people what they can equally well do for themselves. Right-grounded duties are, at the earliest, a second wave of action on behalf of people who cannot act effectively for themselves. However, right-violating institutions often leave people precisely unable to act for themselves, either by depriving them of effective channels for action or by actively blocking their action.

On the other hand, a theory of rights may be asocial, or atomistic, in its account if it is simply about individuals demanding things for themselves. This is a picture that omits every wave of action except the first, in contrast with the statist picture that omits the first. Such theories result when rights are conceived as concerned with little more than maximum negative liberty and unlimited property accumulation, each construed as mainly involving keeping other people at bay.[30]

So, what should the institutions that implement rights be like? Philosophers alone cannot say. Nor can they leave it entirely to others to say.[31] Philosophers, insofar as they reflect only about concepts and about the basic information about how the world works that is available to any reasonably well-informed person, can reason, as I did in the first edition, that while everyone everywhere might have enjoyed all their rights if everyone else had simply refrained from violating anyone's rights, this is in fact not going to happen. In fact, many individuals, firms, and governments are precisely in the business of violating rights for fun and for profit. Anyone who reads a serious newspaper knows this much. So philosophers can be quite certain that beyond a duty not to deprive people of whatever they have rights to, there must be some kind of duty to protect the victims against the violators.[32] And given the way the world has been going in recent centuries, it is fairly obvious that we do not have the protection of the victims very well organized yet, which means that at least some of us sometimes have a duty to conceive, nurture, and support better institutions.[33]

The Thai government does nothing while Burmese kidnappers deliver Burmese peasant girls to Bangkok brothels to serve as prostitutes until they contract AIDS, whereupon the Thais dump the infected women back into Burma.[34] The U.S. government announces, and aggressively presses, new restrictions on peacekeeping operations, largely motivated by the completely unnecessary deaths of eighteen courageous young Americans in Mogadishu in 1993, just before and during the slow spread through Rwanda in 1994 of gangs of young boys hacking approximately 500,000 of their compatriots to death with machetes.[35] African nations take turns holding famines and civil wars. Wealthy nations spew greenhouse gases into the global atmosphere as if the entire stratosphere were their own national territory exclusively for waste disposal.[36] Meanwhile, our pesticides poison even the songbirds (who, I admit, have no rights that it should be otherwise, although that is hardly the whole story). One could rave on and on, but surely it is clear that while the most advantaged carry human technology and culture to spectacular new heights, the most victimized live and die in beastly conditions. We are not managing the fabulous resources of this planet at all well. We ought to build better institutions.

The question is: how do we bring about the transition? Philosophers and rights theorists working alone cannot design better institutions. Some aspects of institutional design are best understood by, for example, lawyers or economists or historians. Yet philosophers ought not simply to flee the scene when things start getting practical. For practical arrangements involve allocations of burdens (and rights and privileges), and such allocations always raise questions of fairness, which philosophers should be inclined to raise and able to help to answer. Philosophers cannot help, however, merely by formulating some general principles of fairness, or general guidelines for fair procedures, and leaving them behind on the table as they hand the institutional design over to the experts, for at least two reasons.

First, good philosophers should be better than most other specialists at sensing where questions about fairness in the assignment of duties arise. Sooner or later those who by then had been treated unfairly perhaps would, if they were not intimidated by an entrenched allocation of power, raise their own questions about the fairness of their treatment. They would probably, however, by then be at a disadvantage, precisely because of the unfairness of their treatment, that would compound the injustice and multiply the difficulties in undoing it. In general, prevention is much better than cure in cases of unfairness. A philosopher might be able to foresee the unfairness before a victim had to feel it. The specific unfairness of a concrete set of arrangements can be foreseen, of course, only by someone who thoroughly understands, and appreciates the workings of, those arrangements. Philosophers and rights theorists who opt out of the details are no help.

Second, philosophical work does not in any case end with the formulation of general principles or general procedures—interpretation and specification are philosophical tasks too. The specification of concrete embodiments of principles does indeed involve extra-philosophical information and skills in addition to philosophical ones, as I have just been emphasizing, but this only makes the philosophical work more challenging, not less essential.[37] Imaginative construction of alternatives, careful analysis of what is and is not presupposed and implied—the sensitive attention to what is fair as well as what is efficient or customary, which was the previous point—these and the other philosophical talents are at least as valuable in the making of concrete judgments as in more abstract pursuits. The work is not pure philosophy—it is practical philosophy—but philosophy nonetheless.

Institutional design must combine judgments about what it is fair to expect people to do, what it is efficient to ask people to do, and what it is possible to motivate people to do.[38] All this depends upon subtle judgments about sense of duty, sense of fairness, sense of identity, sense of solidarity, self-interest, incentives, and coercion—especially hard choices about which aspects of individuals and societies can be changed while which others remain fixed. For example, one cannot specify and assign duties as if individual people generally embody a moral ideal of a person. Ideal persons would not deprive each other of what they had rights to enjoy, so a simple clarification of the duties not to deprive would be sufficient for such well-motivated people. In that ideal world there would be no point in proceeding to thought about duties to protect against deprivation by the ill-motivated, duties to aid the deprived, and whatever other general categories of duty have point in this nonideal world. In this world we deal, or fail to deal, with "leaders" of ethnic groups who orchestrate the genocide of the rival groups and with "entrepreneurs" who trick trusting peasant girls into brothels where they contract fatal diseases. Such behavior is totally unacceptable and should have been crushed by force long ago; no subtle judgments required. But in the vast middle range between the barbaric and the ideal, and between the way we are now and the best we might actually become, intellectually difficult moral and psychological judgments need to be made about how to arrange to get the necessary transition started, while bearing in mind as the historic transitions are planned that the lives individuals are living now are the only lives they will get.

To be more specific, consider the question that I regularly raise, but never answer, about the limits of right-based duties.[39] I have said above that I think one must think strategically about the assignment of duties, with the full enjoyment of (at least) basic rights as the goal. The duties should, then, be assigned in a manner that will make adequate provision for the rights. One could assign the duties necessary to the enjoyment of a right in such a way that, provided everyone did their duty, the right would be secure. That, however, would be the assignment appropriate to a world that was ideal in at least one respect, namely, that everyone did their duty. Indeed, as we already noticed, if everyone could be counted on to honor their duty not to deprive anyone of the substance of their right, we would not need to assign any other duties at all. Since violations of the duty not to deprive people of their rights are deeply characteristic of the world we live in, we must, in order to be in the least practical, move to the assignment of some later waves of duty: default or back-up duties, like duties to protect, duties to aid, and whatever others are needed.

Yet essentially the same problem (of relatively how ideal or real to make our assumptions about how people will generally behave) reasserts itself at each stage. To be minimally practical, we must specify at least duties to protect and some duties to aid (aid those for whom protection in turn fails). How, then, do we assign each of these kinds of default duties among potential bearers: on the assumption that each bearer will perform the duty assigned, or on the assumption that some will fail to perform it, so that a further assignment to a back-up bearer must be made? On the latter choice, we would specify back-up bearers for default duties, for example, who should aid the victims if the people who originally should have aided the victims do not do it, after the people who should have protected the threatened victims against the original right-violators failed to provide adequate protection? This may sound artificially intricate, but it is perfectly ordinary. Who should now pay the medical expenses of the Burmese women already infected with AIDS in the Bangkok brothels openly tolerated by the Thai authorities and patronized by Japanese business executives on organized sex tours? Who should now pay for the orphanage care for the Rwandan children whose parents were already slaughtered in the 1994 genocide that no major military power was willing to bear the expense and danger of stopping?

Rwanda is a classic case of the greater efficiency, not to mention humanity, of performing earlier waves of duty.[40] The amount of money spent in July 1994 by the U.S. military dealing with the famine and epidemic in the camps of the refugees in Zaire produced by the civil war in Rwanda in response to the genocide would have paid several times over for a military force that very likely could in April 1994 have prevented the genocide—and many of the horrors that continue to unwind, to this day. The question remains: since the young executioners were allowed by the rest of humanity to hack slowly through Rwanda for weeks until half a million lay dead, who ought to aid innocent survivors now that the duties to protect have been definitively ignored? And what if we/they, whoever we/they are, do not fulfill the duties to aid either? Then what, for the orphaned Rwandan children?

If one simply proceeded mechanically to assign backups to the backups, and defaults for the defaults, one would presumably finally zero in on whichever dedicated people were sufficiently committed to human rights that they would do whatever duties remained to be done until whatever remained possible to honor rights was accomplished, irrespective of who the original failed duty-bearers had been. Such specifications and assignments of duties would be at the other extreme from the specifications and assignments that would be reasonable if everyone carried out their initial assignments—these are the assignments for the world in which many fail to carry out their original assignments. We have swung from the assignment for an ideal world to the assignment from Hell.

Manifestly, such a mechanical devolution of duties has gross faults. First, expecting some individuals endlessly to be willing to step into the breaches left by the failures of others to do their prior duties is wildly unfair. These lives would simply be consumed by (default) duties—this is precisely to ignore that for duty-bearers too, as much as for victims of rights violations, this is the only life they will live. Second, expecting some endlessly to pick up whatever others have dropped would ignore normal human motivation, creating a powerful perverse incentive. People surely could reasonably reject any arrangement that effectively counted on the radical inequality embodied in a moral two-class system consisting of one group of people who were allowed to dodge their right-based duties and another group who had to shoulder whatever the first group dodged. And reasonably or not, people with a normally healthy sense of self-interest would refuse to lead default lives, determined by the moral failures of others. Third, for right-bearers, earlier is of course always better. Every devolution to a later duty leaves violated rights, and violated people, in its wake. Prevention is always better than cure, even where there is something resembling a cure. Aid to previously unprotected victims, or to their now orphaned children, is scarcely a cure.

The solution seems to me to be to draw the line, insofar as possible, at the first level of default: at duties to protect, broadly interpreted to include the design and maintenance of institutions that make it as easy as possible for people to honor their duties not to deprive others of the enjoyment of their rights or, put differently, as hard as possible to commit, and to get away with, deprivations. On the one hand, it would be utopian in the worst sense to attempt to hold the line at an even earlier level—all the way back at duties not to deprive. The world contains, and will contain for the foreseeable future, evil people who will violate the most basic human rights. Large numbers of people will ignore their duties not to deprive others of their rights. We can do everything humanly possible to instill respect for rights and to punish violators, but it would be truly unrealistic to expect that attempts at violation will cease. On the other hand, it does not seem unrealistic to dig in hard at the next level, the level of designing institutions that protect potential victims against, first, those who would violate their rights and, second, those who would neglect their duties to protect them against the violators, rather than falling back entirely beyond protecting potential victims to aiding actual victims. This requires that many decent people not only fulfill their own negative duties not to violate rights but also take on positive duties to block violations against which others had the primary duties to provide protection, that is, also take on default duties to protect. This involves genuine double duty: the negative duties not to deprive that fall upon everyone and some positive duties to provide protection that should have been provided by others.[41] Yet it need not involve endless duties.

Conditional Sovereignty

These positive duties to protect are duties to conceive and nurture institutions that, taking people as they are, and as they can next be brought to be, make at least the basic rights of all reasonably secure. We have only begun to think seriously about institutional forms for the possibilities here, and my own suggestions are completely tentative. It seems to me, however, that one plausible step would be building a general, global consensus that state sovereignty is conditional upon the protection of at least basic rights and that the international community not only may but ought to step in when the failures of states to protect rights become egregious, as happened in the early 1990s in, for example, both the disintegrating Yugoslavia and the imploding Rwanda. When a state utterly or egregiously fails to protect the rights of the people residing within its jurisdiction, the rest of humanity must have capacities to do more than sit idly by until the slaughter is finished or merely assist the victims after they are violated without resisting the violators.[42] It is not permissible to substitute fulfillment of duties to aid that came into play only because victims went unprotected, for fulfillment of back-up duties to protect.

I am still talking about a back-up arrangement for the failure of so-called national governments—few sovereign states consist of precisely one nation, patriotic myths to the contrary notwithstanding—rather than a replacement for the current state system. This is a practical judgment, and an especially shaky one. Others have long ago made the cleaner and more radical suggestion that we work to replace the modern state system with a world government of some sort. Quite apart from the dangers inherent in such a centralization of power, I simply see not the slightest prospect of its happening. Although it is hard to imagine that anyone creating a world from scratch would have made one dominated by any institution remotely resembling the modern state, this is what we nevertheless have.[43] If the state cannot be eliminated, as one certainly might wish, the question becomes whether it can be civilized. Is there some way that the modern state can become more of an instrument of good than most states have so far been, or, at least, pressured into protecting the rights of the human beings who live under its sway?

The basic idea is that states should have to behave with minimal decency if they want any respect.[44] Sovereignty should be conditional upon performance, and performance should be judged by international norms: *conditional sovereignty, judged by minimal international standards, including the provision of protection for basic rights.* Rather than global institutions, which may be dangerous and are in any case most unlikely, we would pursue minimal global standards for national institutions. Different states can have different institutions in whatever respects, and to whatever degree, they like, short of failure to protect basic rights. It is unacceptable, however, for whichever bunch of thugs has a monopoly of force within a particular territory simply to allow people to be murdered, raped, or herded around like animals, as has been happening in recent years in some parts of both Europe and Africa, including Bosnia and Rwanda.

Anyone can see that the current practice of leaving people to the mercy of their own government is barbaric. The challenge is to come up with a cure that is not worse than the disease, as critics of intervention regularly note. This is why I emphasized at the beginning of this Afterword that the original human-rights impulse in the U.S. Congress in the 1970s, which predated the Carter campaign in 1976 and of course the Carter presidency, was an anti-interventionary impulse. The congressional leaders, like Donald Fraser of Minnesota, were first of all repelled by U.S. complicity in violations of human rights by regimes we had been supporting, most of all in South Vietnam but also in Chile, Iran, South Korea, and elsewhere. The initial congressional demand, relentlessly resisted by Henry Kissinger in the executive, was simply that the United States stop providing economic and military assistance to gross and systematic violators of human rights (in the name of building alliances against communism). The general principle was merely that where a government was violating the basic rights of the people living under it, no other government, like ours, should strengthen the hand of the violators. The U.S. government was not being asked to take the side of the victims—only to stop taking the side of the victimizers. When President George Bush in 1991 actually took the side of the Kurdish victims of the Iraqi state, by establishing a no-fly zone to protect them, he was taking a more positive action than most people would have dreamed of requesting in the 1970s—and was of course severely compromising Iraqi sovereignty.

One way of putting our question is: is U.S. protection for the rights of the Kurds against the depredations of the state that had power over them a paradigm for the future? Is this the model that should be generalized? Should we simply wish that President Bush had done essentially the same for the Bosnian Muslims against the Bosnian Serbs and Serbia in April 1992, and that President Clinton had done the same for Tutsis and moderate Hutus in Rwanda in April 1994? Not exactly, although I believe that action ought to have been taken in each case to prevent what predictably followed.

I believe that the Bush decision to protect the Kurds was commendable, and that the Clinton decision to write off the Tutsis was despicable, all the more contemptible for having been carefully considered and coldly calculated. Each of these U.S. presidents, however, was probably attempting to do mainly what he took, correctly or incorrectly, to be in the U.S. national interest, on some understanding of it. That is one underlying problem. We do not have adequate institutions if other states intervene or not to protect people against genocidal assaults by their own state depending upon whether it is believed to be in the national interest of the potential intervenor. It appears especially likely that in a world with a single superpower, the superpower will act irresponsibly.

It is, as I have been emphasizing, far from a purely philosophical question which alternative arrangement to embrace. One might, for example, work toward some kind of monitoring system for violations of rights around the world—intergovernmental or nongovernmental—that might alert some agency to act at a sufficiently early stage that action other than military intervention would be effective. One might hope that some nonnational agency—either a United Nations agency or a less than global but still multilateral agency—could be created to conduct any interventions that are called for. Or one might urge that national actors base their decisions on considerations broader than exclusively national ones. Or all the above. In large part this depends upon other, deeper trends, some of which may not be amenable to conscious human design.

The various measures that may be taken can serve either of two different intermediate goals on the way to the ultimate goal of individuals' enjoyment of their rights. First, some measures need to provide backup in the most literal sense: where the state with the primary duty to protect rights fails—for lack of will or of capacity—to fulfill its duty, some other agent at least sometimes must step in and provide the missing protection. Where the failure is from want of capacity, not want of will, the state may invite the external agent in. Invited or uninvited, the external agent is engaged in intervention, which carries with it myriad difficulties irrespective of the worthiness of its goal. While I certainly believe that military intervention is fully justified by a systematic pattern of gross violations of basic rights of the magnitude of, for example, the genocidal slaughter in Rwanda in 1994, external military intervention is always the last resort because of its inherent tendencies to be self-defeating.

Better, then, would be measures designed, not to take over from the state with primary responsibility the protective duties that it so far failed to perform, but to stimulate the will or provide the capacity for the original state to carry out its own duties. Now, states usually pay remarkably small prices for utter failures to carry out their primary duties. Where those residing on the state's territory somehow happened to enjoy basic rights to political participation, while other basic rights were violated, they might be able to replace a corrupt or otherwise ineffective government with one competent to protect their other basic rights. But, as I emphasized in chapters 1 and 3, the basic rights tend to go together: it is almost unimaginable that during genocide (failure to protect security rights) or famine (failure to protect subsistence rights), rights to political participation will be protected. People *may* nevertheless in rare cases be able to engage in political participation—not the same as enjoying the right to political participation, of course—by overthrowing the government by force, but the question is whether the rest of us should allow their enjoyment of their basic right routinely to depend entirely upon their own might.[45]

Instead of supplying arms to revolutionaries or intervening militarily on their side—the first option discussed above—we should be able to design less violent means of raising the price for governments that fail to protect the rights of the people over whom they claim jurisdiction. Thomas Pogge has made some imaginative suggestions about a different but somewhat parallel problem: how the international community could reduce the benefits to those who overthrow democratic governments, for example, "proposing, as a principle of international law, that a people need not repay loans incurred by a government that ruled them in violation of constitutionally recognized democratic procedures."[46] Just as this suggestion is intended to make unconstitutional seizure of power a little less appealing, we could attempt to make failure to protect basic rights less costless, short of launching military interventions. I do not have a well-conceived institutional proposal to offer. The United Nations is currently considering, for instance, a permanent International Criminal Court that might be able to try politicians implicated in major violations of rights. In any case, we clearly need more middle ways between sitting idly by while horrors are perpetrated, under which I include toothless U.N. Security Council resolutions, and full-scale military interventions. *Decisive action short of military intervention,* for at least some cases, should not be beyond human powers of imagination and institutional innovation.

What I am calling default duties to protect come, then, in two kinds. Less desirable is literally stepping in to provide protection where those with the primary duty to protect fail to provide it. Often those who will have failed are a government, and stepping in involves military intervention. Hard thought needs to be given to the best agents for such interventions. Far more desirable are institutions that pressure those with the primary duties to protect to perform their duties, especially institutions that impose severe costs upon governments that fail to perform this first duty of government: the protection of basic rights.

This all presupposes logically that the division of moral labor for the protection of basic rights does not respect state boundaries. Does it presuppose it chronologically as well? That is, does a consensus about implementing institutions—for example, arrangements for decisive action short of military intervention—have to wait upon a prior consensus on principle? This is a position held by many and perhaps most forcefully presented by Michael Walzer. It is premature, Walzer has argued, to try to discuss global institutions until there is, if ever there actually will be, a global community whose shared values could be embodied in the institutions: "The only plausible alternative to the political community is humanity itself, the society of nations, the entire globe. But were we to take the globe as our setting, we would have to imagine what does not yet exist: a community that included all men and women everywhere. We would have to invent a set of common meanings for these people, avoiding if we could the stipulation of our own values."[47] In short, "there cannot be a just society until there is a society."[48]

The warning against the danger of simply stipulating our own view as the universal one cannot be repeated too often, especially for Americans with our tendency to overmoralize international affairs. However, the stipulation of our own view and the passive wait for a globally shared view to emerge on its own are far from the only alternatives. Indeed, the initial apparent necessity of "there cannot be a just society until there is a society" rests upon a false dichotomy: an artificially constricted picture in which there can be no chicken until there is an egg. In fact, international society and just international society can be built at the same time through the same activities.[49] A large part of what makes a collection of people a society is, precisely as Walzer maintains, shared understandings about matters like rights and justice. Rather than waiting for a society somehow to emerge on its own before asking its members to think about what would make it a just society, one can attempt to build a society through agreement in theory or practice on just arrangements. And nothing prevents attempts to seek agreement among those who initially disagree, not that the attempts to reach agreement are guaranteed to succeed.

I think it is clear that this world's institutions for the protection of rights are grossly inadequate. Conceiving of institutions that could function more effectively while making only reasonable demands upon those who would make them function is challenging and controversial. It is too difficult to be accomplished by isolated theorists, who individually do not know enough and have not experienced enough—this kind of institutional design is a social task. For the foreseeable future, much of the protection of individual rights will, like it or not, depend upon national governments, but national governments seem to me to be among our most inadequate institutions. Institutions that cannot perform deserve little respect, and they certainly are not entitled as a matter of principle to sovereignty.

What can we do to make the protectors protect? And how long do we stand by after it is clear that they never will? In the most extreme situations, like famine in Somalia in 1992 and genocide in Rwanda in 1994, outsiders must step in and do with military force what the national state has failed to do: protect the utterly vulnerable against relentless forces of death. Military force is blunt and negative—it can protect some (by killing others, including innocent bystanders), but it cannot plant or build. Everyone, and most of all professional military people, can see that military force is the last resort. We need, as I noted above, decisive action short of military intervention. For that we need better international institutions. We will not know what our duties are, nor will we know what rights people can expect to enjoy, until we have constructed these institutions. Meanwhile, our common humanity requires at the very least, I would suggest, that we participate in the conversations about the institutions that might protect basic rights.

·8·

BASIC RIGHTS AND CLIMATE CHANGE (2020)

The general structure of a basic right presented here rests on the conviction, shared with Thomas Hobbes, of the significance for human life of helplessness and vulnerability: "for everyone healthy adulthood is bordered on each side by helplessness, and it is vulnerable to interruption by helplessness, temporary or permanent, at any time. . . . To be helpless they [infants and the aged] need only to be left alone" (19). Acknowledgment of basic rights is an expression of human solidarity. "The honoring of basic rights is an active alliance with those who would otherwise be helpless against natural and social forces too strong for them" (33). Individual persons control what they can when they can, but when they are in danger of suffering at the mercy of forces they cannot control, they need to rely on others, including the strangers who inevitably constitute the vast majority of humanity. This solidarity among strangers can build institutions structured by rights and duties that will protect us each, as needed, against some of the threats that are liable to confront us.[1] The implementation of rights through the performance of duties blocks threats—not all threats, of course, but "standard threats" that are "ordinary and serious but remediable" (32). We do not control which threats arise or when they arise, so we need to do our best to foresee them and to build in advance strong social institutions that will be ready to provide social guarantees for the most fundamental human interests against standard threats if and when they occur. Chapter 7 further explores "the institutional turn" required by basic rights.

Changing Threats

Two crucial features of the standard threats against which rights-based duties can protect are that they must be determined empirically and that they change.[2] This account of basic rights was specifically designed to deal with the contingent and variable character of human threats. Some accounts of rights have tried to specify rights a priori based on putatively unchanging features of humans. This produces static lists of rights that gain immunity to change through vagueness about implementation. That is not the approach here. While human fragility and vulnerability, in general, may be about as constant as anything can be, the salient particular threats vary over time. We need to confront their specificity, which means that arguments about rights cannot be purely conceptual but need to respond to historical context. Effective protections must be specific to threats. We have to investigate what is happening in order to determine what the crucial threats are and how institutions can be designed to block them.[3]

In the late 1970s when I was writing this book, it was virtually unimaginable, for example, how much of a threat to the basic right to security and the basic right to liberty that digital surveillance and manipulation, subsequently perfected through the revolution in information technology, would become. Facebook, Google, and Amazon had not been created, and it did not occur to us then that such organizations would eventually be compiling all the information and meta-information about every person that they could grab with, at best, meaningless pseudo-consent and often entirely without their targets' knowledge. Uncontrolled social media have, I think, become standard threats, and the design of social guarantees to protect personal security and individual liberty is one major current challenge for institutional imagination.

The greatest threat to basic rights in the twenty-first century, however, is most likely uncontrolled climate change. The other greatest threat is the reckless abandonment of the treaty architecture that partially restrained nuclear weapons, but for reasons I will explain presently, I will focus here on accelerating climate change. Forty years ago when I was writing *Basic Rights*, the human institutions and practices driving climate change—the global energy regime dominated by fossil fuels and the industrialization of agriculture—were growing from strength to strength. Scientists employed by the major oil companies had realized in the 1950s and 1960s that business-as-usual was a threat to the climate.[4] The U.S. government had been informed of the climate threat from continued sale and use of fossil fuels in the 1960s and 1970s.[5] I, however, was not yet alert to the threat of climate change—it was simply in one of my personal blind spots—and it was not mentioned in the first edition. I have been studying climate change since 1991 and hope to some degree to remedy that omission here.

Forty years later, now that the danger of indefinitely worsening climate change is evident to all but the willfully blind, it is a legitimate question whether the general structure of basic rights originally laid out in 1980 can cast any light on how we should respond. Is it perhaps necessary to articulate an additional basic right—say, a basic right to a healthy environment or a basic right to a stable climate? Others are advancing such formulations, and I have little interest in quarreling with them.[6] My standard for judging proposed additional rights, however, is that if rights are to be "justified demands . . . not . . . merely requests, pleas, petitions" (14), and basic rights "are everyone's minimum reasonable demands upon the rest of humanity" (15), it is essential for theorists not to multiply rights beyond necessity, to adapt Ockham's phrase. In the economistic jargon often used now, we must avoid "rights inflation" by not adding supposed new rights too readily. So, the question becomes: Is what is threatened by climate change sufficiently new or different that it cannot be accounted for by reference to the familiar rights?

The answer, I think, is a resounding no. In fact, what are endangered by climate change are those very most fundamental human interests that must be protected if any rights at all are to be enjoyed or exercised. Climate change has become a pervasive standard threat. "The substance of a basic right is something the deprivation of which is one standard threat to rights generally"

(34). Consequently, climate change is a threat not only to widely acknowledged basic rights but also to all other rights, the protection of which depends on fulfillment of basic rights.

For example, the basic right to physical security has always seemed to me, as I think it did to Hobbes as well, to be the right that it would be most difficult to doubt seriously. And dozens of people in Paradise, California, in 2018 were incinerated in a flash inside their own homes by a then-unusual wildfire—the Camp Fire—that, even if one of its contributing causes was corporate negligence, was also partly caused by prolonged drought exacerbated by worsening climate change. Climate change threatens physical security—and not only through forest fires, but also through flash floods that can also come quickly in the night, sea-level rise and consequent storm surges that rush farther inland, the extension of the habitable territories of vectors of deadly diseases (like mosquitoes and ticks), severe storms on land and sea, extreme heat, and other phenomena.[7]

The basic right to subsistence is at least equally obviously threatened by the global energy regime of fossil fuels that is forcing the climate to change.[8] The definition of subsistence, as used here, begins: "unpolluted air, unpolluted water, adequate food . . ." (23). With regard to air, it is extraordinary that millions of people are killed every year by the polluting effects of the combustion of fossil fuels, even before the indirect effects of combustion by way of climate modification are taken into account. Calculating the effects on life expectancy of particulate air pollution, Michael Greenstone and Claire Qing Fan conclude: "particulate matter (PM) air pollution is the greatest current threat to human health globally," and they emphasize that "energy production is the primary source of particulate pollution."[9] The death toll from long-term exposure to outdoor fine particulate matter is several million people every year globally.[10] Americans account for more than twenty thousand of these deaths annually.[11]

With regard to water, the burning of coal by electricity-generating plants routinely leads to the dumping of the ashes into unlined pits that then chronically leak dangerous chemicals, including arsenic, into groundwater.[12] And the enormous surge in hydraulic fracturing of shale rock—fracking—for either oil or gas consumes gigantic volumes of water that in many cases might otherwise have been available for drinking and other household uses or for irrigation of crops. The intensity of water use for fracking has increased many times over and "ubiquitously in all US shale basins," producing up to 1,440% larger volumes of wastewater, which contains "salts, toxic elements, organic matter, and naturally occurring radioactive material," and which would have to be managed meticulously if it were not to contaminate groundwater and streams.[13]

The most dangerous effects for humans of the combustion of fossil fuels, however, come indirectly by way of the dynamics of rapid climate change and the effects of climate change on the fundamental interests that basic rights are intended to safeguard—on none more than on the food at the heart of subsistence.[14] The disruption of agriculture by extreme weather, like the March 2019 flooding in the U.S. Midwest and in Mozambique and Zimbabwe after cyclone Idai, can cause bankruptcies for farmers, transportation blockages, spikes in food prices, and absolute shortages of food, as well as drownings and the destruction of homes. For those who are sufficiently poor to begin with, even temporary food price rises can damage nutrition, particularly in children, by making food unaffordable. In *Climate Change and Poverty*, the UN's Special Rapporteur on Extreme Poverty and Human Rights, distinguished international lawyer and scholar Philip Alston, embraces the shocking conclusion that "climate change threatens to undo the last fifty years of progress in development, global health, and poverty reduction".[15]

As I emphasize in chapter 2, the first duty correlative to any right is the negative duty not to deprive anyone of the focus of the right, such as unpolluted air, unpolluted water, or adequate food. Through the example of the flower-growing contract, I highlight the danger that economic and political arrangements made by others will make it impossible for ordinary people to provide such elements of subsistence for themselves by trapping them inside social structures that conflict with their fundamental interests. The most striking feature of the current climate change is that it is anthropogenic: human arrangements, specifically the choices over the last two centuries that have produced and preserved the global energy regime dominated by fossil fuel, are forcing the climate to change by expanding the cumulative concentration of carbon dioxide in the atmosphere. One might say that climate change is a threat that humanity (collectively) is imposing upon itself (collectively).

It is far more accurate to say, however, that climate change is a threat that those (relatively few) with vested interests in fossil fuel are imposing upon those (many millions) whose air is being polluted with particulate matter from combustion, those (many millions) whose supply of fresh water is being endangered, and those (many millions) whose food is likely to become scarce or unaffordable if the energy business-as-usual persists. Those who are fighting to maintain the dominant position of fossil fuel in the global economy, including their financial enablers in banking, are imposing increasing dangers on everyone else (including their own descendants). As Alston's UN report puts it, "climate change is, among other things, an unconscionable assault on the poor".[16]

Climate change will not stop becoming more severe until the addition of carbon dioxide to the atmosphere stops, because the atmospheric concentration cannot stop expanding until we stop adding to it. This means we must reach net zero carbon as quickly as possible. Reaching net zero carbon means escaping from the grip of the current global energy regime and making a rapid transition to new sources of energy that do not inject carbon dioxide into the earth's atmosphere. This means nothing less than an historic global Energy Revolution on the same scale as the Industrial Revolution or the Agricultural Revolution, but much more quickly carried out. Part of what is initially difficult to grasp is that this Energy Revolution is required for the protection of basic rights.

The continued use of fossil fuels for energy has become a pervasive standard threat to basic human rights. Many people will be left unable to provide healthy air, healthy water, healthy food, and physical safety for themselves and their families if societies do not stop obtaining their energy by burning fossil fuels and releasing the carbon dioxide. Every human has a negative moral duty to stop depriving others of the essentials of life, and those of us who are not helpless have the duty to protect those who are.

The current global energy regime is a social institution that is causing harms that its builders mostly did not foresee or intend. In order to protect basic rights, now that we understand the mushrooming magnitude of the harms that are in fact being caused by this institution, we must replace it with institutions that do not undercut the capacity of ordinary people to enjoy their basic rights—with energy systems that do not undermine the planet's climate.

Smart electricity grids, wind turbines, solar power farms, modified agricultural techniques, electric cars—these and many other such possibilities are matters of technology policy and energy policy. It may seem genuinely weird to suggest that they are matters of human rights as well. But they are. Standard threats change over time, and we have to look and see what they are. Severe climate change can undercut the necessary conditions for stable and sustainable human economies and societies in which people can enjoy their basic rights. Changes are being imposed on the climate because societies are so far clinging to primitive and dirty sources of energy when superior energy technology has emerged and become affordable. We need to face reality and promptly abandon the carbon-based energy technology that previous generations blundered into without understanding its destructive cumulative effects.

Three Special Features of Climate Change

This is not the place for anything like an adequate account of the significance of climate change.[17] However, three special features of climate change must at least be noted: the urgency of vigorous mitigation because of the likelihood of our soon passing points of no return, or tipping points, for positive feedbacks and even cascades of positive feedbacks; the threat to the human solidarity that is the ground of commitments to human rights; and the threats to human rights posed by strategies for controlling climate change that attempt to make up for inaction now with dreamed-of technological fixes later.

Tipping Points and Positive Feedbacks

Action to fulfill the duties required by basic rights should always be considered to have urgency because basic rights "specify the line beneath which no one is to be allowed to sink" (18). However, dealing with the threat posed by worsening climate change has a special additional kind of urgency. Earlier I promised to explain why I couple nuclear weapons with climate change as the two greatest threats facing humanity in the twentieth-first century. The basis for singling out these two is that each provides a clear path to—at the extreme—human extinction. Mutual escalation in the use of nuclear weapons, the danger of which provides nuclear deterrence with its distinctive character, is capable of resulting in a certain kind of runaway war. Specifically, if each side rushes to try to preempt the next attack by the other, both sides may unleash more weapons than, in a cooler hour, they would have known to be prudent.[18] Mutual attempts at escalation dominance may thus produce runaway exchanges that are mutually destructive. However, without wishing in any way to minimize the nuclear dangers, it is worth observing that this kind of military runaway is still a process mediated by human decisions. No external force seizes control of the escalation and removes it from human management. The process goes out of control while being decided about by humans. This runaway is a social, psychological, and political process. If the escalation goes wild, it will be humans who drive it there. The result would be an entirely man-made catastrophe.[19]

By contrast, climate change is capable of breaking into a natural, not a social, escalation in which human decisions can no longer significantly affect the process.[20] This is especially ironic in that the origin of contemporary climate change is anthropogenic. Like Dr. Frankenstein's monster, this century's climate change is man-made, but it can escape human control and follow a path of its own that humans can no longer block. Two underlying features are that many of the natural processes involved in climate change are not linear and that some changes in natural processes generate positive feedbacks. Nonlinear change and positive feedbacks are conceptually separate, but they can occur together.

Nonlinear change is abrupt, not gradual—for example, the melting of an Antarctic ice sheet may not simply become progressively faster, but instead become irreversible and even lead to rapid collapse of the ice sheet. The melting of Antarctic sea ice reduces its buttressing effect on marine ice sheets (sheets that rest on land that is below sea-level) and increase the likelihood of glacier instability and rapid collapse.[21] The point at which a nonlinear change will occur is often referred to as a threshold or tipping point. Positive feedbacks, on the other hand, consist of an effect that enhances the causal efficacy of its own cause. The melting of Arctic sea ice uncovers dark ocean water that absorbs more of the heat from sunlight than white sea ice does; the warming of the water speeds the melting of the sea ice, which uncovers dark water even faster, which warms the water still more, and then makes the sea ice melt faster still.[22] Although nonlinear change and positive feedbacks are conceptually separable, one kind of nonlinear change is a change from a process that does not generate any positive feedback to one that does. In addition, one positive feedback can produce a nonlinear change that brings about a second feedback. If such a sequence should continue, it could become a cascade.

If and when any changes of these kinds occur is of course an empirical matter—in the previous paragraph I have mainly been laying out conceptual possibilities. But the possibility that a tipping point for either a large abrupt change, an initiation of a powerful positive feedback, or both will be reached soon means that the climate system contains important points of no return. It is strongly in the human interest—not to mention the interest of thousands of other species that are already becoming extinct left and right—for the climate not to pass such points. Because there are points of no return, there are last chances for human action—times after which greater severity of change is locked-in and cannot be reversed. "Social and technological trends and decisions occurring over the next decade or two could significantly influence the trajectory of the Earth System for tens to hundreds of thousands of years and potentially lead to conditions . . . that would be inhospitable to current human societies and to many other contemporary species."[23]

The existence of such thresholds, or points of no return, gives great urgency to reaching the point of net zero carbon emissions at the earliest possible time and thus at the smallest possible atmospheric concentration of carbon dioxide (and therefore smallest temperature rise). Steep reductions in carbon emissions are urgent, but instead carbon emissions continue to rise globally: "more than half of the carbon exhaled into the atmosphere by the burning of fossil fuels has been emitted in just the past three decades. Which means we have done as much damage to the fate of the planet and its ability to sustain human life and civilization since Al Gore published his first book on climate than in all the centuries—all the millennia—that came before."[24] Throughout the four decades since this book first appeared we have been squandering our opportunity to act. At some point, not precisely predictable but possibly soon, we will be out of time to preserve the physical preconditions for basic rights and the social institutions that protect them.

The Threat to the Ground of Human Rights

The effective implementation of basic rights rests on some form of human solidarity, reciprocity, or deep cooperation. A right is an entitlement to action by others. Invocation of a right is not a plea for help but a justified demand for others to perform their rights-based duties. The performance of duties can sometimes be enforced upon reluctant or unwilling duty-bearers, but institutions constituted by rights and duties can function only if most people willingly cooperate most of the time. And in normal circumstances the willingness, and even readiness, of ordinary decent people to accord others their rights, even at some inconvenience and cost to themselves, is impressive and indeed admirable.

In extreme circumstances such institutions can break down because social ties fray and individuals lapse into the attitude of "every man for himself." For example, it is not unusual to have a panicked rush to escape after the sounding of an alarm or to have looting after a hurricane. Many of the threats posed by climate change are physical: fires, floods, drinking water shortages, failed crops, extreme heat, extreme storms, unfamiliar diseases. Many of these physical phenomena, especially failed crops that lead to either food shortages or spikes in food prices, sometimes have social and political consequences like protests, riots, or revolutions. It seems reasonable to conjecture that at some point the worsening physical dangers from climate change may generate sufficient social disruption that significant numbers of people will abandon their willingness to cooperate with social institutions like practices centered on rights and lapse into ruthless—if, very likely, self-defeating—pursuit of their own immediate interests. If so, the social grounding of all rights may be weakened or undercut, and the institutions embodying them may be destabilized.

Such conjectures are empirically supported by a growing, fascinating, and disturbing historical literature on the most recent previous instance of climate change, the "Little Ice Age" of the long seventeenth century, when global temperature moved approximately 1°C downward. In his monumental study, Geoffrey Parker concludes that "few areas of the world escaped the consequences of global cooling" and notes that "the most celebrated description of the consequences of the fatal synergy between natural and human disasters" was the famous paragraph by Thomas Hobbes that ordinarily is mistakenly assumed to be a hypothetical speculation rather than an analysis of observed historical circumstances: "[T]here is no place for industry, because the fruit thereof is uncertain, and consequently no culture of the earth. . . . And, which is worst of all, continual fear and danger of violent death; and the life of man, solitary, poor, nasty, brutish, and short."[25]

Obviously one cannot readily infer any particular conclusions about social disruption from future global warming from these studies of seventeenth-century disruptions from global cooling. Parker argues explicitly that well-functioning modern welfare states provide an institutional safety margin that was unknown in the 1600s. Nevertheless, contemporary climate change has already moved 1°C, and further rises are firmly locked into the climate system by the carbon dioxide and other greenhouse gases (notably, methane) already released, not to mention the additional gases certain to be released in coming years. The system is already inexorably committed to additional centuries of sea-level rise—as MIT physicist Susan Solomon puts it, "the ocean never forgets."[26] The resulting inundation of coastal areas and infiltration of salt into groundwater will certainly drive millions from their homes, and these migrants are liable to be seen by the current residents of whatever territory they flee to as encroaching on, if not "invading," that territory.[27] One can hope that up to some point the current residents will see the climate refugees as fellow humans with basic rights toward which they bear duties, not as threatening invaders.

But beyond that unpredictable point the current residents may feel as overwhelmed as the refugees feel, and desperation may take over on both sides, with rights ignored and order collapsing. The inability of both Europe and the United States to accommodate comparatively small numbers of refugees in recent years, for instance, is not encouraging. Philip Alston's special report warns about such danger: "consideration of the likely risks that will flow from climate change invariably focuses primarily if not exclusively on rights to life, water and sanitation, health, food, and housing. Yet democracy and the rule of law, as well as a wide range of civil and political rights are every bit [as much] at risk . . . . The risk of community discontent, of growing inequality, and of even greater levels of deprivation among some groups, will likely stimulate nationalist, xenophobic, racist and other responses".[28] The seeds of these responses are sprouting.

Already in 2007, intellectuals in U.S. military and intelligence circles were contemplating U.S. military responses to state collapse in poorer countries as a result of climate change, observing with studied understatement that "altruism and generosity would likely be blunted. In a world with millions of people migrating out of coastal areas and ports across the globe, it will be extremely difficult, perhaps impossible, for the United States to replicate the kind of professional and generous assistance provided to Indonesia following the 2004 tsunami."[29] It is vital that climate change be brought under control before military responses appear to be all that are left.

The Threat to Rights from Attempted Later Fixes for Current Delays

As I mention in a note, my Maryland colleague Paul Vernier liked to say that every silver lining has a cloud (227). Climate scientists realized some years ago that one of the clearest and firmest relationships in climate dynamics is between a particular probability of a particular amount of increase in the average annual global air temperature and the total cumulative atmospheric concentration of carbon dioxide. This led to a helpful conceptual barometer: the cumulative carbon budget. For a specific probability of a given rise in the average annual global air temperature chosen by policymakers as the goal of action to deal with climate change, say, a 66% probability of a rise no greater than 1.5° C, scientists can calculate the approximate total cumulative atmospheric concentration of carbon dioxide compatible with this probability of this rise. This concentration of carbon dioxide is then the cumulative carbon budget for a rise of no more than this probability of this many degrees. This is nicely captured on a website maintained by the Department of Physics at the University of Oxford.[30] Carbon budgets for various temperature rises provide relatively clear and firm targets for policymakers who need to decide how aggressively to cut carbon emissions (although the carbon budget abstracts from the effects of other greenhouse gases like methane, which make climate change worse than the accumulation of carbon dioxide alone would have).

A critical feature of the carbon budget is that it specifies the *cumulative* total of additional carbon dioxide retained in the atmosphere since human activity started adding to that total around the time of the Industrial Revolution. However, it is physically possible to subtract from that total by removing carbon dioxide from the atmosphere, as trees and all other plants performing photosynthesis do. Afforestation, for example, reduces atmospheric carbon dioxide, as do other "carbon sinks." Basically, this is good news—the silver lining—because it means that there can be what has come to be called, rather clumsily, "negative emissions," that is, subtractions from accumulated emissions. These proposed processes have come to be called carbon dioxide removal (CDR), or negative emissions technologies (NETs).

The cloud in the silver lining, however, is that awareness by policymakers of the possibility of CDR later may increase their so far almost incorrigible tendency to do little or nothing to corral the fossil fuel regime driving climate change, on the basis of the totally false, but deeply seductive, assumption that inaction now can always be repaired later.[31] But in fact it cannot be repaired later, and it is crucial to understand why this assumption is not true, even though carbon can in fact be subtracted or removed from the atmosphere. There are more than three reasons why not, but I must restrict consideration here to three.

First, while there are proven natural mechanisms for CDR like photosynthesis by trees, current levels of carbon emissions from persistent reliance on fossil fuels are so vast that such natural mechanisms cannot even begin to keep pace with the ongoing new anthropogenic emissions, much less produce significant net reductions in the cumulative concentration. Several reasons account for this, including the fact that deforestation exceeds afforestation, and the fact that enough afforestation to take a significant bite out of the now-expanding cumulative concentration would require much more land and water than can be spared by current societies for additional forests. Stopping deforestation is vital—"the Amazonian ecosystem is far closer to an existential tipping point than previously thought," with Brazilian President Jair Bolsonaro promoting deforestation as an expression of a right of national sovereignty.[32] And increasing afforestation is valuable—both are necessary—but they are nowhere near sufficient.

Sufficiently great CDR would be possible only by using human technologies designed for the purpose. Several infant technologies look theoretically possible, but none have been tested or deployed at the vast scale that would be necessary to affect total global concentration.[33] The corporations that continue to enrich themselves by extracting and selling fossil fuels for combustion have not made the investments in CDR that would have been necessary for the continued use of the products they sell to be made safe for the climate. Some venture capital is supporting experimentation, but CDR technologies at a scale adequate to make a global difference remain largely wishful thinking. Carbon corporations ought to have invested in making the use of their commodities safe fifty years ago when they realized that they are selling unsafe products.[34] If they had, some of the technologies might be mature now.

Second, even the large reductions in atmospheric carbon that are (merely) theoretically possible could not produce a significantly lower atmospheric concentration until carbon emissions end. This is simple arithmetic. If carbon emissions pour out from our right hand, while we pull them back using CDR with our left hand, we are basically spinning our wheels and going nowhere. Large negative emissions could make a difference, but only in the context of sharply reduced emissions. Negative emissions are at best a supplement to, not a substitute for, zero emissions, given the gigantic existing concentration and all the additional emissions that will inevitably flow between now and the date of net zero.

Third, and most important, are the features of climate dynamics sketched in the previous section regarding nonlinear change, positive feedbacks, and tipping points. It is true that an atmospheric concentration of carbon dioxide that had previously been expanded can subsequently be contracted. "Overshoot" in emissions, as it has come to be called, can be corrected, and the atmospheric concentration can be returned to an earlier, lower level. What is emphatically not possible, however, is to reverse all the physical changes that were meanwhile forced to occur by the expanded atmospheric carbon concentration while it endures. For instance, suppose the carbon concentration grows large enough to trap enough heat on the planet to cause widespread melting of the Arctic tundra and the release of the monumental amounts of methane and carbon dioxide currently trapped there. Later, the carbon concentration might in principle be reversed back below the threshold for the melting of the tundra. The original "overshoot" in emissions (including the additional carbon emissions from the tundra) might eventually be corrected.

The only problem is that the tundra may already have melted and released its methane and carbon during the period while the greenhouse gas concentration was large enough to drive the temperature above the threshold for melting; and any positive feedbacks produced by the presence of the additional carbon and methane in the atmosphere, while they persist, may be irreversible. The carbon concentration itself is reversible, and the methane decomposes over a few years, but some of the physical effects of the larger concentration of greenhouse gases, while it lasts, may be irreversible.[35] Negative emissions later are by no stretch of the imagination equivalent in their effects to emissions reductions now that prevent temperature from ever rising above the melting threshold. If policymakers take the possibility of later negative emissions as a pretext for less radical emissions cuts now, the consequent undermining of basic rights by the resulting much more severe climate change could be disastrous, rendering large numbers of people helpless as their economies and the stability of their societies are undermined.

The Struggle for Control of the Climate

Many of those whose wealth and power rests on the continued extraction and sale of fossil fuels are fighting ferociously and viciously to obscure the facts about climate change and to prevent effective action toward a rapid transition out of the fossil fuel regime.[36] Many banks flagrantly ignore the Paris Agreement and continue to provide loans enabling the expanded long-term use of fossil fuels, with the world's most egregious offenders being JPMorgan Chase, Wells Fargo, Citi, and Bank of America.[37] Continuing to practice their dog-eat-dog version of capitalism, the major oil and gas companies are employing a slick camouflage of PR greenwash to disguise their business plans to extract the maximum possible carbon in coming decades: "The world's 50 biggest oil companies are poised to flood markets with an additional 7m[illion] barrels a day over the next decade . . . . New research commissioned by the *Guardian* forecasts Shell and ExxonMobil will be among the leaders with a projected production increase of more than 35% between 2018 and 2030 . . . . The acceleration is almost the opposite of the 45% reduction in carbon emissions by 2030 that scientists say is necessary to have any chance of holding global heating at a relatively safe level of 1.5C."[38] We urgently need to develop vigorous and effective ways to counterattack this heedless, heartless, and remarkably greedy aggression against the climatic conditions necessary for the satisfaction of basic rights.[39] No one ought to be allowed social license to underwrite such further deprivation of basic rights.

I conclude in chapter 5 that "property laws can be morally justified only if subsistence rights are fulfilled. . . . The moral acceptability of the enforcement of property rights depends upon the enforcement of subsistence rights" (124–125); and I emphasize that "to protect non-vital interests by means that preclude the satisfaction of vital interests is to treat non-vital interests as if they are as important as—actually, as more important than—vital interests" (127).[40] JPMorgan Chase, "the only bank leading financing for all four key tar sands expansion companies," would likely contend that it has a perfect right to invest as much as it pleases of the wealth it controls in the extraction of oil from the Canadian tar sands.[41] But the combustion of the exceptionally high carbon oil from the tar sands throughout the typical lifetime of a loan for extraction will undercut the stability of the climate and be a contributing cause of the deprivation of subsistence rights. It is not possible to acknowledge both basic rights to subsistence and a purported property right to continue indefinitely to finance the reckless extraction of fossil fuels for combustion that releases carbon dioxide. Everyone must choose a side now in the struggle for the fate of the earth and the lives of its vulnerable inhabitants.

Fossil fuels are becoming our contemporary plague, and those whose air, water, and food are most vulnerable to climate change are becoming the victims of this plague. Perhaps decent people can at least adopt the guideline of Albert Camus's character Tarrou: "All I say is that on this earth there are pestilences and there are victims—and as far as possible one must refuse to be on the side of the pestilence."[42] Better, we can vigorously defend basic rights. Fossil fuel interests are extremely powerful and deeply entrenched, but they are not invulnerable. Some hard-headed analysts see hopeful signs for the future.[43] On the other hand, the rate of growth in carbon emissions in 2018 was shockingly high, establishing a new record for carbon dioxide from coal-burning plants of more than ten billion tons.[44] Many utilities that are abandoning coal are making the disastrous choice to switch to gas and to install long-lived pipeline infrastructure instead of switching to non-carbon energy and building its infrastructure.[45] The struggle is on, and even when we cannot find grounds for hope, we can still fight with courage.

October 2019, Merton College

Notes

Preface to the 40th Anniversary Edition

1. Charles R. Beitz and Robert E. Goodin, "Introduction: *Basic Rights* and Beyond," in *Global Basic Rights*, edited by Charles R. Beitz and Robert E. Goodin (Oxford: Oxford University Press, 2009), 1–24, at 17–23; and Simon Caney, "Human Rights, Responsibilities, and Climate Change," in *Global Basic Rights*, 227–247, at 228.

2. I have meanwhile written in passing about climate change and human rights in (1) "Changing Images of Climate Change: Human Rights and Future Generations," *Journal of Human Rights and the Environment* 5 (2014): 50–64; reprinted in Anna Grear and Conor Gearty, eds., *Choosing a Future: The Social and Legal Aspects of Climate Change* (Cheltenham, UK: Edward Elgar, 2014), 50–64; (2) "Human Rights in the Anthropocene," in *Encyclopedia of the Anthropocene*, edited by Dominick A. DellaSala and Michael I. Goldstein (Oxford: Elsevier, 2018), 4:103–109; also available online as a chapter in *Reference Module in Earth Systems and Environmental Sciences*, Science Direct, doi:10.1016/B978-0-12-409548-9.10480-4; and (3) "Last Opportunities: Future Human Rights Generate Urgent Present Duties," in *Global Policy* (November 26, 2015): http://www.globalpolicyjournal.com/blog/26/11/2015/last-opportunities-future-human-rights-generate-urgent-present-duties; part of *Global Policy*'s e-book, *Climate Change and Human Rights: The 2015 Paris Conference and the Task of Protecting People on a Warming Planet* (2015), edited by Marcello di Paola and Daanika Kamal.

Introduction

1. The label "International Bill of Human Rights" very usefully groups together the Preamble and Articles 1, 55, and 56 of the Charter of the United Nations; the Universal Declaration of Human Rights; the International Covenant on Economic, Social and Cultural Rights; the International Covenant on Civil and Political Rights; and the Optional Protocol to the International Covenant on Civil and Political Rights. Although the U.S. Senate has failed to ratify the two Covenants and the Optional Protocol, they all entered into force internationally in 1976. The Carter Administration has failed even to submit to the Senate for ratification the Optional Protocol, which contains the most important mechanism for the enforcement of civil and political rights. The protocol is "optional" only in the sense that it requires separate ratification. To

this grouping probably should be added the most widely ratified UN human rights treaty currently in force (once again, without United States ratification or participation): the International Convention on the Elimination of all Forms of Racial Discrimination, in force since 1969.

On the role of the United States government in promoting within the International Bill of Human Rights the artificial division between civil and political and economic, social and cultural rights, see below, chapter 7, n. 7. On why the division is artificial, see chapter 2.

2. Secretary of State Cyrus R. Vance, "Human Rights Policy," April 30, 1977 (Washington: Office of Media Services, Bureau of Public Affairs, Department of State), PR 194, p. 1. The inclusion of "the right to the fulfillment of such vital needs as food, shelter, health care, and education" was re-affirmed by Deputy Secretary of State Warren Christopher in "Human Rights: Principle and Realism," August 9, 1977 (Washington: Office of Media Services, Bureau of Public Affairs, Department of State), PR 374, p. 1.

3. For my account of subsistence rights, see chapter 1.

4. By focusing discussion upon positions taken by elements of the State Department I do not intend to encourage the false impression that State is the leading force in the Executive Branch on foreign policy. In recent decades the Department of Defense and National Security Advisers to the President (namely McGeorge Bundy, Henry Kissinger, and Zbigniew Brzezinski) have often exerted far more influence—see, for stimulating reflections about this, Graham Allison and Peter Szanton, *Remaking Foreign Policy: The Organizational Connection* (New York: Basic Books, 1976). State is simply the portion of the Executive Branch that makes more of its positions public than others usually do, with the result that citizens can examine them, unlike the more often secret positions pursued by the National Security Council.

5. One published account says that the legal analyses of the International Covenants, signed by Deputy Secretary of State Christopher, were "drafted" by the White House, not by the Office of Legal Advisers, and were forwarded without consultation with the Bureau of Human Rights—see Thomas M. Franck and Edward Weisband, *Foreign Policy by Congress* (New York: Oxford University Press, 1979), p. 96. For some of the reasons why it would not be surprising if no one wanted to take responsibility for the destructive collection of reservations, understandings, and declarations that would turn Senate ratification of the Covenants into a farce, see the first section of chapter 7.

6. See Senate Comm. on Foreign Relations and House Comm. on Foreign Affairs, 96th Cong., 1st Sess., *Report on Human Rights Practices in Countries Receiving U.S. Aid* (Joint Comm. Print, February 8,

1979), *passim*. For the PQLI scores, see pp. 666–673. For a thorough discussion of the PQLI by its developer, see Morris D. Morris, *Measuring the Condition of the World's Poor: The Physical Quality of Life Index*, Pergamon Policy Studies, No. 42 (New York: Pergamon Press for the Overseas Development Council, 1979).

7. See Donald M. Fraser, "Freedom and Foreign Policy," *Foreign Policy*, No. 26 (Spring 1977), p. 144.

8. An example of this traditional way of fudging the issue is: "the right to the satisfaction of basic human needs—such as food, shelter, and essential medical care—when resources are available," United Nations Association of the United States of America, National Policy Panel, *United States Foreign Policy and Human Rights* (New York: UNA-USA, 1979), p. 35. Must any effort be exerted to make resources available, or shall we just use what turns out to be left over after business as usual?

1 • Security and Subsistence

1. Obviously this is not the usual North Atlantic account of what a right is, although it incorporates, I think, what is correct in the usual accounts. Perhaps the most frequently cited philosophical discussion is the useful one in Joel Feinberg, *Social Philosophy* (Englewood Cliffs: Prentice-Hall, Inc., 1973), pp. 55–97. A more recent and extended account is A. I. Melden, *Rights and Persons* (Oxford: Basil Blackwell, 1977). The best collection of recent English and American philosophical essays is probably *Rights*, edited by David Lyons (Belmont, Calif.: Wadsworth Publishing Co., Inc., 1979). For a broader range of views, in less rigorous form, see *Human Rights: Cultural and Ideological Perspectives*, edited by Adamantia Pollis and Peter Schwab (New York: Praeger Publishers, 1979). For additional references, mostly to work in English, see Rex Martin and James W. Nickel, "A Bibliography on the Nature and Foundations of Rights, 1947–1977," *Political Theory*, 6:3 (August 1978), pp. 395–413. Some older but more wide-ranging bibliographies are *International Human Rights: A Bibliography 1965–1969* and *International Human Rights: A Bibliography 1970–1976*, both edited by William Miller (Notre Dame: University of Notre Dame Law School, Center for Civil Rights, 1976).

2. In saying that these three features constitute "the general structure of a moral right" I do not mean that every moral right always has every one of the three. Wittgenstein, for one, has argued persuasively that we have no particular reason to expect all authentic instances of any concept to have all features—indeed, to have any one feature—in common and that what instance A shares with instance B need not be the same as what instance B shares with instance C. See Ludwig Wittgenstein, *Philosophical*

Investigations, Third Edition (Oxford: Basil Blackwell, 1967), Part I, paragraphs 66–67. What we are left with is the more realistic but more elusive notion of standard, central, or typical cases. The danger then rests in the temptation to dismiss as deviant or degenerate cases what ought to be treated as counter-examples to our general claims. We have no mechanical method for deciding what is standard and what is deviant and so must consider individual cases fairly and thoroughly, as we shall soon be trying to do.

Two important characteristics of this list of features should be emphasized. First, the list of features is, not the premises for, but the conclusion from, the detailed description of individual rights considered in the body of the book. Thus, the order of presentation is not the order of derivation. These general features were distilled from the cases of security rights, subsistence rights, and liberty rights discussed in the first three chapters. These general conclusions are presented here as a means of quickly sketching the bold outlines of what is still to be justified.

Second, most of the argument of the book depends only upon its being correct to say that all *basic* rights have these three features. Since the features are derived from the detailed consideration only of basic rights, it would be conceivable that basic rights were peculiar in having all three. Yet, many other rights obviously do have this same structure. So I advance the less fully justified broader claim, not merely the safer, narrower claim.

3. Feinberg, pp. 58–59. The terminology of "claim-rights" is of course from Wesley Hohfeld, *Fundamental Legal Conceptions* (New Haven: Yale University Press, 1923).

4. Standard moral rights are, in the categories devised by Hohfeld for legal rights, claim-rights, not mere liberties. Certainly all basic rights turn out to be moral claim-rights rather than moral liberties. See chapter 2.

5. This becomes clearest in the discussion of rights to liberty in chapter 3.

6. Who exactly are the relevant people is an extremely difficult question, to which chapter 6 is devoted.

7. See chapter 2.

8. For his clearest single presentation of this analysis, see Friedrich Nietzsche, *On the Genealogy of Morals*, edited by Walter Kaufmann and translated by Walter Kaufmann and R. J. Hollingdale (New York: Vintage Books, 1967). Much, but not all, of what is interesting in Nietzsche's account was put into the mouth of Callicles in Plato's *Gorgias*.

9. Many legal claim-rights make little or no contribution to self-respect, but moral claim-rights (and the legal claim-rights based upon them) surely do.

10. Nietzsche was also conflating a number of different kinds of power/weakness. Many of today's politically powerful, against whom

people need protection, totally lack the kind of dignified power Nietzsche most admired and would certainly have incurred his cordial disgust.

11. Anyone not familiar with the real meaning of what gets called "infant mortality rates" might consider the significance of the fact that in nearby Mexico seven out of every 100 babies fail to survive infancy—see United States, Department of State, *Background Notes: Mexico*, Revised February 1979 (Washington: Government Printing Office, 1979), p. 1. For far worse current children's death rates still, see below, chapter 4, note 13.

12. It is controversial whether rights are claims only upon members of one's own society or upon other persons generally. For some support for the conclusion assumed here, see chapter 6.

13. Since the enjoyment of a basic right is necessary for the enjoyment of all other rights, it is basic not only to non-basic rights but to other basic rights as well. Thus the enjoyment of the basic rights is an all-or-nothing matter. Each is necessary to the other basic ones as well as to all non-basic ones. Every right, including every basic right, can be enjoyed only if all basic rights are enjoyed. An extended discussion of a case of this mutual dependence is found in chapter 3.

At the cost of being somewhat premature it may be useful to comment here on an objection that often strikes readers at this point as being a clear counter-example to the thesis that subsistence rights are basic rights in the sense just explained. Mark Wicclair has put the objection especially forcefully for me. The arguments for the thesis have of course not yet been given and occupy much of the remainder of the chapter and, indeed, of the book.

Suppose that in a certain society people are said to enjoy a certain security right—let us say the right not to be tortured. But they do not in fact enjoy subsistence rights: food, for example, is not socially guaranteed even to people who find it impossible to nourish themselves. The thesis that subsistence rights are basic means that people cannot enjoy any other right if subsistence rights are not socially guaranteed. It follows that the people in the society in question could not actually be enjoying the right not to be tortured, because their right to adequate food is not guaranteed. But—this is the objection—it would appear that they could enjoy the right not to be tortured even though they were starving to death for lack of food they could do nothing to obtain. The objection grants that starvation is terrible. The theoretical point is, however, said to remain: starvation without torture is preferable to starvation with torture, and the right not to be tortured is still worth something even in isolation and, in particular, even in the absence of subsistence rights. Subsistence rights are, therefore, not necessary for the enjoyment of all other rights and thus not basic in the relevant sense.

But could there actually be a case of the kind brought forward as a counter-example? Could there actually be a right not to be tortured in the absence of a right to subsistence? The difficulty is that a person who had no social guarantee of, say, food and was in fact deprived of food might, without other recourse, be willing to submit to limited torture in exchange for food. In other words, what is being called a right not to be tortured is open to being undermined by the threat of doing nothing about a shortage of food. If this perverse trade of submission to torture for receipt of food were possible, it would be accurate to say that although the person may *have* a right not to be tortured, he cannot actually *enjoy* the right because he must choose between undergoing torture and undergoing starvation, or malnutrition (to make the alternative involving subsistence more like much torture: painful and damaging but not fatal). Insofar as the person has anything approximating a right not to be tortured, the "right" is a merely conditional one—conditional upon the person's not in fact being without some necessity for subsistence for which the substance of the "right" not to be tortured could, in effect, be sold.

Three ways of trying to save the original objection come to mind. First, it might be suggested that trading the immunity to torture for the means to eat is not an instance of failing to enjoy a right, but an instance of renouncing a right. Only because one has the right not to be tortured does one have something to trade for food.

This response is fairly obviously mistaken. If one's only hope of eating adequately is to submit to torture, one is being coerced into submitting to torture, not renouncing one's right not to be tortured. This is a case of coercion analogous in the relevant respects to the demand, your money or your life. One is not renouncing one's right to the money—one is being forced to surrender one's money in order to stay alive. In prisons, where people are already deprived of the freedom of physical movement ordinarily needed for obtaining their own food, the threat to withhold food as well is in fact a common means of coercion.

Second, it could be noted that the torture-for-food exchange might simply not be available. Certainly in light of the perversity of the bargain, there might be no one in the business of supplying people with food in exchange for the privilege of torturing them. Only some sort of wealthy sadist would engage in this transaction.

Now, of course the exchange described is in fact very unlikely, as is the original situation that constitutes the counter-example. The response to the objection is as fantastical as the objection, but the objector cannot expect otherwise. (In what country are people both provided guarantees against torture and denied guarantees of food for subsistence?) But this second response misses the point. That people were not in fact undergoing torture in order to obtain food (or for any other reason) would not constitute their enjoying a right not to be tortured. Enjoying any right includes, among other things, some social guarantees. It is not merely that one does not undergo objectionable events or that one does undergo desirable events—it includes provisions having been made to see to it that the objectionable does not occur and the desirable does.

Hence, the third way to save the counter-example would be to add to it a prohibition against trading the right not to be tortured for anything else, including what was needed to meet an even more serious threat. The counter-example would have to say: one may not be tortured and one must not surrender, trade, renounce, etc. this right for anything else. This would be a weak version of something roughly like what was traditionally called inalienability, except that as traditionally understood inalienability was essential to or inherent in a right: it was thought to be somehow absolutely impossible to alienate or trade the right. In the objector's counter-example anyone obviously *could* trade the right not to be tortured for something else. The best that could be done would be an exceptionless and enforceable prohibition against trading away this right. The trade would, perhaps, be illegal. We can call this an alienation-prohibition, in order to distinguish it from the traditional notion of intrinsic inalienability.

With the inclusion of the alienation-prohibition the case may be an actual counter-example, but it is difficult to tell. Possibly one is enjoying a right not to be tortured when one is not only protected against torture but also prevented from exchanging that protection for protection against other threats. As the argument of the book unfolds, two of the main contentions will be (a) that in order to enjoy any right one must be protected against the standard threats to the right and (b) that the best way to be protected against a standard threat is to have social guarantees for the absence of the threat. Thus, the way to enjoy a right to subsistence is to be guaranteed that no torture, among other things, will be used to implement an economic strategy that produces malnutrition, and the way to enjoy a right not to be tortured is to be guaranteed that no deprivations of subsistence needs like food, among other things, will be used to implement a political strategy that includes torture (not that the latter is a realistic case).

Now instead of protecting the enjoyment of one right against standard threats by also protecting the other rights the enjoyment of which includes social guarantees against the standard threats, one could conceivably "protect" one right in isolation by prohibiting the use of that right to fend off threats against which one has no guarantees because one lacks other rights. This is what is done by the right not to be tortured that includes the alienation-prohibition. But the attempted counter-example has now become quite contorted and exotic. One is being prohibited from saving one's own life (from lack of subsistence) at a cost of pain and damage that one is willing to accept if one must. Is this an example of enjoying one right (not to be tortured) in the absence of the enjoyment of another right (subsistence)? This case is now so different from an ordinary case of enjoying a right (in which, I will contend, part of the right is social guarantees against standard threats) that it is uncertain what to say. Obviously I could not without circularity invoke what I take to be the normal and adequate conception of enjoying a right in order to judge the proffered case not to be a case of enjoying a right and therefore not a counter-example to the thesis that subsistence rights are basic. However, treating this eccentric example as a clear case would be question-begging against my view, I think. So, I leave it to the reader—and to the argument in the text.

14. It is odd that the list of "primary goods" in Rawlsian theory does not mention physical security as such. See John Rawls, *A Theory of Justice* (Cambridge, Mass.: The Belknap Press of Harvard University Press, 1971), p. 62 and p. 303. The explanation seems to be that security is lumped in with political participation and a number of civil liberties, including freedom of thought, of speech, of press, et al. To do this is to use "liberty" in a confusingly broad sense. One can speak intelligibly of "freedom from" almost anything bad: the child was free from fear, the cabin was free from snakes, the picnic was free from rain. Similarly, it is natural to speak of being free from assault, free from the threat of rape, etc., but this does not turn all these absences of evils into liberties. Freedom from assault, for example, is a kind of security or safety, not a kind of liberty. It may of course be a necessary condition for the exercise of any liberties, which is exactly what I shall now be arguing, but a necessary condition for the exercise of a liberty may be many things other than another kind of liberty. The most complete indication of why I believe physical security and liberty—even freedom of physical movement—need to be treated separately is chapter 3.

15. At considerable risk of encouraging unflattering comparisons I might as well note myself that in its general structure the argument here has the same form as the argument in H.L.A. Hart's classic, "Are There Any Natural Rights?" *Philosophical Review*, 64:2 (April 1955), pp. 175-91. That is, Hart can be summarized as maintaining: if there are any rights, there are rights to liberty. I am saying: if there are any rights, there are rights to security—and to subsistence. The finer structures of the arguments are of course quite different. I find Hart's inference considerably less obvious than he did. So, evidently, do many thoughtful people in the Third and Fourth Worlds, which counts against its obviousness but not necessarily against its validity. My struggle with the place of some kinds of liberty, construed more narrowly than Hart's, constitutes chapter 3.

16. In originally formulating this argument for treating both security and subsistence as basic rights I was not consciously following any philosopher but attempting instead to distill contemporary common sense. As many people have noted, today's common sense tends to be yesterday's philosophy. I was amused to notice recently the following passage from Mill, who not only gives a similar argument for security but notices and then backs away from the parallel with subsistence: "The interest involved is that of security, to everyone's feelings the most vital of all interests. All other earthly benefits are needed by one person, not needed by another; and many of them can, if necessary, be cheerfully foregone or replaced by something else; but security no human being can possibly do without; on it we depend for all our immunity from evil and for the whole value of all and every good, beyond the passing moment, since nothing but the gratification of the instant could be of any worth to us if we could be deprived of everything the next instant by whoever was momentarily stronger than ourselves. Now this most indispensable of all necessaries, after physical nutriment, cannot be had unless. . . ." John Stuart Mill, *Utilitarianism* (Indianapolis: Bobbs-Merrill Co., 1957), p. 67 (chapter V, 14th paragraph from the end).

17. "Many people, therefore, economically dependent as they are upon their employer, hesitate to speak out not because they are afraid of getting arrested, but because they are afraid of being fired. And they are right." Ira Glasser, "Director's Report: You Can Be Fired for Your Politics," *Civil Liberties*, No. 327 (April 1979), p. 8.

18. Exactly how and why Western liberalism has tended to overlook subsistence is another story, but consider, simply as one symptom, the fact that a standard assumption in liberal theory is that there is only moderate scarcity. This has the effect of assuming that everyone's subsistence is taken care of. You must have your subsistence guaranteed in order to be admitted into the domain of the theory. Today this excludes from the scope of liberal theory no fewer than 1,000,000,000 people.

The figure of over one billion is generally accepted as the minimum number of desperately poor people. The U.S. government's World Hunger Working Group, for example, gave "1.2 billion" as the number of "persons without access to safe drinking water"—see United States, White House, *World Hunger and Malnutrition: Improving the U.S. Response* (Washington: Government Printing Office, 1978), p. 9. This is, roughly, 25% of all the people there are—and a much higher percentage of the children, since in many very poor countries most people are young.

I am not criticizing only people who call themselves "liberals" but also, for example, "neoconservatives." For, as Michael Walzer has perceptively observed, "neoconservatives are nervous liberals, and what they are nervous about is liberalism"—see Michael Walzer, "Nervous Liberals," *New York Review of Books*, 26:15 (October 11, 1979), p. 6.

19. James C. Scott, *The Moral Economy of the Peasant: Rebellion and Subsistence in Southeast Asia* (New Haven: Yale University Press, 1976), pp. 40–41. Scott analyzes the "normative roots of peasant politics" (4) with subtlety and clarity, displaying a coherent and rational conceptual framework implicit in the moral consensus across several peasant societies. I do not mean to suggest, nor does Scott, that all is well in Southeast Asia. For one thing, many traditional village institutions are being eliminated by "modernizing" regimes. With Scott's theory, compare Joel S. Migdal, *Peasants, Politics, and Revolution: Pressures toward Political and Social Change in the Third World* (Princeton: Princeton University Press, 1974); and Samuel L. Popkin, *The Rational Peasant: The Political Economy of Rural Society in Vietnam* (Berkeley: University of California Press, 1979).

For defenses of the suspension of the fulfillment of subsistence rights during an indefinite development period, see Lt. Gen. Ali Moertopo, "Political and Economic Development in Indonesia in the Context of Regionalism in Southeast Asia," *Indonesian Quarterly*, 6:2 (April 1978), pp. 30–47, esp. pp. 32–38; and O. D. Corpuz, "Liberty and Government in the New Society" (Quezon City: University of the Philippines, Office of the President, 1975), photocopy. For cautions from a nutritional anthropologist about the effects of U.S. aid programs on traditional societies, see Norge W. Jerome, "Nutritional Dilemmas of Transforming Economies," in *Food Policy: The Responsibility of the United States in the Life and Death Choices*, ed. by Peter G. Brown and Henry Shue (New York: Free Press, 1977), pp. 275–304.

20. Benedict J. Kerkvliet, *The Huk Rebellion: A Study of Peasant Revolt in the Philippines* (Berkeley: University of California Press, 1977), p. 252. On the importance for Philippine peasants of their deep belief in a right to subsistence, see pp. 252–255. The most comprehensive legal and normative analysis of economic rights in developing countries is "The International Dimensions of the Right to Development as a Human Right in Relation with Other Human Rights," United Nations, Economic and Social Council, Commission on Human Rights, E/CN.4/1334 (35th Sess., Agenda item 8, 2 January 1979), (Geneva: Division of Human Rights, 1978).

21. I am grateful to Douglas MacLean for emphasizing the similarity between the notion toward which I am groping here and the one in Thomas M. Scanlon, "Human Rights as a Neutral Concern," in *Human Rights and U.S. Foreign Policy: Principles and Applications*, edited by Peter G. Brown and Douglas MacLean (Lexington, Mass.: Lexington Books, 1979), pp. 83–92. The Brown and MacLean volume and this

volume are products of the same research effort and are designed to complement each other. On nearly every major issue discussed here, alternative views appear in Brown and MacLean, and I am to some degree indebted to the author of almost every chapter of that companion volume, including those with which I am in sharp disagreement philosophically or politically.

22. Although this admission opens a theoretical door to a certain amount of "relativism," I suspect the actual differences across societies in the standard preventable threats are much less than they conceivably might be. Compare Barrington Moore's thesis that although differences in conceptions of happiness are great and important, virtually everyone agrees upon the "miseries"—Barrington Moore, Jr., *Reflections on the Causes of Human Misery and Upon Certain Proposals to Eliminate Them* (Boston: Beacon Press, 1972), especially chapter I, and *Injustice: The Social Bases of Obedience and Revolt* (White Plains: M. E. Sharpe, 1978). Here, as in many other places, philosophical analysis and political analysis need each other.

The unavoidable mixture of the analytic and the empirical in an element like standard threats is obviously difficult to characterize with any precision. On the one hand, it is clearly part of the meaning of a right that the right-holder may insist that other people take measures to protect the enjoyment of the substance of the right against ordinary, non-inevitable threats—this much is analytic. But which threats are pervasive, which are serious, and which can feasibly be resisted must be discovered from particular situations. Naturally, what is, for example, feasible is a function of how much of the available resources are devoted to the task, as chapter 4 will emphasize, and that is a heavily value-laden question, not a mere question of efficiency to be left to the economists. So we can draw no neat line between aspects that require philosophical argument and aspects that require economic and political investigation.

23. The coherence of the account of the general structure of a moral right and the account of a basic right with each other is one consideration in favor of both, although coherence is, needless to say, not enough. I am grateful to Charles R. Beitz for perceptively pressing me to make these underlying connections clearer.

Since fulfilling any one basic right involves creating safeguards for the enjoyment of the substance of that basic right against the other standard threats that are the respective concerns of the other basic rights, no basic right can be completely fulfilled until all basic rights are fulfilled. See note 13 above and, for an extended example, chapter 3, and especially note 14. It would appear that just as (and, because?) deprivations of rights tend to be systematically interrelated, the fulfillment of at least the basic rights also comes in a single package.

2 • Correlative Duties

1. See the Introduction.

2. For a forceful re-affirmation of this view in the current political context (and further references), see Hugo Adam Bedau, "Human Rights and Foreign Assistance Programs," in *Human Rights and U.S. Foreign Policy*, ed. by Peter G. Brown and Douglas MacLean (Lexington, Mass: Lexington Books, 1979), pp. 29–44. Also see Charles Frankel, *Human Rights and Foreign Policy*, Headline Series No. 241 (New York: Foreign Policy Association, 1978), especially pp. 36–49, where Frankel advanced a "modest list of fundamental rights" that explicitly excluded economic rights as "dangerously utopian." A version of the general distinction has recently been re-affirmed by Thomas Nagel—see "Equality," in *Mortal Questions* (New York: Cambridge University Press, 1979), pp. 114–115. An utterly unrealistic but frequently invoked version of the distinction is in Maurice Cranston, *What Are Human Rights?* (London: The Bodley Head, 1973), chapter VIII. An interesting attempt to show that the positive/negative distinction is compatible with economic rights is John Langan, "Defining Human Rights: A Revision of the Liberal Tradition," Working Paper (Washington: Woodstock Theological Center, 1979). For a provocative and relevant discussion of "negative responsibility" (responsibility for what one fails to prevent), see Bernard Williams, "A Critique of Utilitarianism," in *Utilitarianism: For & Against* (New York: Cambridge University Press, 1973), pp. 93 ff.

3. Naturally my use of the same argument for the basic status of both security and subsistence is at least an indirect challenge to (1) (b). No question is raised here, however, about (1) (a): the thesis that subsistence and security are sharply distinguishable. People who should be generally sympathetic to my fundamental thesis that subsistence rights are basic rights, do sometimes try to reach the same conclusion by the much shorter seeming route of denying that security and subsistence are importantly different from each other. For example, it is correctly observed that both security and subsistence are needed for survival and then maintained that both are included in a right to survival, or right to life. Though I am by no means hostile to this approach, it does have three difficulties that I believe can be avoided by my admittedly somewhat more circuitous path of argument. First, it is simply not correct that one cannot maintain a clear and useful distinction between security and subsistence, as, in fact, I hope to have done up to this point. Second, arguments for a general right to life that includes subsistence rights appear to need some premise to the effect that the right to life entails rights to at least some of the means of life. Thus, they face the same "weakness of too much strength"—straining

credulity by implying more than most people are likely to be able to believe—that we tried to avoid at the end of chapter 1. A right-to-the-means-of-life argument might be able to skirt the problem equally well by using a notion of a standard threat to life, analogous to our notion of a standard threat to the enjoyment of rights, but this alternative tack seems, at best, no better off. Third, the concept of a right to life is now deeply infected with ambiguities concerning whether it is a purely negative right, a purely positive right, or, as I shall soon be maintaining with regard to both security and subsistence, an inseparable mixture of positive and negative elements. The appeal for many people of a right to life seems to depend, however, upon its being taken to be essentially negative, while it can fully include subsistence rights only if it has major positive elements.

4. I think one can often show the implausibility of an argument by an exhaustive statement of all the assumptions it needs. I have previously attempted this in the case of one of John Rawls's arguments for the priority of liberty—see "Liberty and Self-Respect," *Ethics*, 85:3 (April 1975), pp. 195–203.

5. I have given a summary of the argument against 3 and arguments against thinking that either the right to a fair trail or the right not to be tortured are negative rights in "Rights in the Light of Duties," in Brown and MacLean, pp. 65–81. I have also argued directly against what is here called 2b and briefly introduced the account of duties presented in the final sections of this chapter. My goal, which I have no illusions about having attained, has been to do as definitive a job on positive and negative rights as Gerald C. MacCallum, Jr. did on positive and negative liberty in his splendid article, "Negative and Positive Freedom," *Philosophical Review*, 76:3 (July 1967), pp. 312–334.

6. See note 3 above.

7. Elsewhere I have briefly queried the moral significance of the action/omission distinction—see the essay cited in note 5 above. For a fuller discussion, see Judith Lichtenberg, "On Being Obligated to Give Aid: Moral and Political Arguments," Diss., City University of New York, 1978.

8. In FY 1975 in the United States the cost of the "criminal justice system" was $17 billion, or $71 per capita, *New York Times*, July 21, 1977, p. A3. In several countries that year the total annual income was less than $71 per capita. Obviously such isolated statistics prove nothing, but they are suggestive. One thing they suggest is that adequate provisions for this supposedly negative right would not necessarily be less costly than adequate provisions for some rights supposed to be positive. Nor is it evident that physical security does any better on what Frankel called the test of being "realistically deliverable" (45) and Cranston called "the test of practicability" (66). On Cranston's use of the latter, see chapter 4.

9. "To have a right, then, is, I conceive, to have something which society ought to defend me in the possession of"—John Stuart Mill, *Utilitarianism* (Indianapolis: Bobbs-Merrill Co., 1957), p. 66 (chapter V, 14th paragraph from the end).

10. This is not a point about ordinary language, in which there is obviously a significant difference between "leave me alone" and "protect me against people who will not leave me alone." My thesis is that people who are not already grinding axes for minimal government will naturally and reasonably think in terms of enjoying a considerable degree of security, will want to have done whatever within reason is necessary, and will recognize that more is necessary than refraining campaigns—campaigns urging self-restraint upon would-be murderers, muggers, rapists, et al. I am of course not assuming that existing police and penal institutions are the best forms of social guarantees for security; I am assuming only that more effective institutions would probably be at least equally complex and expensive.

11. Therefore, as we shall see below, the complete fulfillment of a subsistence right may involve not the actual provision of any aid at all but only the performance of duties to avoid depriving and to protect against deprivation.

12. The literature on underdeveloped countries in fact abounds in actual cases that have the essential features of the so-called hypothetical case, and I have simply presented a stylized sketch of a common pattern. Most anecdotes are in the form of "horror stories" about transnational corporations switching land out of the production of the food consumed by the local poor. See, for example, Robert J. Ledogar, *Hungry for Profits: U.S. Food and Drug Multinationals in Latin America* (New York: IDOC, 1976), pp. 92–98 (Ralston Purina in Colombia) and Richard J. Barnet and Ronald E. Müller, *Global Reach: The Power of the Multinational Corporations* (New York: Simon and Schuster, 1974), p. 182 (carnations in Colombia). For a gargantuan case on a regional scale involving cattle-ranching, see Shelton H. Davis, *Victims of the Miracle: Development and the Indians of Brazil* (New York: Cambridge University Press, 1977). To a considerable extent the long-term development policy of Mexico for at least thirty of the last forty years has followed this basic pattern of depriving the rural poor of food for subsistence for the sake of greater agricultural production of other crops—see the extremely careful and balanced study by Cynthia Hewitt de Alcantara, *Modernizing Mexican Agriculture: Socioeconomic Implications of Technological Change 1940–1970*, Report No. 76.5 (Geneva: United Nations Research Institute for Social Development, 1976); and Judith Adler Hellman, *Mexico in Crisis* (New York: Holmes & Meier Publishers, Inc., 1978), chapter 3. For a sophisticated theoretical analysis of some of the underlying dynamics, see Jeffery M. Paige, *Agrarian Revolution: Social Movements*

and Export Agriculture in the Underdeveloped World (New York: Free Press, 1975), which has case studies of Angola, Peru, and Vietnam.

13. That is, they are conceptually distinct; whether this distinction makes any moral difference is another matter. See above, note 7, and the distinctions at the beginning of this chapter.

14. The increasingly frequent and facile appeal to "overpopulation" as a reason not to prevent preventable starvation is considered in chapter 4.

15. This much of the analysis is derived from the following important article: Onora O'Neill, "Lifeboat Earth," in *World Hunger and Moral Obligation*, edited by William Aiken and Hugh La Follette (Englewood Cliffs: Prentice-Hall, Inc., 1977), pp. 140–164. I return to discussion of the causal complexity of such cases below, pp. 58–60.

16. For example, land-use laws might prohibit removing prime agricultural land from food production. Alternatively, land might be allowed to be used in the manner most beneficial to the national balance of payments with tax laws designed to guarantee compensating transfers to increase the purchasing power of the villagers (e.g., food stamps), etc. I return in chapter 5 to the question of how to apportion the duties to prevent such social disasters.

17. There are of course non-human threats to both security and subsistence, like floods, as well. And we expect a minimally adequate society also to make arrangements to prevent, to control, or to minimize the ill effects of floods and other destructive natural forces. However, for an appreciation of the extent to which supposedly natural famines are the result of inadequate social arrangements, see Richard G. Robbins, *Famine in Russia 1891–92* (New York: Columbia University Press, 1975); and Michael F. Lofchie, "Political and Economic Origins of African Hunger," *Journal of Modern African Studies*, 13:4 (December 1975), pp. 551–567. As Lofchie says: "The point of departure for a political understanding of African hunger is so obvious it is almost always overlooked: the distinction between drought and famine. . . . To the extent that there is a connection between drought and famine, it is mediated by the political and economic arrangements of a society. These can either minimize the human consequences of drought or accentuate its effects" (553). For a demonstration that the weather and other natural factors actually played fairly minor roles in the Great Bengal Famine, see the analysis by Amartya Sen cited in note 17 to chapter 4, and chapter 4 generally. To treat the *absence* of adequate social arrangements as a cause of a famine precipitated by a natural event like a drought or a flood, as these writers and I do, is to assume that it is reasonable to have expected the absent arrangements to have been present.

18. See note 12 above.

19. See below, chapter 7, notes 26–28.

20. Richard R. Fagen, "The Carter Administration and Latin America: Business as Usual?" *Foreign Affairs*, 57:3 (America and the World 1978), pp. 663–667. These policies are very similar to those imposed as conditions for loans by the International Monetary Fund. See William Goodfellow, "The IMF and Basic Human Needs Strategies," Paper prepared for Seminar on "Basic Human Needs: Moral and Political Implications of Policy Alternatives," Woodstock Theological Center, Georgetown University, February 26, 1979; mimeo., p. 4.

With Fagen's analysis, compare Guillermo A. O'Donnell, *Modernization and Bureaucratic-Authoritarianism*, Politics of Modernization Series, No. 9 (Berkeley: University of California, Institute of International Studies, 1973); Fernando Henrique Cardoso and Enzo Faletto, *Dependency and Development in Latin America*, expanded and emended version (Berkeley: University of California Press, 1979), pp. 177–216; and Albert O. Hirschman, "The Turn to Authoritarianism in Latin America and the Search for Its Economic Determinants," in David Collier, ed., *The New Authoritarianism in Latin America* (Princeton: Princeton University Press, 1979), pp. 61–98. Also see Steven Jackson, Bruce Russett, et al., "An Assessment of Empirical Research on *Dependencia*," *Latin American Research Review*, 14:3 (1979), pp. 7–28.

21. On whether an adequate definition can be literally exceptionless, see note 2 to chapter 1.

22. I take the need for the qualification "not necessary to the satisfaction of one's own basic rights" to be fairly obvious. However admirable self-sacrifice may be, it is surely not a basic duty owed to people generally, and the surrender of one's right to subsistence—or security—would in many circumstances constitute a literal sacrifice of oneself, that is, one's life. Unfortunately, the content of a duty does not dictate the identity of its bearers. Chapter 5 discusses how to assign in a reasonable way the responsibility for fulfilling various duties.

23. How to bring transnational corporations under some constraints in order to prevent great social harms, like violations of basic rights, is one of our great political challenges. See the discussion in chapter 7 of recommendation (4) and the relevant notes.

24. I am, of course, not proposing that we start calling it murder, but I am proposing that we acknowledge the parallels and act in appropriately parallel ways.

25. Without becoming anti-intellectual, or even atheoretical, we theorists might remember that a crystal-clear abstract distinction may not only have no positive practical value but may sometimes contribute to vice. Writing about an entirely different matter, Barrie A. Paskins has put the general point eloquently: "We can imagine and describe cases in

which we would think torture justified and unjustified. We can state the grounds on which we are making the discrimination. But what we cannot do is this: *we cannot provide for ourselves, or for those who must act for us in real situations, any way of making our notional distinctions in reality.* What might be claimed about the imaginary example is not that something significantly analogous could not occur but that in reality we cannot enable those who must act to recognize the case for what it is and other cases, by contrast, for what they are. In a real situation we can never be certain that the case in hand is of this kind rather than another. A too vivid imagination blinds us to the dust of war that drifts into the interrogation centre." Barrie A. Paskins, "What's Wrong with Torture?" *British Journal of International Studies*, 2 (1976), p. 144. I think this is a profound methodological point with strong implications concerning the now virtually incorrigible habit among moral and political philosophers of relying upon imaginary cases and concerning the "strict compliance" situations and "ideal theory" discussed by John Rawls and Kantians generally. I am trying to develop the methodological point in an essay with the working title, "Extreme Cases."

26. On the rationality of peasants, see James C. Scott, *The Moral Economy of the Peasant: Rebellion and Subsistence in Southeast Asia* (New Haven: Yale University Press, 1976), chapters 1 and 2.

27. See note 12 above.

28. I am indebted to John Langan for having emphasized this point. For a different argument, see his paper cited in note 2 above, p. 25.

29. For the classic account, see Clifford Geertz, *Agricultural Involution: The Processes of Ecological Change in Indonesia* (Berkeley: University of California Press for the Association of Asian Studies, 1963), chapters 4 and 5. Although various aspects of Geertz's analysis are naturally no longer accepted, the main points relevant here still stand.

3 • Liberty

1. The classic justification for prescribing the "trade-off" of liberty for development is Samuel P. Huntington, *Political Order in Changing Societies* (New Haven: Yale University Press, 1968), pp. 1–92. Compare Samuel P. Huntington and Joan M. Nelson, *No Easy Choice: Political Participation in Developing Countries* (Cambridge, Mass.: Harvard University Press, 1976). A perceptive analysis of the normative assumptions of Huntington's theory is: Mark Kesselman, "Order or Movement? The Literature of Political Development as Ideology," *World Politics*, 26:1 (October 1973), pp. 139–154.

For a lively critique exposing the naiveté of seven of the common arguments in favor of making the trade-off, and for further references see Robert E. Goodin, "The Development-Rights Trade-Off: Some Unwarranted Economic and Political Assumptions," *Universal Human Rights*, 1:2 (April–June 1979), pp. 31–42. For a recent protest against the "trade-off," see Sidney Liskofsky, "Human Rights Minus Liberty?" *Worldview*, 21:7–8 (July/August 1978), pp. 26 and 35–36.

2. Jahangir Amuzegar, "Rights, and Wrongs," *New York Times*, January 29, 1978.

3. Jose W. Diokno, untitled lecture, International Council of Amnesty International, Cambridge, September 21, 1978, pp. 11–12, mimeo.

4. Goodin, p. 31n. The Rawlsian reference is of course to *A Theory of Justice* (Cambridge, Mass.: The Belknap Press of Harvard University Press, 1971), Section 82. My own suspicion is that Rawlsian theory is especially congenial to the notion of exchanges of liberty for economic growth because the Rawlsian conceptual framework artificially separates liberty and the value of liberty. Since the value of liberty is determined by economic factors like subsistence, which are thought to be fairly cleanly separable from liberty itself (whatever that would be), it is easier to believe that liberty and the material goods that are treated as contributing to the value of liberty are sufficiently distinct from each other that one might be traded for the other. I have suggested this point previously by observing that Rawlsian theory encourages a treatment of primary goods that is "very mechanical and rather like trading marbles for tennis balls"; see "The Current Fashions: Trickle-Downs by Arrow and Close-Knits by Rawls," *Journal of Philosophy*, 71:11 (June 13, 1974), p. 327. The tendency to separate the inseparable is, I believe, an almost irresistible force flowing from the distorting atomism at the heart of liberalism.

5. See above, p. 19.

6. This chapter is intended to be, among other things, a reply to the Rawlsian doctrine of the priority of liberty, as it is normally understood. But this does not mean that I will argue that liberty is secondary—only that liberty has no priority over subsistence, security, and any other basic rights. For a decisive internal argument against the doctrine of the priority of liberty, see Norman Daniels, "Equal Liberty and Unequal Worth of Liberty," in *Reading Rawls: Critical Studies of* A Theory of Justice, edited by Norman Daniels (New York: Basic Books, 1974), pp. 253–281.

7. It is for that kind of argument that one turns to the classics of liberalism like John Stuart Mill's *On Liberty*, although not to liberalism only, as provocatively demonstrated in Steven Lukes, *Individualism* (New York: Harper & Row, 1973).

8. For accounts of the little-discussed forms of participation in the People's Republic of China, see Marc Blecher, "Consensual Politics in

Rural Chinese Communities: The Mass Line in Theory and Practice," *Modern China*, 5:1 (January 1979), pp. 105–126; John P. Burns, "The Election of Production Team Cadres in Rural China: 1958–74," *China Quarterly*, No. 74 (June 1978), pp. 273–296; and Victor C. Falkenheim, "Political Participation in China," *Problems of Communism*, 27:3 (May-June 1978), pp. 18–32. For a review of the development literature, see John M. Cohen, Gladys Culagovski, Norman T. Uphoff, and Diane Wolf, *Participation at the Local Level: A Working Bibliography* (Ithaca: Cornell University, Center for International Studies, Rural Development Committee, 1978); and Norman T. Uphoff and John M. Cohen, *The Feasibility and Application of Rural Development Participation: A State of the Art Paper*, Rural Development Committee, Monograph No. 2 (Ithaca: Cornell University, Center for International Studies, 1978). For other suggestions about the relation between subsistence and participation, see Donald Curtis et al., *Popular Participation in Decision-Making and the Basic Needs Approach to Development: Methods, Issues and Emergencies*, World Employment Programme Working Paper (WEP 2-32/WP 12) (Geneva: International Labor Organization, 1978).

9. See Carole Pateman, *Participation and Democratic Theory* (New York: Cambridge University Press, 1970), pp. 67–71. As she notes, Pateman is here following Sidney Verba. Also see Arend Lijphart, *Democracy in Plural Societies: A Comparative Exploration* (New Haven: Yale University Press, 1977).

10. In other words, *this* argument does not in itself establish, for example, a need for democratization of the workplace, as opposed to more indirect controls over one's own work. For one brief point about economic institutions, see the discussion of recommendation (4) in chapter 7.

11. Charles Frankel, *Human Rights and Foreign Policy*, Headline Series No. 241 (New York: Foreign Policy Association, 1978), p. 45. Frankel's second test was mentioned in note 8 to chapter 2. Thomas Nagel invokes "a kind of unanimity requirement," which means that "each of us must limit our actions to a range that is not unacceptable to anyone else in certain respects." See "Equality," in *Mortal Questions* (New York: Cambridge University Press, 1979), pp. 114 and 115 respectively. I assume, however, that this unanimity is a Kantian hypothetical unanimity not incompatible with the general point in the text. It would surely not be sufficient to prevent an action from being the violation of someone's right that the person did not in fact find the action unacceptable.

12. For a sensitive and balanced account of some traditional Asian arrangements for subsistence, and what happened when they failed, see James C. Scott, *The Moral Economy of the Peasant: Rebellion and Subsistence in Southeast Asia* (New Haven: Yale University Press, 1976).

13. I do not mean, of course, that moral beliefs can be shown to be false by exactly the same methods as any other kind of beliefs. For some stimulating reflections on what is actually a very long story, see Bernard Williams, *Morality: An Introduction to Ethics* (New York: Harper & Row, 1972). This little book is also relevant to the remarks in the succeeding paragraph.

14. Full consideration of this point in the case of liberty will greatly strengthen the general argument for taking correlative duties to be necessary constituents of rights. See above, pp. 54–55. Indeed, this chapter as a whole is probably the best explanation I have been able to give of why moral rights normally involve correlative duties and how those duties in turn involve other basic rights—why, in short, there must be a system of basic rights if there are to be any rights at all. The importance of this systematic character of rights first came clear to me in a conversation with Drew Christiansen, although I do not think he would characterize it in the same way.

15. For a full account, see Richard Millett, *Guardians of the Dynasty: A History of the U.S.-Created Guardia Nacional de Nicaragua and the Somoza Family* (Maryknoll, N.Y.: Orbis Books, 1977). Brief references are in Karen DeYoung, "Somoza's Nicaragua," *Washington Post*, October 16, 1977, pp. A1 and A30; and Alan Riding, "Respectable Rebels Threaten Somoza Dynasty," *New York Times*, January 29, 1978, p. E4. The overthrow of Somoza by his subjects and the "profoundly interventionist and self-defeating" Carter/Brzezinski policy during his final months, are recorded in Richard R. Fagen, "Dateline Nicaragua: The End of The Affair," *Foreign Policy*, No. 36 (Fall 1979), pp. 178–191.

16. See *Political Imprisonment in South Africa*, An Amnesty International Report (London: Amnesty International Publications, 1977), pp. 7–36; and Albie Sachs, *Justice in South Africa* (Berkeley: University of California Press, 1973).

17. See Sidney Bloch and Peter Reddaway, *Psychiatric Terror* (New York: Basic Books, 1977).

18. This is not without its own difficulties, of course, on which see Bruce Ennis and Loren Siegel, *The Rights of Mental Patients*, revised edition, American Civil Liberties Union Handbook (New York: Avon Books, 1978).

19. The definitive study of the Chinese program is Thomas P. Bernstein, *Up to the Mountains and Down to the Villages: The Transfer of Youth from Urban to Rural China* (New Haven: Yale University Press, 1977). On U.S. conscription see Robert K. Fullinwider, "Some Issues about Conscription," Working Paper (College Park: Center for Philosophy and Public Policy, 1980), photocopy.

20. Issues about the right to emigrate, the right of asylum, and other related matters are very important, but require separate treatment because of the complexities introduced by travel that crosses national boundaries. These will be treated in two volumes I am co-editing with Peter G. Brown for the Center for Philosophy and Public Policy under the working titles, *Boundaries: National Autonomy and Its Limits* and *The Border That Joins: Mexican Migrants and U.S. Responsibility*.

21. I hope that it is not necessary to say that ordinary prisons housing political prisoners bear little resemblance to this idyllic picture. Under the Marcos regime Philippine prisons, for example, are so terrible that prisoners who can afford to are willing to pay bribes in order to be used as houseboys by Philippine army officers—see Task Force Detainees of the Philippines, Association of Major Religious Superiors, *Political Detainees of the Philippines, Quarterly Report*, 4:2 (April–June 1979), "Mindanao Area," pp. 43–44. This practice of the Philippine military is a form of slavery, which, needless to say, violates even the laws of war. The Carter/Brzezinski foreign policy has included lavish support for the Marcos regime—see Henry Kamm, "Ex-President of Philippines Attacks Carter Over U.S. Support of Marcos," *New York Times*, September 18, 1979, p. A6.

In Indonesian prisons under the Suharto regime neither ordinary criminals nor political prisoners are guaranteed any food they do not pay for, except that ordinary criminals who can be trusted to return are often released for a few hours in the evening to steal food for themselves—interview with Yap Thiam-Hien, Indonesian member, International Commission of Jurists, June 28, 1979, Bellagio, Italy. On Indonesia especially, compare the grossly misleading report by the U.S. Department of State—Senate Comm. on Foreign Relations and House Comm. on Foreign Affairs, 96th Cong., 1st Sess., *Report on Human Rights Practices in Countries Receiving U.S. Aid* (Joint Comm. Print, February 8, 1979), pp. 360–363 and 364–365. State Department reporting on Indonesia has since its beginning consistently been evasive to the point of distortion; see, for example, House Comm. on International Relations, 94th Cong., 2d Sess., *Human Rights and U.S. Policy: Argentina, Haiti, Indonesia, Iran, Peru, and the Philippines* (Comm. Print, December 31, 1976), pp. 12–17; and compare the sources in note 28 to chapter 7. On the general problem of the adequacy of information for policy-making, see John Salzberg, "Monitoring Human Rights Violations: How Good Is the Information?" in Brown and MacLean, especially pp. 178–181 on State Department testimony and reports.

22. One of John Rawls's two main arguments for the priority of liberty would actually establish the importance only of the solitary intellectual liberties, and not all the other liberties to which he would also like to

assign first rank. See Rawls, pp. 205–211. Rawls concedes: "I have tried to show, by taking liberty of conscience as an example, how justice as fairness provides strong arguments for equal liberty. The same kind of reasoning applies, I believe, in other cases, though not always with similar force" (209). This is, I believe, another major difficulty for Rawlsian theory. For an analysis of the other main Rawlsian argument for the priority of liberty, see Henry Shue, "Liberty and Self-Respect," *Ethics*, 85:3 (April 1975), pp. 195–203.

23. Unfortunately they may also be the fate of the non-arbitrarily imprisoned as well. Once again the issue of the other rights of criminals quite properly deprived of their freedom of movement is important but so complex as to require separate treatment. As the succeeding paragraph makes clear, deep problems haunt any attempt to guarantee effective rights to prisoners deprived wrongly or *rightly* of their freedom of movement because of the systematic interrelationship of rights and of the protection for one right with another right. One can hope that where people are put into prison in less arbitrary ways, they will be treated less arbitrarily while there. But there is no necessary connection.

24. See the studies cited in note 16 above and compare John Dugard, *Human Rights and the South African Legal Order* (Princeton: Princeton University Press, 1978). I do not intend to imply that the Botha regime is now better.

25. Contemporary North Atlantic philosophers tend, I believe, seriously to underestimate how misleading about actual cases the consideration of imaginary cases often is, in part because imaginary cases are often extreme, exceptional, or both. Also see note 25 to chapter 2.

26. Among the many "other things" that are not equal, but are also not within the scope of the present argument, are the relative tendencies of participatory and non-participatory governments to chronic corruption and the relative merits of participatory and non-participatory societies considered in terms of very appealing moral ideals. I have restricted myself here to only the argument for liberty that is exactly parallel to my argument for security and subsistence. That argument by itself seems to me to be strong enough. On participation as an ideal see the books by Lukes and Pateman cited above, and the references there.

27. Popular writers often present the People's Republic of China since liberation in 1949 as an obvious counter-example allegedly constituting a form of non-participatory economic development. This is a complex case, needless to say, but the force of the PRC as a counter-example often depends upon wildly exaggerated accounts of the violence during the transition period. The supposed levels of violence are then taken to be evidence that the process was totally coercive and non-participatory. For

a careful and balanced assessment of the extent of violence, see Benedict Stavis, *The Politics of Agricultural Mechanization in China* (Ithaca: Cornell University Press, 1978), pp. 23–32. As Stavis notes, some of the more exaggerated early accounts were accepted by the *New York Times*, which went on to offer the racist observation: "It is an axiom that life is cheap in crowded and undeveloped countries" (Stavis, p. 27, n. 10). Although the violence tends to be overestimated, the participation tends to be underestimated—see n. 8 above. For a more general analysis of the forces at work in the early years after the revolution, see Vivienne Shue, *Peasant China in Transition: The Dynamics of Development Toward Socialism, 1949–1956* (Berkeley: University of California Press, 1980).

4 • Realism and Responsibility

1. Those who would prefer, or feel compelled, not to take seriously any economic rights, even basic rights to subsistence, sometimes take comfort in one possible interpretation of the *International Covenant on Economic, Social and Cultural Rights*, Article 2, Section 1, which says that every State party to the covenant will "take steps . . . with a view to achieving progressively the full realization of the rights recognized. . . ." If one ignores the much tighter language of Article 1, Section 2, which insists that "in no case may a people be deprived of its own means of subsistence," one can construe Article 2, Section 1, as saying, in effect: "take your time, even about subsistence." Without debating the intention (or the wisdom) of the drafters of the *Covenants* in including this "gradualism" clause in this *Covenant* but not in the *International Covenant on Civil and Political Rights* (Were civil and political rights to be fulfilled instantaneously?), I think we can say that if the *International Covenant on Economic, Social and Cultural Rights* does not mean that supreme priority is to go to the fulfillment of subsistence rights, then it is more like a list of wishes than a bill of rights and does not deserve much attention, unless it is in fact unrealistic to make the social guarantee of subsistence anything more than a somewhat dreamy distant hope.

2. The most dynamic academic advocate of this position has probably been Garrett Hardin, several of whose main recent essays are collected along with related essays by others, in *Managing the Commons*, edited by Garrett Hardin and John Baden (San Francisco: W. H. Freeman and Company, 1977). For philosophical discussion of some of the issues involved see *Ethics and Population*, edited by Michael D. Bayles (Cambridge, Mass.: Schenkman Publishing Company, 1976). A less good collection, because so many contributors uncritically accept the terms of the question as set by Hardin, is *Lifeboat Ethics: The Moral Dilemmas of*

World Hunger, edited by George R. Lucas, Jr. and Thomas Ogletree (New York: Harper & Row, Publishers, 1976). Also see the Sikora and Barry volume cited below in note 10.

This view also has powerful advocates and opponents in the U.S. Agency for International Development and the Congress.

3. Why always other people? Why don't more people conclude that, for example, they ought to commit suicide by fasting, or refrain from having children of their own? The answer is, of course, that they have a perfect right to continue to live, to eat, and to have children if they want to. But if they have this right, why don't others?

4. Blaming the victims in this way is at the other extreme from the searching for villains that Charles Frankel feared would result from the acknowledgment of any economic rights: "Corruption, callousness, a desire to maintain positions of privilege, are surely among the causes of poor countries' problems. But the language of rights gives them excessive attention. It simplifies and obscures the underlying issues. It suggests that peoples' [sic] deprivations are due in the main neither to the scarcities of nature nor to their own habits and preferences but to the misdeeds of others. It encourages a search for villains, and an impatience with the slow ways of freedom." See Charles Frankel, *Human Rights and Foreign Policy*, Headline Series No. 241 (New York: Foreign Policy Association, 1978), p. 41.

Frankel's view depends upon an empirical assumption about the main causes of deprivation, not upon any strictly philosophical point. Indeed, this is a very clear example of how moral analysis depends upon correct social analysis. And there is considerable evidence "that peoples' deprivations are due in the main neither to the scarcities of nature nor to their own habits and preferences. . . ." It does not follow, however, that the deprivations must then be due "to the misdeeds of others," taken to be "villains." The correct one of several possible alternative explanations seems to me to be inadequate social institutions (local, national, and international) that do not provide the kinds of social guarantees like grain reserves against standard threats like crop failures that basic rights justify. I am, of course, making an alternative empirical assumption to Frankel's about the main causes of deprivation. For supporting evidence see the studies cited in chapter 2 and later in this chapter. For an excellent brief summary of the causes of malnutrition see Cheryl Christensen, "World Hunger: A Structural Approach," *International Organization*, 32:3 (Summer 1978), Special Issue: The Global Political Economy of Food, ed. by Raymond F. Hopkins and Donald J. Puchala, pp. 745–774; also see her forthcoming book on the international political economy of food (New York: Free Press).

If relying upon "the slow ways of freedom" includes relying upon the free market in food, chronic malnutrition will persist indefinitely—see

Christensen; Lyle Schertz, "World Needs: Shall the Hungry Be With Us Always?" in *Food Policy: The Responsibility of the United States in the Life and Death Choices*, ed. by Peter G. Brown and Henry Shue (New York: Free Press, 1977), pp. 13–35, esp. pp. 30–34; and Donald J. Puchala and Raymond F. Hopkins, "Toward Innovation in the Global Food Regime," *International Organization*, 32:3 (Summer 1978), pp. 855–868.

5. Garrett Hardin is certainly committed to a challenge that is at least this strong. See Hardin's essays "Living on a Lifeboat," in Hardin and Baden, pp. 261–279; and "Carrying Capacity as an Ethical Concept," in Lucas and Ogletree, pp. 120–137.

6. Henry Shue, "Torture," *Philosophy & Public Affairs*, 7:2 (Winter 1978), pp. 124–143. On artificial examples, see esp. pp. 141–142.

7. Richard D. Lyons, "World Hunger to Impact on U.S.," *The Journal of the Institute for Socioeconomic Studies*, 4:3 (Autumn 1979), 57–65. The quotations, in the order quoted, are from pp. 65, 63, 61, and 57; emphases in the original. Lyons, who is described by *The Journal* as "national science correspondent for *The New York Times*," expects "pandemic famine" (57) and "the slow etiolation of American prosperity" (62). An A.I.D. press release attributes to the Administrator of A.I.D., John J. Gilligan, the simplistic opinion that "by 1985 a global food deficit of one hundred million tons is anticipated, *directly attributable to population growth* outstripping agricultural production" (emphasis added)—"World Population Growth, Food Shortages Adversely Affect Americans, Says Gilligan," *A.I.D. News*, AID-79-4 (Washington: Office of Public Affairs, A.I.D., 1979), p. 3. Every study I have ever seen indicates that *food* production—much agriculture is not food—in the poor countries has generally kept pace with population growth. On the future, see *Food Needs of Developing Countries: Projections of Production and Consumption to 1990* (Washington: International Food Policy Research Institute, 1977), which contains careful country-by-country projections.

8. I am not saying that specific people have raised one but not the other of the specific versions I am distinguishing. Analysis is often the key to refutation, and I hope that people who carefully consider the alternative versions of the diffuse initial worry will, for the reasons I will be giving, decline each.

9. International issues are the subject of chapter 6.

10. On inter-generational (temporal) and international (spatial) questions, respectively, see John Rawls, *A Theory of Justice* (Cambridge, Mass.: Belknap Press of Harvard University Press, 1971), pp. 284–298 and 377–382. More recent work on inter-generational questions includes Brian M. Barry, "Justice Between Generations," in *Law, Morality, and Society: Essays in Honour of H.L.A. Hart*, edited by P.M.S. Hacker and

J. Raz (Oxford: Clarendon Press of Oxford University Press, 1977), pp. 268–284; and *Obligations to Future Generations*, edited by R. I. Sikora and Brian Barry (Philadelphia: Temple University Press, 1978), especially the essay by Barry. The questions of inter-temporal allocation, as they apply to U.S. energy policy, are being analyzed in a study directed by Douglas MacLean—see his perceptive essay, "Benefit-Cost Analysis, Future Generations, and Energy Policy: A Survey of the Moral Issues," *Science, Technology, and Human Values*, No. 31 (Spring 1980), forthcoming.

A recent work that I have regrettably not been able to take into account here, but that promises certainly to make a major contribution on the international questions, is Charles R. Beitz, *Political Theory and International Relations* (Princeton: Princeton University Press, 1979).

11. Contrary to what may appear to be common sense, this assumed prediction is by no means clearly true. Much depends, as we shall see below, upon the effects upon fertility rates of any lowered infant mortality rates that may result from fulfilling subsistence needs. Compare Michael F. Brewer, "Slowing Population Growth with Food Aid," in Brown and Shue, pp. 259–274; and Beverly Winikoff, "Nutrition, Population, and Health: Some Implications for Policy," *Science*, 200 (26 May 1978), pp. 895–902.

12. "One-half of child deaths are in some way attributable to malnutrition," United Nations, Food and Agricultural Organization, "Assessment of the World Food Situation: Present and Future," E/Conf. 65/3, United Nations World Food Conference, November 1974, p. 67. This figure is accepted by the U.S. Department of Agriculture's leading specialist on the question, Lyle Schertz—see "World Needs: Shall the Hungry Be With Us Always?" in Brown and Shue, p. 20 and p. 32. Also see A.K.M. Alauddin Chowdhury and Lincoln C. Chen, "The Interaction of Nutrition, Infection, and Mortality during Recent Food Crises in Bangladesh," *Food Research Institute Studies*, 16:2 (1977), pp. 47–61.

13. Alan Berg, *The Nutrition Factor: Its Role in National Development* (Washington: The Brookings Institution, 1973), Table B-1, p. 222. The age by which the same percentage of the U.S. population will have died as have already died in Guinea by the age of 5 is 68 (Egypt, 61; Guatemala, 57). This might be called inequality in life prospects. Also see Shlomo Reutlinger and Marcelo Selowsky, *Malnutrition and Poverty: Magnitude and Policy Options*, World Bank Staff Occasional Papers, No. 23 (Baltimore: Johns Hopkins University Press for the World Bank, 1976), pp. 29–38 (analysis of Calcutta Food Survey).

14. Fyodor Dostoyevsky, *The Brothers Karamazov*, Book V, chapter 4, "Rebellion."

15. See Maurice Cranston, *What Are Human Rights?* (New York: Taplinger Publishing Co., 1973), chapter VIII.

16. Cranston, pp. 66–67. Also see note 8 to chapter 2.

17. All references to the Bengal famine, which may have been the worst of this century, rest upon a brilliant article that establishes, among other conclusions, that the more fundamental problem was not the quantity of food, but the level of wages: Amartya Sen, "Starvation and Exchange Entitlements: A General Approach and Its Application to the Great Bengal Famine," *Cambridge Journal of Economics*, 1:1 (1977), pp. 33–59. The Governor's comment is quoted on p. 52. It is fascinating to compare Sen's analysis of Bengal in 1943 with Schertz's analysis of the global situation now—see the Schertz article in Brown and Shue, cited in note 4 above. To put it crudely, Sen and Schertz agree that levels of income, not quantities of food, are the dominant obstacle to adequate nutrition. Famines tend to be social, not natural, disasters.

One of the unwritten chapters of 20th-century history concerns what might be called the Holocaust of Neglect in Asia. While 6 million Jews were being executed in Europe, well over 6 million Asians were being allowed to starve in Asia. Why the Holocaust of Neglect was also allowed to happen (for example, the relative importance of the World War), and why these appalling tragedies have gone virtually unnoticed in the North Atlantic scholarly community, would make a fascinating but sobering tale, I think. For 1943–1945 the toll was over 3 million Bengalis in British India—see the study by Amartya Sen, and further references there; over 2 million in French Indochina—see Tran Van Mai, "Who Committed This Crime?" in *Before the Revolution: The Vietnamese Peasants Under the French*, Ngo Vinh Long, ed. (Cambridge, Mass.: MIT Press,1973); and 2 or 3 million Honanese in Nationalist China—see Theodore H. White and Annalee Jacoby, *Thunder Out of China* (New York: William Sloane Associates, Inc., 1946), Chapter II, "The Honan Famine."

As this book goes to press, the widows and orphans of Kampuchea eat the last bark from the last trees and sink toward their places in the fourth historic famine in Asia since 1940. This time the major powers lack the excuse that they were having a war among themselves. The list of "statesmen," governments, and armies who have created this famine—if ever a famine is not natural but man-made, this is it—is long and illustrious. But anyone doubting that the U.S. played a role might look at William Shawcross, *Sideshow: Kissinger, Nixon and the Destruction of Cambodia* (New York: Simon and Schuster, 1979).

For a description of the subsequent step in the decimation of the Kampucheans, see François Ponchaud, *Cambodia: Year Zero* (New York:

Holt, Rinehart and Winston, 1978). A recent, understated account is in Murray Hiebert and Linda Gibson Hiebert, "Famine in Kampuchea: Politics of a Tragedy," Indochina Issues, No. 4 (Washington: Center for International Policy, 1979). The many-sided debate about the Vietnamese conquest of Kampuchea, the effect of the fighting in deepening the famine, and the roles being played by the major powers is only beginning at this point. Useful articles, including some giving the Vietnamese point of view, are in *Southeast Asia Chronicle*, No. 68, "Vietnam-China War" (December 1979), and in *Bulletin of Concerned Asian Scholars*, 11:4 (October-December 1979), pp. 2–25.

18. Thomas Nagel, "Poverty and Food: Why Charity Is Not Enough," in Brown and Shue, pp. 54–62.

19. Once again, the moral argument depends upon the causal analysis. An earlier attempt to criticize Nagel's, and Peter Singer's, argument on this point somewhat differently is, I think, less clear—see Henry Shue, "Distributive Criteria for Development Assistance," in Brown and Shue, pp. 313–314.

20. This is now generally accepted, as are most of the points in this paragraph. For a clear argument and extensive references, see John Osgood Field and Mitchel B. Wallerstein, "Beyond Humanitarianism: A Developmental Perspective on American Food Aid," in Brown and Shue, pp. 234–258. The Field/Wallerstein diagnosis is separable from their prescription, which is more optimistic about U.S. A.I.D. than I am. Also see United States, Department of State, *World Population: The Silent Explosion*, Bulletin Reprint, DOS Publication 8956 (October 1978), pp. 10–14; Radha Sinha, *Food and Poverty* (New York: Holmes & Meier, 1976); Christensen; Winikoff; Berg; Reutlinger and Selowsky; James E. Kocher, "Socioeconomic Development and Fertility Change in Rural Africa," *Food Research Institute Studies*, 16:2 (1977), pp. 63–75; and Donald Warwick, "Draft Recommendations: Project on Cultural Values and Population Policy," Papers prepared for the Institute of Society, Ethics, and the Life Sciences (March 1979), photocopy.

21. In addition to the items cited in the previous note, see Mahmood Mamdani, *The Myth of Population Control* (New York: Monthly Review Press, 1972). On the general rationality of peasants, see James C. Scott, *The Moral Economy of the Peasant* (New Haven: Yale University Press, 1977), pp. 35–55, and references cited there. In United States, Department of State, see esp. p. 22: "In the desperately poor circumstances of wide areas of Africa, Asia, and Latin America parents may be powerfully motivated to have many children. From the perspective of their own private interests . . . surviving children are highly desirable. . . ."

22. Indonesia is now being touted as a possible first exception—see United States, Department of State, p. 23. But the trends are so far short-lived, and there are disturbing questions, not least of which is whether drops in fertility rates prior to economic development for the poorest depend upon the high level of repression in Indonesia. On the repression, see *Indonesia: An Amnesty International Report* (London: Amnesty International Publications, 1977).

23. For a responsible attempt to tell us what we need to know, which is the effects of various rates and sizes of transfers, see the study by Leontief discussed below.

24. For the recent levels of assistance transfers, see Organisation for Economic Co-operation and Development, *Development Co-operation: Efforts and Policies of the Members of the Development Assistance Committee*, 1978 Review (Paris: OECD, 1978), which includes statistical annex. To allow everything to depend upon the unaided growth of the economies of the individual poor countries is to beg the question of transnational duties to aid in favor of the affluent countries—see chapter 6. It is essential, however, not to assume that the most effective form of assistance is "aid," bilateral or multilateral. Trade arrangements designed to slow the growth in the inequality among nations could be significant. Many poor countries' comparative positions in the world economy are so weak that "free trade" simply leaves them further and further behind. Also see Harrington's impressions cited in the next note.

25. The logical point is that to will the end is to will the means. The economic point is probably best made by studies of the distortions produced in individual LDCs, and the diversions of their resources away from sustaining the lives of their own people, like Jeffery M. Paige, *Agrarian Revolution: Social Movements and Export Agriculture in the Underdeveloped World* (New York: Free Press, 1975), especially chapters 1 and 2. An explicitly impressionistic argument is given in Michael Harrington, *The Vast Majority: A Journey to the World's Poor* (New York: Simon and Schuster, 1977).

26. See Harden, in Lucas and Ogletree, pp. 125–131.

27. With thanks to the whimsicality of my colleague Paul Vernier, who also taught me, among other things, that every silver lining has a cloud.

28. Major challenges, which I take up in chapter 5, lie in the way of specifying who more exactly the sources of aid ought to be, but on the assumption that the apportionment of duties to aid will to a considerable degree be based upon ability to pay, I can for now refer loosely to the sources of the aid as "the affluent." The division of burdens between the

affluent of the same nation as the deprived and the affluent of other nations, for example, is obviously one major issue, and I discuss it at some length in chapter 6.

Clearly, if subsistence rights are basic rights and if the fulfillment of basic rights takes priority, when a choice must be made, over both the fulfillment of non-basic rights and the satisfaction of preferences to the enjoyment of which people have no right, any unavoidable conflict between the subsistence rights of some people and the preferences or non-basic rights of other people ought to be settled in favor of the subsistence and other basic rights. Positive arguments for this assignment of priorities are given in the next chapter. In the face of the arguments already given to establish that subsistence rights are basic rights, however, most of the burden of proof in the case of this broad objection, as in the case of the earlier narrow population objection, already rests upon the challenger.

29. Harry Walters, "Difficult Issues Underlying Food Problems," in *Food: Politics, Economics, Nutrition, and Research*, ed. by Philip H. Abelson (Washington: American Association for the Advancement of Science, 1975), pp. 22–28.

30. See Wassily Leontief, Ann P. Carter and Peter A. Petri, *The Future of the World Economy: A United Nations Study* (New York: Oxford University Press, 1977). Obviously no one study settles such matters, and I discuss this one more by way of illustration than of proof. The point is to establish that the case for the broader population objection remains to be made, not to make the empirical case for the opposite view.

31. Leontief et al., p. 3.

32. Leontief et al., pp. 10–11.

33. For further discussion of why the affluent and the poor, and who is meant, see pp. 114–120 below.

34. Leontief et al., p. 11.

35. I have analyzed the disguised moral character of judgments about overpopulation at greater length in "Food, Population and Wealth: Toward Global Principles of Justice," in *Proceedings of the American Political Science Association, 1976* (Ann Arbor: University Microfilms, 1977).

5 • Affluence and Responsibility

1. See above, pp. 94–95 and 104–110.

2. I am grateful to Peter G. Brown for insisting from the beginning that if a right has a correlative duty, the account of the right is incomplete without an account of the duty.

3. Where economic interactions are complex and cessation of ac-

tivities by any one of several major actors would stop the deprivation of people's subsistence, it may be difficult to decide who ought to stop. In the destruction of indigenous societies in the Amazon, for example, is it Brazilian government policy, the foreign ranching, or both? On this case, see Shelton H. Davis, *Victims of the Miracle: Development and the Indians of Brazil* (New York: Cambridge University Press, 1977); and Anthropology Resource Center, *The Geological Imperative: Anthropology and Development in the Amazon Basin of South America* (Cambridge, Mass.: ARC, Inc., 1976). Compare Hugh O'Shaughnessy, "What Future for the Amerindians of South America?" Report No. 15 (London: Minority Rights Group, 1973), pp. 20–24; and Roger Fox, *Brazil's Minimum Price Policy and the Agricultural Sector of Northeast Brazil*, Research Report 9 (Washington: International Food Policy Research Institute, 1979).

On the principles, I have two suggestions. The principle suggested later in this chapter is probably equally as applicable to avoidance as to protection and aid. Second, and this is the point in the text here, however difficult it may be to decide who should stop, no one is entitled to continue. Therefore, in case of doubt, more rather than fewer operations ought to stop until people are again secure in their food supplies and other subsistence needs.

4. On essential deprivations and accidental deprivations see above, p. 47.

5. See above, p. 56. As explained there, this merely relies upon the way such matters are now organized, on the whole. Exceptions occur now, for instance, the basic economic policies of the government of Indonesia are dictated to it by a consortium of its creditors, known as the Inter-Governmental Group on Indonesia (IGGI) and dominated by the World Bank and the governments whose citizens have the largest private investments in Indonesia: the Netherlands, Japan, and the U.S. See Ho Kwon Ping, "Back to the Drawing Board," *Far Eastern Economic Review*, 104:17 (April 27, 1979), pp. 86–93. Also see "The Failure of the Berkeley Mafia Technocracy," *Southeast Asia Record*, 1:23 (November 9–15, 1979), p. 11, translated by Marie Mohr from the last issue of *Matahari* (Jakarta), now banned by the Suharto government.

For the full list of categories of duties, see above, p. 60.

6. Thus, I think one can reasonably conclude that no government pursuing a strategy of essential deprivation of its own people can be considered legitimate or deserving of respect or obedience.

7. Questions about duty III-1 and duty III-3 could obviously be fruitfully discussed also. I take issues about duty III-2, however, to be both

more controversial and more central to questions of U.S. foreign policy. The arguments in chapter 6 have implications for the relation between duty III-1 and duty III-2.

8. One might dignify this task of explaining which possibly non-universal duties fall upon which individuals and institutions as the beginnings of a theory of responsibility. On the one hand, a theory of rights is needed to explain what rights are, which rights belong to which people, which rights take priority over others, and so on. But just as not all rights are universal—although all basic rights are universal—not all duties are universal either. And we have no *a priori* guarantee that even the duties correlative to universal rights are themselves universal—on the contrary, no subsistence duties except duties to avoid depriving seem to be universal. So, one needs some explanation of who is and who is not responsible for performing the non-universal duties.

9. This raises the question whether one ought to do one's duty *only if* other people also do theirs. The question deserves fuller discussion, but the short answer is: no. People have a right—in the cases we are discussing, a basic right—that one do one's duty. It is not unfair that one should do one's part in fulfilling other person's rights, even if third parties are not doing theirs, any more than it is unfair to punish the criminals who are caught, even if others who have committed the same crimes get away.

It would of course be unfair to expect one to do one's part if doing it would have no effect unless others also did theirs, since it cannot be a requirement to perform costly actions that are predictably of no benefit. Compare note 11 below.

10. See Michael D. Bayles, *Principles of Legislation: The Uses of Political Authority* (Detroit: Wayne State University Press, 1978), chapter VI and further references there; and Gerald Dworkin, "Paternalism and Welfare Policy," in *Conceptual and Moral Issues in Welfare Reform*, edited by Peter G. Brown, Conrad Johnson, and Paul Vernier (Totowa, N.J.: Rowman and Littlefield, forthcoming).

11. The thesis (I) that one need not do more than one's minimum duty until others have done their minimum duty, must be distinguished from the thesis (II) that one need not do one's minimum duty unless others do theirs. On the value of coercion in enforcing fairness to bearers of duties, see below, pp. 118–119.

12. How much priority? At the considerable risk of not being very helpful, I am inclined to say: an almost lexical priority. The priority must be very strong in order to express the significance of something's being a right, but literally lexical priorities yield absurd results—see Brian Barry's critique of Rawls's use of lexical orderings in *The Liberal Theory of Justice*

(Oxford: Clarendon Press of Oxford University Press, 1973), chapter 7. Thomas Nagel speaks of rights as "a limited veto"—"Equality," in *Mortal Questions* (New York: Cambridge University Press, 1979), p. 114. I am not sure how much more definite than saying "almost lexical" and "limited veto" one can be in the abstract, but it is worth further efforts. Douglas MacLean has emphasized the extent of the indeterminacy here.

13. An additional element of the reason for legal requirements is the complexity of the arrangements often needed to insure fairness. For example, if the mechanism for some of the transfers were a general commodity agreement covering a variety of commodities and designed to have a redistributive effect on international transactions from wealthier nations to poorer ones, the people with interests in one of the commodities covered would sometimes find that they had to sell for less than they could have obtained outside the agreement, if they are exporters, or that they had to buy for more than they would have had to pay outside the agreement, if they are importers, because of the price ceilings and floors built into the agreement. But it may not be fair for only the individuals who happen to deal in the richer countries with the commodities that are vital to the poorer countries to bear all the burden borne by their nation. This can sometimes only be prevented by carefully designed transfers within the wealthier nation to those directly hurt by the international agreement from those not directly affected. Therefore, the tax laws need to take this particular kind of fairness into account.

14. Standard utilitarian assumptions about diminishing marginal utility, for instance, yield a fairly obvious argument that might in practice have the same implications. Also, Thomas Nagel has developed a striking notion of "radical inequality" on which I have drawn in what follows—see "Poverty and Food: Why Charity is Not Enough," in *Food Policy: The Responsibility of the United States in the Life and Death Choices*, ed. by Peter G. Brown and Henry Shue (New York: Free Press, 1977), pp. 54–62. A third, very different, and important argument is the one in T. M. Scanlon, "Preference and Urgency," *Journal of Philosophy*, 72:19 (November 6, 1975), pp. 655–669. Although the policy implications of the views of both Nagel and Scanlon would also be similar to the implications of the priority principle, neither of them concludes with me that urgent economic needs (Scanlon) and radical economic inequalities (Nagel) are, strictly speaking, matters of rights and violations of rights, respectively.

15. Compare the finding, already quoted in chapter 1, by James C. Scott for the case of peasants in Southeast Asia: "Village egalitarianism in this sense is conservative not radical; it claims that all should have a

place, a living, not that all should be equal." See *The Moral Economy of the Peasant: Rebellion and Subsistence in Southeast Asia* (New Haven: Yale University Press, 1976), p. 40.

16. This is obviously not the whole answer. The next degree of specificity would require criteria for pairing affluent duty-bearers with deprived right-bearers, e.g., nation by nation (We take care of our deprived, and you take care of your deprived.). Chapter 6 considers such a division according to national boundaries.

17. See text and citation above, p. 8.

18. The argument in this section has benefited greatly from the perceptive critique provided by Drew Christiansen of a quite different earlier version of it. For a fresh approach to many of these same issues, and an extremely careful handling of the concept of basic needs, which often seems to inspire sloppy thinking, see Drew Christiansen, "Basic Needs: Criterion for the Legitimacy of Development," Working Paper (Washington: Woodstock Theological Center, 1979).

19. I am appealing here to essentially the same consideration that John Rawls calls "the strains of commitment"—see *A Theory of Justice* (Cambridge, Mass.: The Belknap Press of Harvard University Press, 1971), pp. 175–177.

20. This tie to self-respect and dignity is one reason for the doubt expressed earlier that the arguments from degradation and from fairness are independent of each other.

21. There is always the hypothetical benefit for any property one might live to acquire, but perhaps it can be agreed that this is too slender a reed on which to lean a requirement that people actually deteriorate physically rather than steal.

22. Compare Gilbert Harman's account of what could be expected to be the content of a compromise between rich and poor in "Moral Relativism Defended," *Philosophical Review*, 84:1 (January 1975), pp. 3–22, and, of course, Rousseau's classic account of the social contract in the *Discourse on the Origins of Inequality*.

23. Hence, this principle could have been called the principle of the Pareto-optimality of vital interests: never choose an arrangement that sacrifices vital interests when an arrangement that does not sacrifice any vital interest is available. This seems to me to be far more reasonable as a normative guide than is the standard rule of Pareto-optimality, which this rule contradicts, because the standard rule allows vital interests to be sacrificed in order to preserve trivial interests. The substance of this principle, although not this name or the analogy with Pareto, may have been whispered to me in Manila by Robert E. Goodin.

Peter G. Brown has observed that "the concept of 'national interest' lumps together under one word [interest] matters of very different moral standing as if, in all relevant ways, they are homogeneous"—see ". . . in the National Interest," in Brown and MacLean, p. 163. Economists often create the same mush by calling all sorts of different things "preferences"—this is part of the problem with the ordinary Pareto rule. Distinguishing the vital from the non-vital is one very small step back from abstractions toward reality. For other problems with the Pareto rule, see Amartya Sen, "Utilitarianism and Welfarism," *Journal of Philosophy*, 76:9 (September 1979), esp. pp. 479–487.

24. I will, as has become customary, assume a general familiarity with *A Theory of Justice* and not rehearse points that are clear from a careful reading. Since I will now for the most part be criticizing Rawls's theory, I am glad also to acknowledge that Part Three of *A Theory of Justice* has done much to encourage a return by social philosophers to examination of topics like self-respect, dignity, and degradation, which play a critical role in my own argument. Indeed, I think the psychology of self-respect plays a much more significant role in the underlying structure of Rawlsian theory than is usually recognized by those friends and foes of the theory who, as it were, get stuck in the original position—see Henry Shue, "Justice, Rationality, and Desire: On the Logical Structure of Justice as Fairness," *Southern Journal of Philosophy*, 13:1 (Spring 1975), pp. 89–97. A printer's error in this article omitted a critical part of my definition of Rawls's Aristotelian Principle; the second and third lines from the bottom of p. 93 should read: "People tend to desire that people (themselves and others) follow PI.[7]"

25. R. H. Tawney, *Land and Labor in China* (Boston: Beacon Press, 1966), p. 77.

26. I am assuming that the Rawlsian difference principle is to be applied only prospectively: that existing inequalities are to be left in place and only institutions that would otherwise produce greater future increases in inequality are to be constrained by the difference principle. If the difference principle were applied retrospectively and the inequalities already produced by institutions that did not satisfy the difference principle at the time they were functioning were now eliminated, the implications would be radically different from those belonging to the prospective interpretation—and radically redistributive. But I see no evidence that the theory is intended to receive this more egalitarian retrospective interpretation. Such difficulties in application are inherent in, and are strong disadvantages of, strict compliance theory.

For an attempt to formulate a Rawlsian approach to distributions across national boundaries, see Charles R. Beitz, *Political Theory and International Relations* (Princeton: Princeton University Press, 1979), Part Three.

27. For an imaginative and provocative discussion of the case for thinking people may sometimes be justified in going to war to obtain subsistence, see David Luban, "Just War and Human Rights," *Philosophy & Public Affairs*, 9:2 (Winter 1980), pp. 160–181.

28. Rawls, pp. 122 and 139. The unanimity requirement, which is of course not unusual among consent theorists, also smuggles in Pareto optimality. Why is unanimity required unless it is required that no one should lose anything? And why should no one lose anything, however superfluous, to anyone, however deprived?

29. Rawls eliminates this possibility from consideration by assuming only moderate scarcity, pp. 127–128. On the significance of dealing with this by assumption, see note 18 to chapter 1, as well as the next note here.

30. Rawls of course excludes such specific information as whether a fight for survival would likely succeed, by means of the veil of ignorance. This assumption, along with the unanimity requirement and the assumption of moderate scarcity, add force to Ronald Dworkin's methodological question: why should I willingly abide in this situation by principles that would have been agreed to in a situation so unlike this one? See Ronald Dworkin, "The Original Position," in *Reading Rawls: Critical Studies of A Theory of Justice*, ed. by Norman Daniels (New York: Basic Books, 1974), pp. 16–19. These are fundamental difficulties for Kantian approaches to moral and political theory.

6 • Nationality and Responsibility

1. Someone who thought that only duties to aid, and neither duties to avoid depriving nor duties to protect, stopped at national boundaries would probably be relying heavily upon some analogue of the distinction between "negative" and "positive" rights criticized above in chapter 2. Thus, confronting duties to aid is confronting the more difficult case.

2. As indicated below, a *locus classicus* for a description of this kind of view is Book III of David Hume's *Treatise*. However, I will in this chapter rarely attribute a particular justification for the priority of compatriots to a particular thinker, because I am less interested in the scholarly originals than in the popular copies of the various arguments. I am primarily trying to articulate the somewhat inchoate reasons that seem to lie behind deep public attitudes that are not usually fully reasoned and are sometimes, of course, mere bigotry and chauvinism. For provocative reflec-

tions on the difference between unacceptable bigotry and admirable loyalty, see Samuel Gorovitz, "Bigotry, Loyalty, and Malnutrition," in *Food Policy: The Responsibility of the United States in the Life and Death Choices*, edited by Peter G. Brown and Henry Shue (New York: Free Press, 1977), pp. 129–142.

3. I used this label at a leadership briefing in 1976, summarized in *Who Shall Eat?: Report on An Inquiry Into U.S. Food Policy Options* (New York: American Friends Service Committee, 1977), pp. 27–28. The basic notion is long familiar, as will be indicated below. For a lively and important current debate on some of these same issues, see Michael Walzer, "The Moral Standing of States: A Response to Four Critics," *Philosophy & Public Affairs*, 9:3 (Spring 1980), pp. 209–229, and the cited work of the four critics in question (Charles R. Beitz, Gerald Doppelt, David Luban, and Richard Wasserstrom).

4. See, for example, the accounts of nationalism cited in note 13, below, especially Smith. Also see the alternative accounts of the international system formulated and assessed in Charles R. Beitz, *Political Theory and International Relations* (Princeton: Princeton University Press, 1979), Parts One and Two.

5. This formulation was suggested by Douglas MacLean.

6. Since one obviously cannot aid all non-compatriots, an adequate account must include principles that serve both the functions served by the priority principle discussed in chapter 5: ranking potential recipients and limiting the extent of duty-bearers' obligatory transfers, if the need is ever overwhelming (contrary to the contention of chapter 4).

7. Once again, no effort will be made to attribute these stylized views to particular people, but the first—the trustee/adversary—view clearly underlies many discussions of acceptable means for the pursuit of national interests. It even underlies U.S. law concerning human rights and arms transfers, which explicitly permits the supply of U.S. arms to regimes violating the rights of the people under them whenever the arms sales or grants are taken to be in the U.S. national interest. For the law, see Foreign Assistance Act of 1961, as amended, Section 502B. For critiques, see Peter G. Brown, ". . . in the National Interest," in *Human Rights and U.S. Foreign Policy: Principles and Applications*, edited by Peter G. Brown and Douglas MacLean (Lexington, Mass.: Lexington Books, 1979), pp. 161–171, and see the third section of chapter 7, below.

8. On the complexities of representation, see Hanna Fenichel Pitkin, *The Concept of Representation* (Berkeley: University of California Press, 1967), especially chapter 9.

9. In the final section of this chapter these are discussed somewhat more fully as "service duties."

10. Lois B. McHugh, "Summary," in Senate Comm. on the Judiciary, 96th Cong., 1st Sess., *World Refugee Crisis: The International Community's Response* (Comm. Print, August 1979), pp. xi–xxvi. For the observation that the majority of refugees are children, see p. xv.

11. This, however, can probably be dealt with in various ways—see, for instance, Joseph Sneed, "A Utilitarian Framework for Policy Analysis in Food-related Foreign Aid," in Brown and Shue, pp. 103–128. What Sneed does not tackle is the next issue mentioned in the text.

12. To see that native stock is not necessarily superior, one need consider only some recent cases: the Amin regime in Uganda, the Pol Pot regime in Kampuchea, the Somoza regime in Nicaragua, the Shah's regime in Iran, and a few others. It by no means follows that intervention of any particular kind is justified. On that difficult issue see Louis Henkin, "Human Rights and 'Domestic Jurisdiction,'" in *Human Rights, International Law and the Helsinki Accord*, edited by Thomas Buergenthal (Montclair, N.J.: Allanheld, Osmun & Co. for the American Society of International Law, 1977), pp. 21–40; and the chapters by Thomas Buergenthal, J. Bryan Hehir, and Mark R. Wicclair in Brown and MacLean.

13. Compare, for example, the respective conceptions of nationalism in Karl Deutsch's *Nationalism and Social Communication: An Inquiry into the Foundations of Nationality*, 2nd ed. (Cambridge, Mass.: MIT Press, 1966); F. H. Hinsley's *Nationalism and the International System* (Dobbs Ferry: Oceana Publications, 1973); Hans Kohn's *The Idea of Nationalism: A Study in Its Origins and Background* (New York: Macmillan, 1944); and J. L. Tamon's *The Origins of Totalitarian Democracy* (New York: Praeger, 1960). Anthony Smith's *Theories of Nationalism* (New York: Harper & Row, 1971), including Appendix B, "Some Ideological Relatives of Nationalism," contains a useful attempt at systematically sorting the varieties of nationalism.

14. Clifford Geertz, "The Integrative Revolution: Primordial Sentiments and Civil Politics in the New States," in *Old Societies and New States: The Quest for Modernity in Asia and Africa*, ed. by Clifford Geertz (New York: Free Press, 1963), p. 109.

15. See, for example, Cynthia H. Enloe, *Ethnic Conflict and Political Development: An Analytic Study* (Boston: Little, Brown and Company, 1973). Enloe concludes:

> Loss of a sense of boundaries, not just territorial but social and psychological, may be at the core of the current outbreak of communal versus nation-state tensions. The fact that the struggle to establish new boundaries for meaningful political action is going on in countries at several different stages of modernization warns against rely-

> ing on the inevitability of the nation-state or assuming that political development leads to modernity. The mobilization of ethnic groups may reflect the traumas of casting off tradition, but it may also portend innovative political forms for the future, beyond modernity. (274)

I realize that the strength of primordial sentiments is, for the position I am defending, a two-edged sword. While such sentiments may undercut nationalistic sentiments (where the two conflict), they may more effectively than nationalism undercut any sense of transnational duties.

16. See Kant's famous footnote to the First Section of *Foundations of the Metaphysics of Morals* at 401 (Beck, p. 17).

17. For rich suggestions about the deeper questions concerning motivation, see the work of Stuart Hampshire generally and especially his essay, "Spinoza and the Idea of Freedom" in *Freedom of Mind and Other Essays* by Stuart Hampshire (Princeton: Princeton University Press, 1971).

18. David Hume, *A Treatise of Human Nature*, Book III, Part II, Section II (Selby-Bigge, p. 488).

19. Rousseau and Kant, each in his own way, also of course retained a special place for the national community. For this other—roughly, nationalistic—side of each see, for example, Rousseau's *Constitution for Poland*, not to mention *The Social Contract*, and some of Kant's explicitly political essays, such as "On the Common Saying: 'This May Be True in Theory, But It Does Not Apply in Practice'" and *The Metaphysical Elements of the Theory of Right*.

20. Jean-Jacques Rousseau, *Émile*, Book IV (Foxley, p. 196).

21. Jean-Jacques Rousseau, *Émile*, Book IV (Foxley, p. 215—translation following Charvet).

22. Immanuel Kant, *Foundations of the Metaphysics of Morals*, 410–411 (Beck, p. 27).

23. Immanuel Kant, *Foundations of the Metaphysics of Morals*, 433 (Beck, pp. 51–52).

24. This utterly fundamental divergence between Hume and Rousseau, on the one hand, and Kant, on the other, about psychological bases for moral conduct is a modern revival of essentially the same debate powerfully and clearly analyzed by Plato in *Protagoras*, esp. 352–355 (and pursued by Aristotle in terms of *acrasia* in the *Nicomachean Ethics*, Book VII).

25. See the framework given by William K. Frankena in "Recent Conceptions of Morality," in *Morality and the Language of Conduct*, ed. by Hector-Neri Castañeda and George Nakhnikian (Detroit: Wayne State University Press, 1963), pp. 1–24, as well as the following chapter

in the same volume, W. D. Falk, "Morality, Self, and Others." Also compare the position taken by Thomas Nagel, *The Possibility of Altruism* (New York: Oxford University Press, 1970) with the critique in Nicholas L. Sturgeon, "Altruism, Solipsism, and the Objectivity of Reasons," *Philosophical Review*, 83:3 (July 1974), pp. 374–402, and the alternative approach in Gilbert Harman, *The Nature of Morality* (New York: Oxford University Press, 1977), esp. chapters 8–12.

7 • Right-Grounded Duties and the Institutional Turn

1. Having mentioned the term in chapter 2 (p. 61), I continued to use it in "The Interdependence of Duties," in *The Right to Food*, ed. by Philip Alston and Katerina Tomasevski, International Studies in Human Rights (Dordrecht: Martinus Nijhoff, 1984), p. 90. I first tried to discuss the division of moral labor systematically, if somewhat murkily, in "Mediating Duties," *Ethics*, 98 (July 1988), pp. 687–704. James W. Nickel has valuable recent discussions in "How Human Rights Generate Duties to Protect and Provide," *Human Rights Quarterly*, 15:1 (February 1993), pp. 77–86; and "A Human Rights Approach to World Hunger," in *World Hunger and Morality*, 2d ed., ed. by William Aiken and Hugh LaFollette (Upper Saddle River, N.J.: Prentice Hall, 1996), pp. 171–185. For a useful overview of recent work, see Jack Donnelly, "Post-Cold War Reflections on the Study of International Human Rights," *Ethics & International Affairs*, 8 (1994), pp. 97–117.

2. For example, John Locke, *Two Treatises of Government*, Book II, Chap. V, Para. 25. Also see, on the intellectual history of subsistence rights, Thomas A. Horne, "Welfare Rights as Property Rights," in *Responsibility, Rights, and Welfare: The Theory of the Welfare State*, ed. by J. Donald Moon (Boulder: Westview Press, 1988), pp. 107–132.

3. See Louis B. Sohn, *The Human Rights Movement: From Roosevelt's Four Freedoms to the Interdependence of Peace, Development and Human Rights* (Cambridge: Human Rights Program, Harvard Law School, 1995), pp. 11–17. In particular, see Franklin D. Roosevelt, "Eleventh Annual Message to Congress," January 11, 1944, reprinted in *State of the Union Messages of the Presidents, 1790–1966*, vol. 3.

4. Quoted on p. 5. A recent, highly accurate account of those times is in Kathryn Sikkink, "The Power of Principled Ideas: Human Rights Policies in the United States and Western Europe," in *Ideas and Foreign Policy: Beliefs, Institutions, and Political Change*, ed. by Judith Goldstein and Robert O. Keohane (Ithaca: Cornell University Press, 1993), pp. 139–170. Two good contemporaneous accounts by participants outside the Carter Administration, the first a legislative assistant to a senator and the second a senator, are Mark L. Schneider, "A New Administra-

tion's New Policy: The Rise to Power of Human Rights," in *Human Rights and U.S. Foreign Policy: Principles and Applications*, ed. by Peter G. Brown and Douglas MacLean (Lexington, Mass.: Lexington Books, 1979), pp. 3–13; and Tom Harkin, "Human Rights and Foreign Aid: Forging an Unbreakable Link," in Brown and MacLean, pp. 15–26.

5. Charles Frankel, *Human Rights and Foreign Policy*, Headline Series 241 (New York: Foreign Policy Association, 1978), p. 38. Frankel wrote here of "the older Lockean rights like free speech or free political association" (39), as if Locke had not mentioned subsistence. Frankel had earlier taken a leave from teaching philosophy and public affairs at Columbia University to serve as assistant secretary of state in 1965–67 in the Johnson Administration; in 1977 he became the first director of the National Humanities Center. Frankel was an important leader in the movement beginning in the 1960s in the United States to return the attention of philosophers to public affairs, and he was taken all the more seriously in some Washington circles because of his experience in the State Department.

While in the early and middle 1940s Franklin, and Eleanor, Roosevelt had supported the balanced view, other U.S. political figures in the late 1940s and 1950s had denigrated economic rights in the same manner as Frankel, lobbying successfully to reverse the position taken by the U.N. General Assembly and split the *Universal Declaration of Human Rights*, which embodied the balanced view, into two separate *International Covenants*, one that they wanted taken seriously and one that they wanted ignored. In debates before the U.N. Economic and Social Council in 1951, "Mr. Kotschnig (United States) underlined the distinction between civil and political rights, on the one hand, and the economic, social and cultural rights, on the other hand. He pointed out that 'civil and political rights were of such a nature as to be given legal effect promptly by the adoption of such legislation or other measures as might be necessary. The economic, social and cultural rights while spoken of as "rights" were, however, to be treated as objectives towards which *States* adhering to the Covenant would *within their resources* undertake to strive, by the creation of conditions which would be conducive to the exercise of private as well as public action, for their progressive achievement.' He suggested, therefore, together with several other delegates, that the Council should recommend to the General Assembly to reconsider its decision on including both categories of rights in one covenant. This proposal was adopted by 11 votes to 7" [emphasis added]—see Louis B. Sohn, "Supplementary Paper: A Short History of United Nations Documents on Human Rights," in *The United Nations and Human Rights*, Eighteenth Report of the Commission to Study the Organization of Peace (Dobbs Ferry, N.Y.: Oceana Publications, 1968), pp. 105–106.

"States . . . within their resources" means, of course, that there is no duty on the part of rich states like the United States to transfer any wealth to poor states, who must make do in fulfilling economic rights with whatever wealth they happen to have ended up with (in many cases after decades of colonial exploitation). Mr. Kotschnig's statement is one classic rich-country position, endlessly repeated ever since, especially the nonsensical notion that civil and political rights are fulfilled simply with the passage of a little legislation. This is why no one is ever robbed or murdered in countries like the United States and Britain, which have good legislation! Charles Frankel simply added some new arguments for this basic position.

6. Frankel, p. 40. Frankel did admit: "Indeed, if the United States were to decide not to use the word 'rights' to designate goals like full employment and the reduction of want, it would simply separate itself from the outlook and feelings of the mass of mankind" (p. 40); also see 33–35. But he considered this "mild overspeak."

7. Jeremy Waldron, *Liberal Rights: Collected Papers, 1981–1991* (Cambridge: Cambridge University Press, 1993), p. 25.

8. Thomas W. Pogge, "How Should Human Rights Be Conceived?" *Jahrbuch für Recht und Ethik*, 3 (1995), pp. 103–120.

9. The first sentence on p. 91 explicitly denies that these are the only basic rights. Since I was defending against attacks by philosophers (like Charles Frankel, Maurice Cranston, and many others) upon economic rights, it is understandable that my defense of subsistence rights in particular has sometimes been misunderstood as saying that subsistence rights are especially basic, or the most basic. Not so—subsistence is simply no less basic than, say, physical security and social participation. But no more basic.

10. It is a historical point of some significance that the congressional impulse in the 1970s to act to defend human rights abroad was, not an interventionary impulse, but an anti-interventionary impulse, directed against the cynical creation and support of authoritarian regimes favored by the "geostrategic" notions of Henry Kissinger and his school. Many critics of the human rights initiatives have attempted to portray them falsely as the interventionary side. For Kissinger's general approach, see Walter Isaacson, *Kissinger* (New York: Simon & Schuster, 1992).

11. I have not brought my empirical research up to date for this edition, but questions certainly continue to be raised about the School of the Americas at Fort Benning in Columbus, Georgia. H.R. 2652, introduced by Rep. Joseph Kennedy, proposes closing the SOA; Maryknoll Productions in Maryknoll, N.Y., has made a documentary about SOA called "School of the Assassins." To this day, the CIA continues to be

complicit in murders in Guatemala, most notoriously including the husband of American Jennifer Harbury, whose hunger strikes brought brief media attention to that particular CIA cover-up; it is especially outrageous that after overthrowing the Guatemalan government in 1954 and ushering in decades of death squads, the CIA's ignorantly out-of-control and murderous meddling in that unfortunate country still blunders on forty years later—see Tim Weiner, "Records Tie C.I.A. Informer to Two Guatemala Killings," *New York Times*, May 7, 1996, pp. A1 and A4. In spite of promises to come clean with the public, the CIA continues to cover up its worst disasters—see Tim Weiner, "CIA Is Slow To Tell Early Cold War Secrets," *New York Times*, April 8, 1996, p. A6. A particularly good account of self-defeating covert action in Asia is Audrey R. Kahin and George McT. Kahin, *Subversion as Foreign Policy: The Secret Eisenhower and Dulles Debacle in Indonesia* (New York: New Press, 1995). More generally, see Evan Thomas, *The Very Best Men* (New York: Simon & Schuster, 1995); and Kathryn Olmsted, *Challenging the Secret Government: The Post-Watergate Investigations of the CIA and FBI* (Chapel Hill: University of North Carolina Press, 1996).

12. Thus, it is not obvious that Pogge is correct in describing my account as "maximalist"—see Pogge, "How Should Human Rights be Conceived?" n. 17.

13. In practice, sadly, it is for the foreseeable future highly relevant to focus on how to enable people to recover from the wrongs already done them, specifically, to recover from the violations of rights that have already occurred and to secure themselves against repeat violations in the future. As I have perhaps too pessimistically suggested elsewhere, "Extriction ethics largely constitutes transition ethics"—see "Environmental Change and the Varieties of Justice," in *Global Environmental Change and Social Justice*, ed. by Fen Hampson and Judith Reppy (Ithaca: Cornell University Press, 1996).

14. Philip Alston, "International Law and the Right to Food," in *Food as a Human Right*, ed. by Asbjorn Eide, Wenche Barth Eide, et al. (Tokyo: United Nations University, 1984), p. 172.

15. Asbjorn Eide, "The International Human Rights System," in *Food as a Human Right*, p. 154.

16. I intended to be recommending strategic reasoning about the institutions to implement rights in "Mediating Duties."

17. James W. Nickel, *Making Sense of Human Rights: Philosophical Reflections on the Universal Declaration of Human Rights* (Berkeley: University of California Press, 1987), pp. 54–55. Nickel has developed this point further in "A Human Rights Approach to World Hunger," pp. 171–85, as I note later.

18. Nickel, *Making Sense*, p. 13. This is what I call the "substance" of the right.

19. I also argue for concrete, partially empirical approaches to rights in "Thickening Convergence: Human Rights and Cultural Diversity," in *Zur Philosophie der Menschenrechte*, ed. by Georg Lohmann and Stefan Gosepath (Frankfurt: Suhrkamp Verlag, in press).

20. Nickel later writes: "A consequentialist theory of moral rights might interpret importance as a purely axiological notion; a claim would be very important if it were closely connected with a very strong interest or value. I propose, however, to interpret importance as having essential deontological elements. Principles of duty as well as considerations of value will be used in judging importance" (p. 109).

21. Thomas W. Pogge, "How Should Human Rights Be Conceived?" esp. pp. 113–116. The distinction between interactional and institutional was introduced in Pogge's important 1992 article, "Cosmopolitanism and Sovereignty," *Ethics*, 103:1 (October 1992), pp. 48–75. I have found this distinction provocative and fruitful to struggle with. I am not confident that I grasp it correctly, but I do not think that my own views are interactional in his sense, as Pogge does.

22. Pogge, "How Should Human Rights Be Conceived?" p. 113.

23. Ibid., p. 115.

24. Ibid., p. 113.

25. Pogge has an important thesis about negative and positive duties that I do not have the space to take up here. Much too briefly, I think that while he may appear to be contradicting my emphasis on widespread positive duties, his point is at a higher, noncontradictory level. Pogge emphasizes the extremely important fact that those who have some influence on how the world operates are imposing fundamental institutions—global "basic structures" in the Rawlsian sense—upon billions of people with no influence on the terms embodied in the institutions. Insofar as these shared institutions are already enforcing unjust terms upon people, those of us who operate the institutions have a negative duty to stop imposing the unjust institutions. The cessation of the imposition will require exertion and expense, but there is a level at which all these exertions—all this "positive" activity—is satisfying a purely negative requirement: stop imposing unjust terms. That I have had my foot on your neck for so long that it will be uncomfortable for me to get off does not make getting off a positive duty. However, I still want to maintain two theses, which I think are complementary to Pogge, not in conflict with his thesis. First, although the requirement is fundamentally negative, its fulfillment is still constituted in practice by challenging and imaginative institutional reform that involves effort and sacrifice. Second, and per-

haps more important, Pogge's point applies only to institutions that already are shared and have in fact been imposed; these basic structures are extremely important and profoundly affect people's lives. Nevertheless, in addition to justifying the lifting of the unjust institutions off people's backs, I am also attempting to justify the creation of new institutions to fulfill rights that have so far gone unfulfilled. Some of what I view as the positive creating of new institutions, Pogge might reasonably take as the elimination or reform of old institutions. But I doubt that it can all be very helpfully so viewed.

26. Nickel, "A Human Rights Approach to World Hunger," p. 172.

27. This may be what Pogge understands by the "interactional" perspective. Clearly the "interactional" view is individualistic, not institutional. However, Pogge sometimes describes it as if it is the view that one somehow specifies a set of rights and then simply insists that individuals' duties are whatever they have to be in order to implement the rights specified. I have tried to emphasize, as on pp. 111–112, that no account of rights can be shown to be reasonable without showing that the duties implied are reasonable.

28. A further complication is that the two tests may not be independent of each other: perhaps what it is fair to demand of duty-bearers cannot be established separately and generally but depends to some extent upon which rights would have to go unfulfilled or unacknowledged if fairness were set at one level rather than another. What counted as fair could be affected or influenced without the fair allocation's simply being defined as whatever must be done to secure the rights.

29. I believe this means that, in Pogge's terms, neither the interactional nor the institutional can replace the other. They are, I think, complementary.

30. I have considered the currently fashionable critique of rights as encouraging an atomistic or excessively individualistic picture of society in "Thickening Convergence."

31. For a beautiful example of both how little is obvious and how much a widely knowledgeable philosopher can contribute, see Jeremy Waldron, "A Right-Based Critique of Constitutional Rights," *Oxford Journal of Legal Studies*, 13:1 (Spring 1993), pp. 18–51.

32. I have also defended the necessity of duties to protect in "Thickening Convergence."

33. Nothing, as far as I can see, turns on whether this is considered a kind of protection—so that this duty is a subcategory of a general duty to protect, as in my original scheme—or a separate duty.

34. See Asia Watch and the Women's Rights Project, *A Modern Form of Slavery: Trafficking of Burmese Women and Girls into Brothels in Thai-*

land (New York: Human Rights Watch, 1993). Also see Human Rights Watch/Asia, *Rape for Profit: Trafficking of Nepali Girls and Women to India's Brothels* (New York: Human Rights Watch, 1995); and Robert I. Friedman, "India's Shame," *The Nation*, 262:14 (April 8, 1996), pp. 11–12, 14, 16, and 18–20.

35. For the U.S. policy of walking by on the other side of the road, see United States, "The Clinton Administration's Policy on Reforming Multilateral Peace Operations" (May 1994) [PDD (Presidential Decision Directive) 25, unclassified version], *International Legal Materials*, 33 (1994), pp. 798–813; rpt. in Richard N. Haass, *Intervention: The Use of American Military Force in the Post-Cold War World* (Washington, D.C.: Carnegie Endowment for International Peace, 1994), pp. 209–221, Appendix H. Also see Henry Shue, "Let Whatever Is Smoldering Erupt? Conditional Sovereignty, Reviewable Intervention, and Rwanda 1994," in *Between Sovereignty and Global Governance: The State, Civil Society and the United Nations*, ed. by Anthony P. Jarvis, Albert J. Paolini, and Christian Reus-Smit (New York: St. Martin's, in press). For events in Rwanda, see Alain Destexhe, *Rwanda and Genocide in the Twentieth Century*, tr. by Alison Marschner (New York: New York University Press, 1995; African Rights, *Rwanda: Death, Despair and Defiance*, rev. ed. (London: African Rights, 1995); African Rights, *Rwanda: "A Waste of Hope"—The United Nations Human Rights Field Operation* (London: African Rights, 1995); African Rights, *Rwanda: Killing the Evidence—Murder, Attacks, Arrests and Intimidation of Survivors and Witnesses* (London: African Rights, 1996); Philip Gourevitch, "After the Genocide: Letter from Rwanda," *The New Yorker*, December 18, 1995, pp. 78–94; and Douglas Jehl, "Officials Told To Avoid Calling Rwanda Killings 'Genocide,'" *New York Times*, June 10, 1994. For earlier events and policy in Somalia, see Mohamed Sahnoun, *Somalia: The Missed Opportunities* (Washington, D.C.: United States Institute of Peace Press, 1994); and John L. Hirsch and Robert B. Oakley, *Somalia and Operation Restore Hope: Reflections on Peacemaking and Peacekeeping* (Washington: United States Institute of Peace Press, 1995). Compare Kent DeLong and Steven Tuckey, *Mogadishu!: Heroism and Tragedy* (Westport, Conn.: Praeger, 1994).

36. I have taken this up in a series of recent articles, including "The Unavoidability of Justice," in *The International Politics of the Environment: Actors, Interests, and Institutions*, ed. by Andrew Hurrell and Benedict Kingsbury (Oxford: Oxford University Press, 1992), pp. 373–397; "Subsistence Emissions and Luxury Emissions," *Law & Policy*, 15:1 (January 1993), pp. 39–59; "Avoidable Necessity: Global Warming, International Fairness, and Alternative Energy," in *Theory and Practice*, NOMOS XXXVII, ed. by Ian Shapiro and Judith Wagner

DeCew (New York: NYU Press, 1995), pp. 239–64; "Equity in International Agreements on Climate Change," in *Proceedings of IPCC Workshop, Nairobi, July 1994* (Nairobi: ICIPE Science Press, 1995), pp. 385–392; and "Environmental Change and the Varieties of Justice," in *Global Environmental Change and Social Justice*, ed. by Fen Hampson and Judith Reppy (Ithaca: Cornell University Press, 1996).

37. For an attempt to work out a methodology, see Henry S. Richardson, "Specifying Norms as a Way To Resolve Concrete Ethical Problems," *Philosophy & Public Affairs*, 19:4 (Fall 1990), pp. 279–310; and "Beyond Good and Right: Toward a Constructive Ethical Pragmatism," *Philosophy & Public Affairs*, 24:2 (Spring 1995), pp. 108–141.

38. In the terms used in the previous section, one must consider both the institutional adequacy of specifying the duties in certain ways and the individual fairness of assigning the duties as specified.

39. I have most recently wrestled with it in Henry Shue, "Solidarity among Strangers and the Right to Food," in *World Hunger and Morality*, pp. 113–132.

40. The case for preventive intervention is argued in Shue, "Let Whatever is Smoldering Erupt?" Also see Stanley Hoffmann, "The Politics and Ethics of Military Intervention," *Survival*, 37:4 (Winter 1995–96), pp. 29–51. I believe that Hoffmann is wrong specifically about Rwanda (p. 48) but share his general emphasis on "quick early use of force" (p. 44).

41. Duties to aid naturally continue to fall upon those complicit in the violations that made the aid necessary.

42. Alain Destexhe has noted the growing pattern of attempting to use humanitarian assistance to victims of unprevented outrages to cover up failures to prevent them in the first place—*Rwanda and Genocide in the Twentieth Century*, chap. 4. Aid is never an excuse for the failed protection that makes it necessary. Many commentators have also made this criticism of the disastrous U.N. policy in Bosnia, which provided food to ravaged areas instead of defending them—see, for example, David Rieff, *Slaughterhouse: Bosnia and the Failure of the West* (New York: Simon & Schuster, 1995).

43. For much kinder words about the nation, and a provocative discussion of the international allocation of duties grounded in basic rights, see David Miller, *On Nationality* (Oxford: Clarendon Press of Oxford University Press, 1995), chap. 3.

44. This fundamental point was powerfully argued by Charles R. Beitz in a book that appeared just as the first edition of this one was in press: *Political Theory and International Relations* (Princeton: Princeton University Press, 1979), part 2.

45. I do not mean to imply that the answer is obvious. Michael Wal-

zer has famously maintained that "it is not true, then, that intervention is justified whenever revolution is; for revolutionary activity is an exercise in self-determination"—*Just and Unjust Wars: Moral Argument with Historical Illustrations*, 2d ed. (New York: Basic Books, 1992), p. 89. This was reaffirmed and elaborated, in response to David Luban, in "The Moral Standing of States," *Philosophy & Public Affairs*, 9:3 (Spring 1980), p. 214. On Rwanda and Bosnia specifically, however, also see Michael Walzer, "The Politics of Rescue," *Dissent*, 42:1 [whole no. 178] (Winter 1995), pp. 35–41. For some of the general issues, see Henry Shue, "Eroding Sovereignty: The Advance of Principle," in *The Morality of Nationalism*, ed. by Robert McKim and Jeff McMahan (New York: Oxford University Press, in press). For reasons why one should not easily assume that economic sanctions are "kinder" than military intervention, see Lori Fisler Damrosch, "The Civilian Impact of Economic Sanctions," in *Enforcing Restraint: Collective Intervention in Internal Conflicts*, ed. by Lori Fisler Damrosch (New York: Council on Foreign Relations Press, 1993), pp. 274–315; and Damrosch, "The Collective Enforcement of International Norms Through Economic Sanctions," *Ethics & International Affairs*, 8 (1994), pp. 59–75.

46. Thomas Pogge, "Human Rights as Moral Claims on Global Institutions," in Lohmann and Gosepath.

47. Michael Walzer, *Spheres of Justice: A Defense of Pluralism and Equality* (New York: Basic Books, 1983), pp. 29–30.

48. Walzer, *Spheres of Justice*, p. 313.

49. I have discussed this more fully in "Thickening Convergence."

8 • Basic Rights and Climate Change

1. John Stuart Mill recognized to some extent the social character of rights—see *Utilitarianism*, chapter 5 (Indianapolis: Bobbs-Merrill Co., 1957), 66: "To have a right, then, is, I conceive, to have something which society ought to defend me in the possession of".

2. Valuable discussions of 'standard threats' are in David Luban, "The Warren Court and the Concept of a Right," *Harvard Civil Rights-Civil Liberties Law Review*, 34 (1999), 7–37, at 18–21; Charles R. Beitz and Robert E. Goodin, "Introduction: *Basic Rights* and Beyond," in Charles R. Beitz and Robert E. Goodin (eds.), *Global Basic Rights* (Oxford: Oxford University Press, 2009), 1–24, at 10; and Jonathan Wolf, "The Content of the Human Right to Health" in Rowan Cruft, S. Matthew Liao, and Massimo Renzo, *Philosophical Foundations of Human Rights* (Oxford: Oxford University Press, 2015), 491–501, at 495–496.

3. Henry Shue, "Making Exceptions," *Journal of Applied Philosophy*, 26:4 (2009), 307–22.

4. Benjamin Franta, "Early Oil Industry Knowledge of CO_2 and Global Warming," *Nature Climate Change* 8 (2018): 1024–1025; doi:10.1038/s41558-018-0349-9. Also see Neela Banerjee, "Exxon's Oil Industry Peers Knew about Climate Dangers in the 1970s Too," *Inside Climate News* (2015): https://insideclimatenews.org/news/22122015/exxon-mobil-oil-industry-peers-knew-about-climate-change-dangers-1970s-american-petroleum-institute-api-shell-chevron-texaco (retrieved March 20, 2019).

5. Roger Revelle, Wallace Broecker, C. D. Keeling, et al., "Atmospheric Carbon Dioxide in United States," in White House, *Restoring the Quality of Our Environment: Report of the Environmental Pollution Panel, President's Science Advisory Committee* (Washington, D.C.: U.S. Government Printing Office, 1965), appendix Y4, 111–133. Also see Kaitlin Sullivan, "U.S. Government Knew Climate Risks in 1970s, Energy Advisory Group Documents Show," *Climate Liability News*, March 18, 2019; https://www.climateliabilitynews.org/2019/03/18/national-petroleum-council-climate-change (retrieved March 19, 2019).

6. For example, the original trial judge in *Juliana v U.S.A.*—the "childrens' lawsuit" - found a "fundamental right . . . to a climate system capable of sustaining human life". See Jacqueline Peel & Hari M. Osofsky, "Litigating the right to a sustainable climate system," *OpenGlobalRights*, 21 March 2019. https://www.openglobalrights.org/litigating-the-right-to-a-sustainable-climate-system/

7. Ove Hoegh-Guldberg, Daniela Jacob, Michael Taylor, et al., "Impacts of 1.5°C of Global Warming on Natural and Human Systems," in Intergovernmental Panel on Climate Change, *Global Warming of 1.5°C: An IPCC Special Report* (2018), 175–311; https://www.ipcc.ch/sr15/chapter/chapter-3.

8. For a development and refinement of the argument in support of subsistence as a basic right, see Elizabeth Ashford, "A Moral Inconsistency Argument for a Basic Human Right to Subsistence," in Cruft, Liao, and Renzo (eds.), *Philosophical Foundations of Human Rights*, 515–534; and a number of other articles by Ashford.

9. Michael Greenstone and Claire Qing Fan, *Introducing the Air Quality Life Index* (Chicago: Energy Policy Institute at the University of Chicago, 2018), 4 and 8; https://aqli.epic.uchicago.edu/wp-content/uploads/2018/11/AQLI-Report.111918–2.pdf. Also see Hilary Brueck, "Pollution Is Killing More People than Wars, Obesity, Smoking, and Malnutrition," *Business Insider*, 24 October 2017. And see more generally Anthony J. McMichael with Alistair Woodward and Cameron Muir,

Climate Change and the Health of Nations: Famines, Fevers, and the Fate of Populations (New York: Oxford University Press, 2017).

10. UN Environment, *Global Environment Outlook—GEO-6: Summary for Policymakers* (Nairobi: UN Environment, 2019), 2.2.1; doi: 10.1017/9781108639217. Also see Richard Burnett, Hong Chen, Mieczyslaw Szyszkowicz, et al., "Global Estimates of Mortality Associated with Long-Term Exposure to Outdoor Fine Particulate Matter," *Proceedings of the National Academy of Sciences of the United States of America* 115 (38) (September 18, 2018): 9592–9597; doi:10.1073/pnas.1803222115.

11. Nicholas Bakalar, "Air Pollution Contributes to More Than 20,000 Deaths a Year," *New York Times*, December 27, 2017.

12. Steven Mufson and Brady Dennis, "Report Finds Widespread Contamination at Nation's Coal Ash Sites," *Washington Post*, March 4, 2019. See more generally UN Environment, *Global Environment Outlook—GEO-6: Summary for Policymakers*, 2.2.5.

13. Andrew J. Kondash, Nancy E. Lauer, and Avner Vengosh, "The Intensification of the Water Footprint of Hydraulic Fracturing," *Science Advances*, 4 (8) (August 15, 2018), 1–8, at 1; doi:10.1126/sciadv.aar5982. Also see Southern Environmental Law Center, "EPA Study Shows Fracking Pollutes Drinking Water," December 22, 2016; https://selc.link/2h5vph7. The original study is: U.S. Environmental Protection Agency, "Hydraulic Fracturing for Oil and Gas: Impacts from the Hydraulic Fracturing Water Cycle on Drinking Water Resources in the United States," EPA-600-R-16–236ES (December 2017); https://www.epa.gov/hfstudy/executive-summary-hydraulic-fracturing-study-final-assessment-2016.

14. Hoegh-Guldberg, Jacob, Taylor, et al., "Impacts of 1.5°C of Global Warming on Natural and Human Systems," 238–240.

15. United Nations, Human Rights Council, 41st Session [24 June - 12 July 2019], Agenda item 3, *Climate Change and Poverty: Report of the Special Rapporteur on extreme poverty and human rights*, A/HRC/41/39 (Advance unedited version), para. 13. Alston cites a 2015 study reported in *The Lancet* and the World Bank's influential 2016 study *Shock Waves: Managing the Impacts of Climate Change on Poverty*.

16. United Nations, Human Rights Council, *Climate Change and Poverty*, para. 87. Also see Committee on the Elimination of Discrimination Against Women; Committee on Economic, Social and Cultural Rights; Committee on the Protection of the Rights of All Migrant Workers and Members of their Families; Committee on the Rights of the Child; and Committee on the Rights of Persons with Disabilities, *Joint Statement on "Human Rights and Climate Change"*, 16 September 2019. https://www.ohchr.org/en/NewsEvents/Pages/DisplayNews.aspx?NewsID=24998&LangID=E.

17. Some diverse, valuable sources include Mike Berners-Lee, *There Is No Planet B: A Handbook for the Make or Break Years* (Cambridge: Cambridge University Press, 2019); Stephen M. Gardiner, A *Perfect Moral Storm: The Ethical Tragedy of Climate Change* (New York: Oxford University Press, 2011); Amitav Ghosh, *The Great Derangement: Climate Change and the Unthinkable* (Chicago: University of Chicago Press, 2016); Dale Jamieson, *Reason in a Dark Time: Why the Struggle against Climate Change Failed—and What It Means for Our Future* (New York: Oxford University Press, 2014); Michael T. Klare, *All Hell Breaking Loose: The Pentagon's Perspective on Climate Change* (New York: Metropolitan/Henry Holt, 2019); Rachel Maddow, *Blowout: Corrupted Democracy, Rogue State Russia, and the Richest, Most Destructive Industry on Earth* (New York: Crown, 2019); and David Wallace-Wells, *The Uninhabitable Earth: A Story of the Future* (New York: Penguin Random House, 2019). Selected essays of mine from 1992 to 2013 constitute *Climate Justice: Vulnerability and Protection* (Oxford: Oxford University Press, 2014). I currently have under way a short book called "Just in Time?: Climate Change and Future Generations."

18. Henry Shue, "Having It Both Ways: The Gradual Wrong Turn in American Strategy," in *Nuclear Deterrence and Moral Restraint: Critical Choices for American Strategy*, edited by Henry Shue, Cambridge Studies in Philosophy and Public Policy (New York: Cambridge University Press, 1989), 3–49.

19. Far and away the best book on nuclear weapons remains Jonathan Schell, *The Fate of the Earth* (New York: Alfred A. Knopf, 1982), which contains a profound meditation on the significance of risking extinction.

20. I am grateful to Eugen Pissarskoi for provocatively laying out this contrast—see his "The Controllability Precautionary Principle: Justification of a Climate Policy Goal under Uncertainty," in *Climate Justice: Integrating Economics and Philosophy*, edited by Ravi Kanbur and Henry Shue (Oxford: Oxford University Press, 2019), 188–208.

21. Oppenheimer, Michael, and Bruce Glavovic (in press). "Sea Level Rise and Implications for Low Lying Islands, Coasts and Communities". In H.-O. Pörtner, D.C. Roberts, V. Masson-Delmotte, *et al.*, *IPCC Special Report on the Ocean and Cryosphere in a Changing Climate*, Sections 4.2.3.1.2 and 4.2.3.4. Cambridge: Cambridge University Press. Also see chapter 3, Cross-chapter Box 8. For a study of why the IPCC has consistently under-estimated the danger of dynamic instability in the West Antarctic Ice Sheet, see Michael Oppenheimer, Naomi Oreskes, Dale Jamieson, *et al.*, *Discerning Experts: The Practices of Scientific Assessment for Environmental Policy* (Chicago: University of Chicago Press, 2019), 127–169, esp. 164–168.

22. Claire L. Parkinson, "A 40-y record reveals gradual Antarctic sea ice increases followed by decreases at rates far exceeding the rates seen in the Arctic," *Proceedings of the National Academy of Sciences of the United States of America* [*PNAS*] (published online July 2019; open access). Doi:10.1073/pnas.1906556116.

23. Will Steffen, Johan Rockström, Katherine Richardson, et al., "Trajectories of the Earth System in the Anthropocene," *Proceedings of the National Academy of Sciences of the United States of America* 115 (33) (August 14, 2018): 8252–8259, at 8253; doi:10.1073/pnas.1810141115. For emphasis on the extent of the uncertainty about where any threshold lies, see Richard Betts, "Is Our Planet Headed toward a 'Hothouse'? Here's What the Science Does—and Doesn't—Say," *Washington Post*, August 13, 2018.

24. Wallace-Wells, *The Uninhabitable Earth*, 4 and 235.

25. Geoffrey Parker, *Global Crisis: War, Climate Change and Catastrophe in the Seventeenth Century*, abridged and rev. ed. (New Haven, Conn.: Yale University Press, 2017), xx and xxi. Also see Sam White, *A Cold Welcome: The Little Ice Age and Europe's Encounter with North America* (Cambridge, Mass.: Harvard University Press, 2017); and Philip Blom, *Nature's Mutiny: How the Little Ice Age Transformed the West and Shaped the Present* (New York: W. W. Norton, 2019). More generally see John L. Brooke, *Climate Change and the Course of Global History: A Rough Journey* (Cambridge: Cambridge University Press, 2014); and Eric H. Cline, *1177 B.C.: The Year Civilization Collapsed*, with a new afterword (Princeton, N.J.: Princeton University Press, 2015), esp. 145–147.

26. Chelsea Harvey, "Methane May Not Last Long in the Atmosphere—but It Drives Sea Level Rise for Centuries," *Washington Post*, January 13, 2017. For the underlying study, see Kirsten Zickfeld, Susan Solomon, and Daniel M. Gilford, "Centuries of Thermal Sea-Level Rise due to Anthropogenic Emissions of Short-Lived Greenhouse Gases," *Proceedings of the National Academy of Sciences of the United States of America* 114 (4) (January 24, 2017), 657–662; doi:10.1073/pnas.1612066114.

27. Jeroen C.J.H. Aerts, "Climate-Induced Migration: Impacts beyond the Coast," *Nature Climate Change* 7 (2017): 315–316; doi:10.1038/nclimate3279. Also see Ghosh, *The Great Derangement*, 37–53; and Jonathan Watts, "Number in danger from rising sea levels trebles to 300 million," *The Guardian*, 30 October 2019.

28. United Nations, Human Rights Council, *Climate Change and Poverty*, para. 65–66.

29. R. James Woolsey, "Security Implications of Climate Scenario 3: Catastrophic Climate Change over the Next 100 Years," in Kurt M. Campbell, Jay Gulledge, J. R. McNeill, et al., *The Age of Consequences:*

The Foreign Policy and National Security Implications of Global Climate Change (Washington, D.C.: Center for Strategic and International Studies and the Center for New American Security, 2007), 79–91, at 85. Woolsey is a former director of the Central Intelligence Agency. Also see Klare, *All Hell Breaking Loose*.

30. http://trillionthtonne.org.

31. Oliver Geden, "Politically Informed Advice for Climate Action," *Nature Geoscience* 11 (June 2018): 378–383; doi:10.1038/s415611-018-0143-3.

32. Anthony Faiola, Marina Lopes, and Chris Mooney, "The price of 'progress' in the Amazon," *Washington Post*, 28 June 2019. Also see Fred Pearce, "Rivers in the Sky: How Deforestation Is Affecting Global Water Cycles," YaleEnvironment360, 24 July 2018. https://e360.yale.edu/features/how-deforestation-affecting-global-water-cycles-climate-change (accessed 3 July 2019).

33. Pete Smith, Steven J. Davis, Felix Creutzig, et al., "Biophysical and Economic Limits to Negative CO_2 Emissions," *Nature Climate Change* 6 (2016): 42–50; doi:10.1038/nclimate2870. Also see Dominic Lenzi, "The Ethics of Negative Emissions," *Global Sustainability* 1 (2018): e7, 1–8; doi:10.1017/sus.2018.5.

34. Henry Shue, "Responsible for What? Carbon Producer CO_2 Contributions and the Energy Transition," *Climatic Change* 144 (4) (2017): 591–596; doi:10.1007/s10584-017-2042-9. Also see Leslie Hook, "Climate Change Fears Spur Investment in Carbon Capture Technology," *Financial Times*, March 23, 2019.

35. Henry Shue, "Climate Dreaming: Negative Emissions, Risk Transfer, and Irreversibility," *Journal of Human Rights and Environment* 8 (2017): 203–216; doi:10.4337/jhre.2017.02.02.

36. Robert J. Brulle, "Institutionalizing Delay: Foundation Funding and the Creation of U.S. Climate Change Counter-movement Organizations," *Climatic Change* 122 (2014): 681–694; doi:10.1007/s10584-013-1018-7. Robert J. Brulle, "The Climate Lobby: A Sectoral Analysis of Lobbying Spending on Climate Change in the USA, 2000 to 2016," *Climatic Change* 149 (2018): 289–303; doi:10.1007/s10584-018-2241-z. Michael E. Mann, *The Hockey Stick and the Climate Wars: Dispatches from the Front Lines* (New York: Columbia University Press, 2012). Jane Mayer, *Dark Money: The Hidden History of the Billionaires behind the Rise of the Radical Right* (New York: Doubleday, 2016). Naomi Oreskes and Erik M. Conway, *Merchants of Doubt: How a Handful of Scientists Obscured the Truth on Issues from Tobacco Smoke to Global Warming* (New York: Bloomsbury Press, 2010), 169–215. Geoffrey Supran and Naomi Oreskes, "Assessing ExxonMobil's Climate Change

Communications (1977–2014)," *Environmental Research Letters* 12:084019 (2017): 1–18; doi:10.1088/1748–9326/aa815f.

37. Rainforest Action Network, *Banking on Climate Change: Fossil Fuel Finance Report Card 2019* (March 20, 2019), 7; https://www.ran.org/bankingonclimatechange2019 (retrieved March 22, 2019). Also see Joe Romm, "The Stunning Hypocrisy of JP Morgan and CEO Jamie Dimon on Climate Change," *ThinkProgress*, March 21, 2019; https://thinkprogress.org/stunning-hypocrisy-of-jp-morgan-jamie-dimon-on-climate-change-a3fd2ecfbbbd (retrieved March 22, 2019).

38. Jonathan Watts, Jillian Ambrose, and Adam Vaughan, "Oil Companies scrambling to raise output in final 'fossil fuel harvest'," *The Guardian*, 11 October 2019.

39. For principled analyses of strategy, see Simon Caney, "Climate Change and Non-ideal Theory: Six Ways of Responding to Non-compliance," in *Climate Justice in a Non-ideal World*, edited by Clare Heyward and Dominic Roser (Oxford: Oxford University Press, 2016), 21–42; Aaron Maltais, "A Climate of Disorder," in Heyward and Roser, 43–63; and Alex Lenferna, "Divest-Invest: A Moral Case for Fossil Fuel Divestment," in Kanbur and Shue, *Climate Justice*, 139–156.

40. An otherwise sometimes generous assessment of *Basic Rights* by Samuel Moyn does not note the radically critical implications of this conclusion for neoliberal claims—see his *Not Enough: Human Rights in an Unequal World* (Cambridge, Mass.: Belknap Press of Harvard University Press, 2018), esp. 162–172. I was trying to say that what Moyn has recently dubbed 'economic libertarianism' is unacceptable—see Samuel Moyn, "We're in an anti-liberal moment. Liberals need better answers," *Washington Post*, 21 June 2019. https://www.washingtonpost.com/outlook/were-in-an-anti-liberal-moment-liberals-need-better-answers/2019/06/21/5f276b26-91f7-11e9-b72d-d56510fa753e_story.html?utm_term=.a68aa2c01163. (accessed 3 July 2019)

41. Rainforest Action Network, *Banking on Climate Change*, 10–12 and 31.

42. Albert Camus, *The Plague* (1947), translated by Robin Buss (London: Penguin Classics, 2013), 195.

43. See Dieter Helm, *Burn Out: The Endgame for Fossil Fuels* (New Haven, Conn.: Yale University Press, 2017); and Carbon Tracker Initiative, *2020 Vision: Why You Should See the Fossil Fuel Peak Coming*, September 10, 2018, https://www.carbontracker.org/reports/2020-vision-why-you-should-see-the-fossil-fuel-peak-coming (retrieved March 25, 2019). Also see Global Commission on the Geopolitics of Energy Transformation, *A New World: The Geopolitics of the Energy Transformation* (International Renewable Energy Agency, 2019); https://www

.irena.org/publications/2019/Jan/A-New-World-The-Geopolitics-of-the-Energy-Transformation (retrieved March 25, 2019).

44. Chris Mooney and Brady Davis, "In Blow to Climate, Coal Plants Emitted More Than Ever in 2018," *Washington Post*, March 25, 2019. .https://www.washingtonpost.com/climate-environment/2019/03/26/blow-climate-coal-plants-emitted-more-than-ever/?wpisrc=nl_green&wpmm=1 (retrieved 31 October 2019).

45. David Pomerantz, "Utility Carbon Targets Reflect Decarbonization Slowdown in Crucial Next Decade," San Francisco: Energy and Policy Institute, 25 June 2019. https://www.energyandpolicy.org/utility-carbon-targets/ (accessed 2 July 2019); and Dan Tong, Qiang Zhang, Yixuan Zheng, et al., "Committed emissions from existing energy infrastructure jeopardize 1.5° C climate target," *Nature* (2019), doi:10.1038/s41586-019-1364-3. Published online, 1 July 2019. For an accessible account of the significance of this *Nature* study, see Chris Mooney, "Existing fossil fuel plants will push the world across a dangerous climate limit, research finds," *Washington Post*, 1 July 2019.

Bibliography

Selected Current Books

Aiken, William, and LaFollette, Hugh, ed. *World Hunger and Moral Obligation*. Englewood Cliffs: Prentice-Hall, Inc., 1977.

Brown, Peter G., and MacLean, Douglas, ed. *Human Rights and U. S. Foreign Policy*. Lexington, Mass.: Lexington Books, 1979.

Brown, Peter G., and Shue, Henry, ed. *Food Policy: The Responsibility of the United States in the Life and Death Choices*. New York: Free Press, 1977.

Chomsky, Noam, and Herman, Edward S. *The Washington Connection and Third World Fascism*, The Political Economy of Human Rights, Vol. I. Boston: South End Press, 1979.

Claude, Richard P., ed. *Comparative Human Rights*. Baltimore: The Johns Hopkins University Press, 1976.

Domínguez, Jorge I.; Rodley, Nigel S.; Wood, Bryce; and Falk, Richard. *Enhancing Global Human Rights*. 1980s Project/Council on Foreign Relations. New York: McGraw-Hill, 1979.

Dworkin, Ronald. *Taking Rights Seriously*, with "A Reply to Critics." Cambridge, Mass.: Harvard University Press, 1978.

Fishkin, James S. *Tyranny and Legitimacy: A Critique of Political Theories*. Baltimore: The Johns Hopkins University Press, 1979.

Frankel, Charles. *Human Rights and Foreign Policy*. Headline Series No. 241. New York: Foreign Policy Association, 1978.

Hampshire, Stuart, ed. *Public and Private Morality*. New York: Cambridge University Press, 1978.

Henkin, Louis. *How Nations Behave*, 2nd Edition. New York: Columbia University Press, 1979.

Hollenbach, David. *Claims in Conflict: Retrieving and Renewing the Catholic Human Rights Tradition*. New York: Paulist Press, 1979.

Honderich, Ted, ed. *Social Ends and Political Means*. Boston: Routledge & Kegan Paul, 1976.

Kamenka, Eugene, and Tay, Alice Erh-Soon, ed. *Human Rights*. New York: St. Martin's Press, 1978.

Kommers, Donald P., and Loescher, Gilburt D., ed. *Human Rights and American Foreign Policy*. Notre Dame, Ind.; University of Notre Dame Press, 1979.

Lillich, Richard B., and Newman, Frank C. *International Human Rights: Problems of Law and Policy*, with "Documentary Appendix." Boston: Little, Brown and Company, 1979.

BIBLIOGRAPHY

Lyons, David, ed. *Rights*. Belmont, Cal.: Wadsworth Publishing Co., 1979.

Melden, A. I. *Rights and Persons*. Values and Philosophical Inquiry. Oxford: Basil Blackwell, 1977.

Morris, Morris D. *Measuring the Condition of the World's Poor: The Physical Quality of Life Index*. Pergamon Policy Studies, No. 42. New York: Pergamon Press for the Overseas Development Council, 1979.

Newberg, Paula R., ed. *The Politics of Human Rights*. New York: New York University Press for UNA-USA, forthcoming.

Pollis, Adamantia, and Schwab, Peter, ed. *Human Rights: Cultural and Ideological Perspectives*. New York: Praeger Publishers, 1979. Contains narrative bibliography.

Said, Abdul Aziz, ed. *Human Rights & World Order*. New Brunswick, N.J.: Transaction Books, 1978.

Scott, James C. *The Moral Economy of the Peasant: Rebellion and Subsistence in Southeast Asia*. New Haven, Conn.: Yale University Press, 1976.

United Nations, Economic and Social Council, Commission on Human Rights. *International Dimensions of the Right to Development as a Human Right*. E/CN. 4/1334. Geneva: Commission on Human Rights, 1978.

Vogelgesang, Sandy. *American Dream /Global Nightmare: The Dilemma of U.S. Human Rights Policy*, New York: W. W. Norton, 1980.

Additional Resources

Martin, Rex, and Nickel, James W. "A Bibliography on the Nature and Foundations of Rights, 1947-1977." *Political Theory*, 6:3 (August 1978), pp. 395-413. Annotated.

Simon, Jackie. "Human Rights: A Resource List of Previewed Films." New York: Amnesty International U.S.A., 1978, photocopy. Annotated.

Index

CPSIA information can be obtained
at www.ICGtesting.com
Printed in the USA
LVHW102207050922
727599LV00002B/215